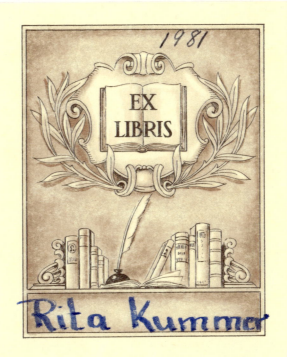

1981

EX
LIBRIS

Rita Kummer

Teaching Reading
to Slow and Disabled Learners

Teaching Reading to Slow and Disabled Learners

Samuel A. Kirk University of Arizona
Sister Joanne Marie Kliebhan Cardinal Stritch College
Janet W. Lerner Northeastern Illinois University

Houghton Mifflin Company   Boston
Dallas   Geneva, Illinois   Hopewell, New Jersey
Palo Alto   London

Library of Congress Catalog Card Number: 77–77655
ISBN: 0-395-25821-9

For the children we have worked with

Contents

Preface

My co-authors, whose efforts have made possible this virtually new book, have urged me to write this preface. I have not been able to determine whether their insistence is out of respect or merely because I wrote the original book, *Teaching Reading to Slow Learning Children* (1940).

For many years our publisher has requested this complete revision, but having concentrated my efforts in other directions, I was not prepared to provide such a revision until I solicited the help of Drs. Kliebhan and Lerner. Our review of the original text in the light of current literature and practices convinced each of us that a much-reworked text, having the earlier version as its genesis, would be a worthwhile contribution to the field. We all agreed, however, that the new book should relate not only to slow learners, but also to disabled learners, since many of the diagnostic and remedial procedures in reading that have been developed over the years often apply to disabled learners just as much as to slow learners.

This decision, proposed by my co-authors, had a strong appeal to me, since my initial work in reading was with disabled readers who were also slow learners. My major activity in this area was in the Research Department of the Wayne County Training School which was then an institution for school-aged delinquent children who were educable mentally retarded. Since many of these children were not functioning up to their capacity in reading, I had the opportunity to assess children who had difficulty in learning, to study basic problems underlying their difficulties, and to evaluate the effectiveness of various methods of remediation. It was through these experiences, and later, the opportunity to apply them to the preparation of teachers, that I received the impetus to write the earlier version of this book.

In this new work my co-authors and I have attempted to describe the characteristics and problems of slow and disabled learners; to discuss procedures and controversies in preparing these children for reading; to explain at some length the stages of development and the needs of children who are not developing at the expected rate; to describe some specialized techniques that have been developed for working with children who have difficulty in learning to read; and also to cover some methods of diagnosing these problems through both formal and informal procedures. The final chapter is a review of reading research dealing with slow and disabled learners.

The authors of this book hope that teachers of reading may glean some insights from the reading programs presented here for slow and disabled learners and can benefit from the detailed methods of diagnosis and remediation presented.

We wish to express our appreciation to the many who have reviewed the book and given valuable suggestions, especially to Professor Tom Becker of John Carroll University, and to those authors and publishers who have given us permission to use quotations from their works. We also wish to express appreciation to the many students the three of us have had over the years, for we have learned much from working with them.

S. A. K.

Teaching Reading
to Slow and Disabled Learners

Our organization of schools into grades for all children of the same age is based on the assumption that all are alike and that all learn at the same rate and by the same methods. The American tradition of equality has often been confused with identical learning ability and learning style.

Actually, children differ biologically, psychologically, and socially, and individual children learn differently and at different rates. It is for this reason that not all eight-year-old children learn to read at the third-grade level and not all children can master first-grade reading materials at the age of 6.

The major goal of education is to develop each child to his or her maximum potential. For a particular child, we do not know what that potential for reading is. Our objective, therefore, must be to provide every child with the widest possible opportunities and to remove if possible any conditions or factors inhibiting the child's ability to learn to read.

This book is concerned with the teaching of reading to children who are slow or disabled learners. Such children deviate from the norm in their learning patterns and have been referred to as *slow learners, mentally retarded, learning-disabled, dyslexic, minimal-brain dysfunctioning,* or simply as *atypical learners.*

The classification and labeling of children has its advantages and disadvantages. Labels and classifications are useful initially in diagnosis and later for communication purposes. Labels and categories, however, have little educational relevance. For example, if an otologist examines a child and finds that the child has no hearing, the otologist classifies the child as *deaf* and refers him or her to a school for the deaf. The personnel in the school for the deaf forget the label of deafness and proceed to evaluate the child for educational purposes. This issue has been discussed by Hobbs (1975) in *The Futures of Children: Categories, Labels, and Their Consequences.*

In this chapter, we offer an overview of the problems involved in teaching reading to slow and disabled learners.

Children Who Are Slow or Disabled Learners

Slow Learners

The term *slow learner* is used in a generalized sense in this book to include children who are borderline in intelligence and those who are classified as mildly or moderately retarded. Slow learners require much repetition in order to learn, require more systematic instructional procedures, and do not reach the levels of reading achievement of other children their age. Slow learning abilities are caused by a number of factors, which probably include biological diversity, genetics, and pathological conditions before, during, or after birth that may affect the integrity of the central nervous system.

While classification and labeling of children may be necessary for communication purposes, a label should be accompanied by a description of the child's learning problems. Children who learn at a slower pace are classified by their degree of slowness or retardation.

The classification and labeling of children who develop at a slower than normal rate has been the subject of much discussion. With the support of the National Institute of Mental Health, the American Association on Mental Deficiency (AAMD) published its concepts of terminology and classification (Grossman, 1973; Heber, 1959, revised in 1961). According to the most recent AAMD classification system, "mental retardation refers to significantly subaverage general intellectual functioning existing concurrently with deficits in adaptive behavior and manifested during the developmental period" (Grossman, 1973, p. 5). In this new definition, mental retardation refers to an IQ of 67 or less, and children above that level are not considered retarded. The new definition establishes four levels of mental retardation:

Mild Retardation	IQ between 67 and 52
Moderate Retardation	IQ between 51 and 36
Severe Retardation	IQ between 35 and 20
Profound Retardation	IQ 19 and below

This book deals with teaching reading to several classifications of slow learners, some in the AAMD category of mentally retarded as well as borderline children who are learning at a slower rate:

Slow Learners

Borderline Child	IQ between 85 and 68
Mildly Retarded Child	IQ between 67 and 52
Moderately Retarded Child	IQ between 51 and 36

The Borderline Child

The *borderline child* (sometimes referred to as the *slow-learning child*) has been variously described as a dull normal or dull average child, or one who is borderline in intellectual functioning, between the mentally retarded and the average child. Generally, these are children with an IQ range roughly below 85 and above 68. Such children, constituting approximately 10 to 15 percent of all school-age children, are among those found at the lower end of their class in academic achievement. Borderline children are not equally slow in all activities or abnormal in all their characteristics. A large proportion of such children are found among the underachievers in school; they tend to be dropouts when they reach secondary school. Johnson (1963) has discussed in depth the characteristics of this group.

It is sometimes difficult to differentiate borderline children and children with specific learning disabilities from underachievers produced by disadvantaged environments. While the mildly retarded child described below may reach third- to fifth-grade level at the age of 16, the borderline learner can complete the sixth to the tenth grade by that age level. At the adult level, borderline learners are found in the unskilled, semiskilled, and sometimes in the skilled trades.

The Mildly Retarded Child

Because of subnormal mental development, a *mildly retarded* child is unable to profit from the program of the regular elementary school but is considered to have the potential for development in three areas: (1) minimal educability in academic affairs, (2) sufficient educability in social adjustment to be taught to get along independently in the community, and (3) sufficient occupational educability to become partially or totally self-supporting as an adult. The mildly retarded child has the following specific growth potentialities:

1. Ability to function at the second-grade level or higher in reading, writing, and arithmetic by the age of 16.
2. Ability to read and to understand formal arithmetic, which begins sometime between the ages 9 and 12.
3. Rate of mental development approximately one-half to two-thirds the rate of an average child.
4. School progress one-half to two-thirds the rate of an average child. For example, after the mildly retarded child learns to read, he or she does not make a full year's progress each year like the normal child, but only about one-half or two-thirds the normal progress each year. If the mildly retarded child begins to learn to read at age 9, he or she can probably make three or four grades' progress in the next six or seven years.
5. Limited vocabulary and language. But speech and language may be adequate in most ordinary situations.

6. Sufficient social skills to permit the child to get along with people in the community independently.
7. Ability to perform unskilled or semiskilled work. Mildly retarded adults can usually learn to support themselves partially or in full.

Often, the mildly retarded child is not known to be retarded during infancy and early childhood. Retardation and delayed growth in mental and social activities can be noted only if the child is observed very closely during the preschool years. Most of the time the growth is normal, and retardation is not evident until poor learning ability is evidenced in school. In many instances, there are no obvious pathological conditions that account for the retardation.

The Moderately Retarded Child

The *moderately retarded* child (often referred to as the trainable child) is one who is not educable in the sense of academic achievement, ultimate social independence in the community, or occupational independence at the adult level. The moderately retarded child, however, has the potential for learning: (a) self-help skills, (b) social adjustment in the family and in the neighborhood, and (c) economic usefulness in the home, in a residential school, in a sheltered workshop, and sometimes, in a job under supervision. Such a child has the following potentialities:

1. Ability to achieve self-care in dressing, undressing, eating, using the toilet, keeping clean, and other necessary skills, which will make the child independent of parents in the routines of living.
2. Ability to learn to get along in the family and in the immediate neighborhood by learning to share, to respect property rights, and in general to cooperate with family and with neighbors. Independent management of affairs in the community is not expected of most moderately retarded persons.
3. Mental development between one-quarter and one-half that of an average child.
4. Ability to learn to assist with chores around the house or to do routine tasks for some remuneration in a sheltered workshop, in a residential school, or in a job under supervision.
5. Little ability to acquire academic skills such as reading and arithmetic—beyond the rote learning of some words or simple numbers. (However, some exceptions are found.)
6. Distinctly limited speech and language.
7. Ability to learn eventually to protect self from common dangers.

Some care, supervision and economic support will be required throughout life. Most such children will be known to be retarded during infancy and early childhood. The retardation is generally noted because of known clinical or physical stigmata or deviations, and because talking and walking are markedly delayed.

Prevalence

How many children in a school system could be classified as slow learning or mentally retarded, requiring special attention? Many studies on the distribution of intelligence have been made, and it appears that among slow learners, the distribution of low intelligence, defined primarily through intelligence tests, is as follows:

Approximate Percentage

Total Population of Slow Learners (IQ of less than 85)		16%
Borderline Children	14 %	
Mildly Retarded	2 %	
Moderately Retarded	.1%	

The figures listed above vary from community to community and are of course dependent on the area and the socioeconomic level of the population. It is known that intelligence tests reveal many more borderline and mildly retarded children among low socioeconomic groups than among higher socioeconomic groups. These intelligence tests are standardized primarily on middle-class white children, and in a sense they discriminate against children from families of a lower socioeconomic level. With moderately retarded children, whose retardation is generally pathological (as in mongolism or Down's syndrome), there is little difference in prevalence among socioeconomic groups.

Distribution of Children with
Low Intelligence

Sometimes the normal curve graph is used to illustrate the distribution of various intelligence levels. With the new definition of mental retardation, the numbers no longer fit the normal curve distribution exactly. However, there is a close enough approximation to the normal distribution that it may be helpful to present it pictorially.

The accompanying Figure 1.1 presents this theoretical distribution of intelligence as measured by standard deviations and IQs. It will be noted that 68 percent, or roughly two-thirds, of the population fall between −1 (standard deviation) and +1 (standard deviation). In other words, two-thirds of the population have an IQ between 85 and 115. This group is considered to be in the average range. Children who have been labeled slow learners or borderline in intelligence are those with an IQ between 68 and 85 as measured by such tests as the *Wechsler Intelligence Scale for Children-Revised (WISC-R)*. Approximately 14 percent of children fall within this range.

Approximately 2 percent of children have an IQ between 52 and 67, that is, between −2 and −3 (standard deviation). This range of intelligence includes mildly retarded children.

The third group, below −3 (standard deviation), or below an IQ of 51, includes .13 percent of children, or approximately 1.3 children per thousand. These children are known as the moderately retarded.

Note that the numbers in the new classification system are slightly different from those in the normal curve distribution. However, the proportion in each category remains the same. It should be noted that the standard deviation using the *Stanford-Binet* is 16, while the standard deviation on the *WISC-R*, represented in Figure 1.1, is 15.

There is danger in the classification and labeling of children through the use of intelligence tests. Much damage has been done to children by placing them in institutions or inappropriate special classes on the basis of their IQ scores. A child may score low on an intelligence test for many reasons unrelated to mental retardation. A foreign language background, a learning disability, or a divergent cultural background are among the factors that can cause a low test score. According to AAMD standards, children cannot be identified as mentally retarded until they have been measured not only with an intelligence test but with adaptive behavior scales as well (Grossman, 1973).

The major drawback of definitions and classifications is that they are based on the concept of interindividual differences, which has limited value. The children represented in Figure 1.1 are placed on a continuum, some with high ability and some with low ability. Saying that a child with an IQ

Figure 1.1   Theoretical Distribution of Intelligence Test Scores

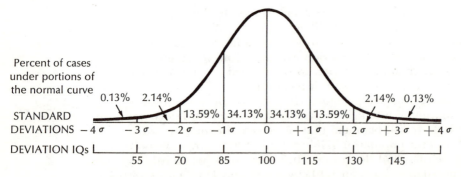

Source: Adapted from *Test Service Bulletin No. 48* (New York: Psychological Corporation, January, 1955). Reproduced by permission of the Corporation.

of 78 is a slow learner may aid in communication or even placement but has very little relevance to the specific educational needs of the child. These needs are best served through intraindividual diagnosis.

As the term is used in this book, the *slow learner* category comprises three subcategories, namely, the borderline child, the mildly mentally retarded child, and the moderately retarded child.

Figure 1.2 illustrates these three subcategories of slow learners, presenting the approximate proportion of the slow-learning population in each subcategory.

Disabled Learners

The concept of the disabled learner is a relatively new one. The *disabled learner* is a child whose learning pattern deviates from the norm to such a degree that it is difficult for the youngster to acquire academic skills such as reading through ordinary classroom instruction.

Historically, this type of child has been given a number of labels, including *brain-injured, minimal-brain dysfunctioning* (MBD), *dyslexic,* and most recently, *learning-disabled.* All of these labels describe a child who learns in a different fashion from the normal learner and therefore requires special teaching techniques. Many disabled learners, though not all, have

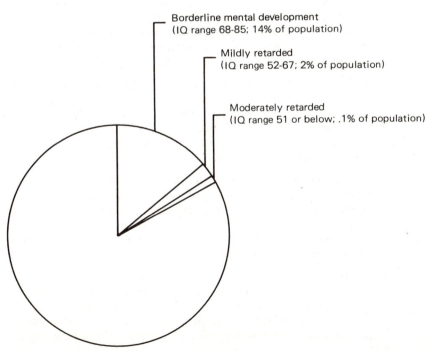

Slow Learners in the Total Population   Figure 1.2

Borderline mental development
(IQ range 68-85; 14% of population)

Mildly retarded
(IQ range 52-67; 2% of population)

Moderately retarded
(IQ range 51 or below; .1% of population)

difficulty learning to read. Although disabled learners are not blind, many cannot see as normal children do; although they are not deaf, many cannot listen or hear normally; although they are neither retarded in mental development nor deprived of educational opportunities, they cannot learn, and many develop personality and social problems as a result.

Definition of Disabled Learners

The disabled learner is the most recently recognized type of exceptional child. The problem of defining learning disabilities has been perplexing. Because learning disabilities is an interdisciplinary field involving many diverse professions, a confusion of terminology and a seeming conflict of ideas pervade current discussions found in the literature. In the various attempts to identify the population of disabled learners, several dimensions of the problem have been considered (Lerner, 1976).

1. *Neurological dysfunction or brain impairment.* Many definitions of learning disabilities either state or imply that the learning impairment is due to some damage or defect of the central nervous system or to a neurological abnormality. This dimension of the definition stresses the physiological cause or etiology of the problem.

2. *Uneven growth pattern.* Many definitions emphasize the irregular development of mental abilities observed in learning-disabled children. An analysis of the subcomponents of mental functioning often reveals that disabled learners are not developing in an even and regular manner. In these children, some subcomponents of mental functioning are very high; others are very low. Such strengths and weaknesses, or unevenness in development, are characteristic of disabled learners.

3. *Difficulty in academic and learning tasks.* Disabled learners come to the attention of parents and school personnel because of the problems they encounter in learning certain tasks, such as talking, arithmetic, reading, spelling, or handwriting. Of major concern to us are the difficulties that disabled learners have learning to read.

4. *Discrepancy between achievement and intelligence.* Another way to identify the population of disabled learners is to determine the difference between what they are judged capable of learning and what they have actually achieved. If this difference is deemed to be significant, then the child may be considered a disabled learner.

5. *Definition by exclusion.* Another way to view the disabled learner is to consider whether the child fits into any other category of exceptionality. That is, disabled learners are not *primarily* mentally retarded, emotionally disturbed, deprived of the opportunity to learn, or sensorially handicapped.

The United States Congress created an official definition of learning disabilities in 1969 when it passed the Children with Specific Learning Disabilities Act. The handicap of specific learning disabilities is further defined in Public Law 94–142, entitled the Education of All Handicapped Children Act of 1975:

> The term 'children with specific learning disabilities' means those children who have a disorder in one or more of the basic psychological processes involved in understanding or in using language, spoken or written, which disorder may manifest itself in imperfect ability to listen, think, speak, read, write or spell, or do mathematical calculations. Such disorders include such conditions as perceptual handicaps, brain injury, minimal brain dysfunction, dyslexia, and developmental aphasia. Such term does not include children who have learning problems which are primarily the result of visual, hearing, or motor handicaps, of mental retardation, of emotional disturbance, or environmental, cultural, or economic disadvantage (Public Law 94–142, Section 5(b)(4), 1975).

A delineation of this definition was proposed by the Office of Education in 1976 (*Federal Register,* Part III, December 29, 1977, pp. 65083). The proposed regulations state that a child can be considered as learning disabled if:

1. The child does not achieve commensurate with his or her age and ability levels in one or more of seven specified areas when provided with learning experiences appropriate for the child's age and ability.
2. There is a severe discrepancy between the child's academic achievement and intellectual ability in one or more of seven areas: (1) oral expression, (2) listening comprehension, (3) written expression, (4) basic reading skill, (5) reading comprehension, (6) mathematics calculation or, (7) mathematics reasoning. Items (4) and (5) relate to the area of reading.

Characteristics of Disabled Learners

The characteristics discussed below are typically used to describe children with learning disabilities. It must be noted that disabled learners are a heterogeneous group and no single set of characteristics can describe all of these children. Each learning disabled individual is unique and may exhibit learning difficulties in one of the following areas but not in the others.

Motor Development. Many disabled learners have difficulty with sensory-motor or perceptual-motor learning. Such children may walk with an awkward gait, be very poor in motor activities such as throwing or catching a ball, or have difficulty with fine motor skills such as buttoning or zipping. The motor development view suggests that the study of human movement is inseparable from the study of learning because as humans move, they learn. An understanding of the dynamics of learning necessarily involves an understanding of movement and motor development. Motor learning thus becomes the foundation for other kinds of later learning. A number of theoretical studies of the disabled learner stress the motor development and motor training of such a child (Barsch, 1967; Getman, 1966; Kephart, 1971).

Another characteristic noted in some disabled learners is *hyperkinesis* or *hyperactivity*. Hyperkinetic children have a tendency to be very restless and are in constant motion. Such children seem unable to concentrate on learning tasks. Hyperkinetic children are easy to spot because they cannot sit in their seats; they are constantly touching things and bumping into furniture or other children.

Perceptual Abilities. The terms *perceptually handicapped* or *perceptually impaired* have been used as synonyms for learning disabled. Disabled learners may have difficulty with visual or auditory perception, both of which will later be discussed as correlates of reading failure. A reading difficulty may reflect a deficit in a perceptual area.

Perception seems to be a learned skill. This implies that the teaching process can have a direct impact on the child's perceptual development. Once an evaluation of perceptual abilities is made, appropriate teaching procedures can improve various perceptual skills, or the learning process can be modified in the light of perceptual difficulties.

Memory. Memory pertains to sensations and data already received and perceived. The ability to receive, store, and retrieve previously experienced sensations and perceptions is called *memory, imagery, or recall.* Children with memory problems seem to forget information shortly after it is learned. They cannot remember oral vocabulary, written words, or computation facts. Disabled learners frequently have difficulty recalling how things looked or sounded.

Memory of past experiences must be retained and compared in order to organize and interpret experience. Otherwise, each experience is unique, with no connection to previous experience and past learning. Memory refers to the recall of nonverbal as well as verbal experiences, to visual as well as to spoken language. Memory problems can be related to a specific perceptual modality, such as visual memory or auditory memory. There are other categories of memory that can be differentiated, such as rote memory, immediate or short-term memory, sequential or serial memory, and long-term memory.

Many disabled learners who have reading difficulties also appear to have memory problems. Instructional activities therefore are designed to help such individuals remember. We assume it is possible to expedite the storage and retrieval of specific kinds of information by improving the techniques of selective observation, organization of materials, and repetition (Chalfant & Scheffelin, 1969).

Language.   The vital role that language plays in learning is under intensive study by a number of disciplines: the language arts and communication specialties, language pathology, linguistics, and psycholinguistics. As we appreciate the importance of language in all aspects of learning, we also realize the consequent intimate relationship between deficits in language development and learning problems. Children with language disorders may have difficulty remembering words or putting words together to make sentences.

It is becoming apparent that language disorders affect many areas of learning. Current research reveals that many children who have difficulty reading suffer from underlying language problems (Vogel, 1975). In many such cases, it is the language problem rather than the reading problem that needs remediation. The study of reading and reading problems, therefore, can be viewed as one aspect of the area of language.

Cognitive Skills.   Some disabled learners have difficulty with cognitive skills. At the apex of the human developmental hierarchy is the acquisition of cognitive skills—the ability to conceptualize, use abstractions, and to think creatively and critically. A disturbance in the thinking process is characteristic of many disabled learners. Furthermore, other disabilities or inadequate development of other abilities—be they motor, perceptual, memory, or language skills—may adversely affect the development of higher cognitive skills.

It is known that even mild brain damage may have severe effects upon concept formation. Impairments in the capacity to categorize and abstract effectively are sometimes among the most easily observed manifestations of brain damage.

Attention.   Disabled learners often have attentional deficits. That is, they have short attention spans and are generally very distractible. They are unable to concentrate on a task for an extended period of time. Such problems require specific teaching techniques.

Maturational, Emotional, and Social Characteristics.   Disabled learners often have the following maturational, emotional, and social characteristics.

1. *Maturation.* Many disabled learners exhibit a slowness in certain specialized aspects of development, which has been termed a *maturational lag* (Bender, 1957). These children may lag in the maturation of certain specific processes that may affect learning to read. It is important for those who have the responsibility of providing the educational environment for such children to be aware of the child's stage of maturation and of any lag that may be present.

2. *Emotional Characteristics.* The personality development of disabled learners may not follow the pattern of the normal child. Children who learn in a normal fashion develop feelings

of self-worth and prideful identity due to their own sense of accomplishment and their awareness that others approve of them. Disabled learners do not follow this pattern. Ego functions are adversely affected if the central nervous system is not intact and if the child is not maturing and learning in a normal and even manner. For disabled learners, their own feelings and feedback from the environment mold a concept of a threatening world and a sense of ineptness and lack of identity. Such children do not receive the normal satisfaction of recognition, achievement, or affection.

The emotional status of the child has an obvious impact on the learning process. Emotional well-being and a favorable attitude are essential for effective learning to take place. The emotional problem must be taken into consideration when plans are made to help the disabled learner who has reading problems. The emotional problem is likely to become acute during the adolescent years.

3. *Social Disabilities.* In addition to all of the problems discussed earlier, the disabled learner often has difficulty learning social skills. It has been suggested that the socially imperceptive child may have a wholly separate learning disability, with characteristics that are different from those of other types of learning disabilities. A deficit in social skills implies a lack of sensitivity to people and a poor perception of social situations. Thus the deficit affects almost every area of the child's life. This kind of disorder may or may not be related to the child's reading difficulty.

Disabled learners are a complex group. Although experts have had much difficulty formulating a definition, every teacher can readily identify the disabled learner in the classroom. The characteristics of the disabled learner include inadequate motor development, including hyperkinetic behavior; perceptual disturbances; memory deficits; language disorders; poor cognitive abilities; and maturational, emotional, and social difficulties. Each disabled learner is different. Some may have several of the characteristics described in this section, while others may exhibit only one. Not all disabled learners have difficulty reading, but many do (Kirk & Elkins, 1975). The concern of this book is solely with the reading problems of slow and disabled learners and not with the other learning difficulties often encountered by children with learning disabilities.

Commonalities in the Teaching of Reading to Slow and Disabled Learners

Two broad categories of handicapped children—slow learners and disabled learners—are described in this chapter. Each type of child is unique: the cause of the problem is different, the characteristics differ, and the training sequence and certification requirements for teachers differ. Yet when it comes to reading, there are many similarities in teaching these two types of exceptional children.

13
Commonalities
in the Teaching
of Reading to
Slow and
Disabled
Learners

First, both groups of children deviate from the norm in the manner in which they learn. There are times when it is difficult in practice to determine if a particular child is primarily a slow learner or a disabled learner. For example, many teachers report that some children who are identified as mentally retarded also exhibit characteristics of those with learning disabilities. In many cases, one diagnostician will classify a child as learning disabled while another will view the child as a slow learner. The labeling process itself has been criticized because it is often used to explain the problems of children rather than offering appropriate ways to instruct the child. A label does not necessarily lead to a useful instructional or remedial program.

A second commonality is the diagnostic procedure. Diagnostic techniques used to analyze the reading problem of the disabled learner are sometimes equally effective in determining the reading difficulties of the slow learner. The same survey and diagnostic tests can be used with both groups. The same informal and observational techniques can be used for both groups. Teachers must ask themselves the same kinds of

Population of Slow and Disabled Learners with Reading Problems   Figure 1.3

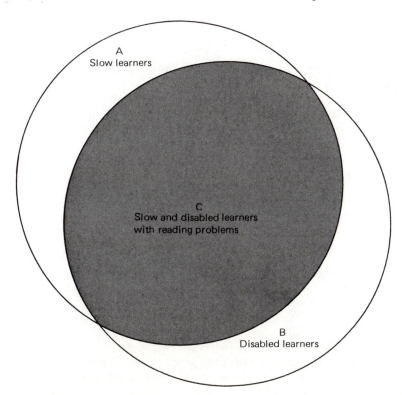

A
Slow learners

C
Slow and disabled learners
with reading problems

B
Disabled learners

questions about a child's reading, whether that child is called a slow learner or a disabled learner.

A third commonality can be found in the instructional methods used for the two groups. There is no single set of techniques for teaching reading to the slow learner or retarded child and no single set of techniques for the disabled learner. Instead, treatment procedures overlap; a particular material or method may be as useful with the slow learner as with the disabled learner.

Finally, there are commonalities between the slow learner and the disabled learner as far as the correlates of reading failure are concerned. Many of the factors that appear to be related to reading failure in one group are also important in the other group. A discussion of these common factors appears later in this chapter.

Thus, it is practical to group the slow and disabled learner together when it comes to the teaching of reading because: (a) it is often difficult to know into which category the child fits, (b) similar diagnostic procedures and tests are used, (c) there is an overlap of instructional methods and materials, and (d) there are commonalities between slow learners and disabled learners in the correlates of reading failure (Dunn, 1971; Keogh & Levitt, 1976; MacMillan, Jones, & Aloia, 1974).

Figure 1.3 illustrates the relationship between slow and disabled learners with reading problems.

Importance of Reading

Why is the teaching of reading to slow and disabled learners important?

After all, it is apparent that in today's world increasing quantities of information come to us through nonprint media. Television has replaced the world of print in many ways. No longer is it necessary to read in order to span either time or distance. Indeed, some educators have suggested that a bookless curriculum be established in our schools. Such an approach to education would provide teaching through the use of nonprint media (such as television, films, audio cassettes, etc.) designed to relate information and to create learning experiences for children (Silberberg & Silberberg, 1969).

Nevertheless, failure to learn to read places severe social and business restrictions upon the individual. While the inability to read and write was both common and acceptable a few generations back, poor reading closes many doors in today's world.

Reading is the basic tool for all other academic learning. The child's ability or inability to read affects learning in all school areas: arithmetic, social studies, English, and science. In fact, all teachers, from preschool through college, teach reading in one way or another. Failure in a subject area is

frequently due not to inability to learn the subject but inability to read the required material.

Reading skills are needed throughout life. With the rapidity of change in today's world, old jobs become obsolete and
there is need for continual retraining for new tasks. It is
predicted that all individuals in every occupational area will
have to retrain themselves to prepare for new jobs many times
during their work careers. Reading is the key tool for retraining and maintaining employable skills. Automation has
resulted in the elimination of many jobs that were filled by
unskilled or semiskilled workers. When such workers are
functionally illiterate, they become chronically unemployable
if they do not possess the minimum reading skills required for
success in other positions. The level of reading competency
required for many occupations is surprisingly high. For example, a recent study showed that an army cook must have
a reading level of 7.0; a repairman or army crewman, 8.0; and
a supply clerk, 9.0 (Sticht, Caylor, Kern, & Fox, 1972).

The *Right to Read* (1972) report made the following comments about the impact of the inability to read:

> Inability to read fluently not only inhibits the effective operation
> of our political system, but contributes substantially to our social
> and economic ills. For example, many of our delinquents and
> criminal offenders have a history of reading difficulties. Our relief
> rolls are filled with people whose lack of adequate reading devel-
> opment renders them almost unemployable in a literature-oriented
> world. Only 25 percent of the jobs now available can be described
> as unskilled or fit for the low achieving reader and by the end of
> the decade the figure is expected to dwindle to less than five
> percent. Jobs cannot be held with yesterday's skills. Without a
> compensating increase in literacy, the rolls of the unemployable
> only continue to swell. The single most frequent cause for referral
> to child psychiatrists and guidance clinics is learning difficulty,
> and a large proportion of those classified as mentally ill are actually
> academically backward . . . the endless facts and statistics which
> document the results of illiteracy cannot express the enormous
> human suffering which accompanies the social and economic
> effects. (p. 592)

The importance of reading skills is highlighted with the
report of lawsuits pending in California, Pennsylvania, and
New Jersey brought by dyslexic adults against the school board
in the districts where they attended school. These individuals
claim that because of the school system's failure to educate
them properly, their earning capacity is decreased. In one
lawsuit, the twenty-year-old victim of dyslexia charges that he
was "socially promoted" and was graduated from high school
at age 18 with a second-grade reading ability. He says that this
has condemned him to pursuing the "most demeaning, unskilled, low-paid manual jobs," despite an above-average
intelligence (*New York Times,* October 4, 1975).

The ability to read is an essential skill for all who live in a
democratic society, including those who are slow or disabled

learners. Reading permits the individual to participate as a citizen in a democratic society; it enables him or her to develop marketable skills; it permits participation in social and cultural affairs; it can fulfill emotional and spiritual needs; and finally, it offers a means of entertainment and enjoyment.

Correlates of Reading Failure

There are many reasons why a child does not learn to read. One reason may be slow learning ability in general, but everyone knows that some children with high IQs have difficulty reading. Consequently, there must be other factors or *correlates* that inhibit learning to read. The correlates of reading failure refer to certain characteristics within the child or in the environment of children who are failing in reading. These correlates are not synonymous with causes, but rather are conditions that often accompany inability to read. The correlates that have been studied may be listed as: (a) physical correlates, (b) environmental correlates, and (c) psychological correlates.

The correlates of reading failure are discussed in this section for the purpose of directing their removal where possible and thereby maximizing reading growth. While these correlates are numerous and deserve extensive examination, this section discusses briefly only *some* of the factors that have been assumed to inhibit the process of learning to read. Many of the correlates not discussed in this section are discussed in other chapters of this book.

Physical Correlates

Neurological Dysfunction

Difficulties in learning to read have been studied for many years. The neurological correlates were studied by Dr. James Hinshelwood, a Scottish ophthalmologist who published extensively on this topic as early as 1905. In his book entitled *Congenital Word Blindness* (1917), he described individuals who had lost the ability to read as a result of acquired brain damage. *Alexia* is the term used to refer to this condition. Hinshelwood concluded that a congenital brain defect that resulted in the loss of the visual memory centers for letters and words, which are situated in the angular supramarginal gyrus of the left side of the brain, could also cause a reading problem. Hinshelwood entitled his book *Congenital Word Blindness* to differentiate the condition he was studying from acquired word blindness and to indicate that it occurs as a congenital defect in children who are otherwise normal.

Many authorities believe that children who are otherwise normal but who have great difficulty learning to read must have something wrong with their neurological make-up. When one uses the term *dyslexia,* one is inferring that the child has some brain pathology that is inhibiting the ability to read. In most cases, neurologists are unable to find a neurological defect; hence the inference of minimal-brain dysfunction is occasionally made.

Dr. Samuel T. Orton (1937), a professor of neurology at the University of Iowa, rejected the concept of dyslexia in children with reading problems. Instead, Orton professed that the inability to learn to read was the result of a lack of cerebral dominance. The reading errors reported in his cases were mainly reversals in reading and writing. He called this condition *strephosymbolia,* meaning "twisted symbols." With this theory he attempted to explain why children read and write letters and words in reverse fashion, such as *on* for *no* and *was* for *saw*.

The work of Hinshelwood and Orton stimulated further investigation and research into neurological dysfunction as a correlate of reading failure. Recent work in this area has been contributed by Critchly (1964), Hermann (1959), Johnson and Myklebust (1967), Money (1966), and others.

Cerebral Dominance and Laterality

Interest in neurological correlates and the hemispheres of the brain as they relate to reading problems led to specific investigations of two more correlates—cerebral dominance and laterality.

The brain is divided into two halves—the right and the left hemispheres. For most people, the left hemisphere is dominant over the right. One theory of reading failure points to the lack of cerebral or *hemispheric dominance*. That is, one half of the brain has failed to take over control of language functions.

Laterality refers to the tendency of individuals to have a preference for using one side of their bodies. For example, an individual may show preference for using the right hand, right foot, right eye, and right ear. A person who fails to establish this preference is said to have mixed or crossed laterality. Some authorities believe mixed laterality, namely, left-eye dominance with right-hand dominance, to be another correlate of reading failure.

Following Orton's work, many studies were done on handedness, eyedness, mixed laterality, and cerebral dominance as factors that inhibit the normal child's ability to learn to read. Despite the many studies of these correlates that appear in the literature, their relationship to reading difficulties has still not been proved conclusively.

In spite of the lack of evidence from research, however, many practitioners still believe that lack of directional orientation, mixed eye-hand dominance, and other laterality factors have inhibited some children's ability to learn to read. It is possible that the so-called controlled experimental studies may not have been sensitive enough in terms of selection of subjects or in the isolation of other variables to find the hypothesized relationship.

It is interesting to note that concepts of mixed laterality and cerebral dominance, which were hypothesized by Hughlings Jackson as early as the late nineteenth century (Taylor, 1932), seem to persist generation after generation—for the theory is reintroduced every decade. Perhaps there is some basis for the theory that has not yet been demonstrated clearly. The fact that many of these children have been taught to read might indicate that it is not laterality alone that is responsible for the reading difficulty, but possibly it is the condition of mixed laterality *plus* inadequate training procedures that contribute to retardation in reading.

Visual Defects

Evidence in the research literature on the relationship between visual defects and reading problems is contradictory (Lerner, 1976; Park, 1968; Robinson, 1946). Comparisons between children with visual defects and those without such defects have not resulted in clear-cut conclusions about visual problems as a correlate of reading disability—for example:

1. Some studies have shown that far-sighted children are found more frequently among reading disability cases.
2. Some studies conclude that eye muscle imbalance is more significantly related to reading failure than are acuity factors.
3. Still other studies indicate that visual defects in children have no direct relationship to failure in reading.

Some clinical studies of individual children, however, do suggest a relationship between reading failure and visual problems. Furthermore, other studies indicate that there are fewer reading problems with visually defective children when they are taught by a specific method. For example, children with severe visual handicaps are generally taught with a phonics method, while deaf or near-deaf children are taught by the sight method.

In conclusion, despite contradictory evidence, it is important that any visual defects be detected and if possible corrected before attempts are made to teach a child to read.

Auditory Defects

Auditory defects refer to problems in acuity—the ability to hear sounds. To measure hearing loss, two dimensions of hearing are used: intensity and frequency. *Intensity,* or loudness, is measured in decibels. Normal conversation measures about 50 decibels. *Frequency* refers to the pitch of the sound and is measured from 500 to 8,000 Hz. Vowels are often the low frequency sounds; consonants (e.g., *s, sh, z, f*) are high frequency sounds. Children with a hearing loss at certain frequencies may miss specific sounds in conversational language.

Generally, marked hearing losses are associated with reading retardation (Dechant, 1970). It has been estimated that 5 percent of the general population have serious hearing impairments (Bond & Tinker, 1967). Among the mentally retarded population, the incidence of hearing loss has been reported to range from 5 to 50 percent. However, little specific information concerning the incidence of hearing loss among the borderline retarded or learning-disabled population has been reported (Siegenthaler, Sallade, & Lordibuona, 1972).

A clear-cut relationship between hearing impairment and reading difficulties has not been documented in the research. Although it is well established that hard-of-hearing children are retarded in reading, the research does not indicate that the hearing acuity of the general population of school children is highly correlated with reading achievement (Bond & Tinker, 1967; Harris & Sipay, 1975; Reynolds, 1953; Robinson, 1946). The studies relating hearing acuity to reading have been conducted with large groups of children, which may account for this lack of correlation. Nonetheless, in individual clinical cases, hearing loss is often noted as a correlate of the reading problem.

Hearing difficulty may be detected in the classroom by observation of the following symptoms: many requests for repetitions, misunderstanding of directions, complaints of ringing or buzzing sounds, turning the ear toward the speaker or cupping a hand behind the ear, a blank expression or scowl while trying to listen, earaches, colds, unusual amounts of ear-wax, monotonous speaking voice, and turning a radio or television up to an unusually loud level (Bond & Tinker, 1967).

Despite lack of conclusive evidence that hearing defects bear a direct relationship to reading failure, it is advisable to have any suspected auditory problems checked. It is best to remove any physical factors that may possibly be contributing to a child's difficulty learning to read.

Heredity and Genetics

Some authorities explain reading disabilities on the basis of inheritability, since several children with severe reading difficulties are sometimes found in the same generation or family (Hallgren, 1950; Hermann, 1959). Other studies of twins and siblings indicate that reading disabilities exist in families. Recently, out of a total of 676 pairs of like-sexed twins Bakwin (1973) found 97 (14.5 percent) that had a history of reading disabilities. Of the monozygotic (identical) twins, 84 percent were concordant, while of the dizygotic (fraternal) twins, only 29 percent were concordant. This study gives support to a genetic etiology of reading disability.

Currently, a study of the inheritability of reading disabilities is being conducted by Professor John Defries at the Institute of Behavior Genetics of the University of Colorado. A part of the study has been reported by Frances Irene Lewitter (1975). Her data support the hypothesis that specific learning disabilities are inheritable.

To the authors' knowledge, no chromosomal aberrations have been found in cases of severe reading disability such as have been found in Down's syndrome. Because it is possible that instructional techniques can compensate for biological diversity, it is difficult to ascribe reading failure to heredity alone until research evidence becomes more conclusive.

Environmental Correlates

A number of correlates related to reading failure can be classified as environmental because they are within the environment in which the child lives and learns. The correlates discussed in this section include: (a) poor school experiences, (b) cultural differences, (c) language problems, and (d) emotional and social problems.

Poor School Experiences

If there is one thing that educational researchers agree on, it is that the teacher is a key ingredient in a child's success in learning to read. Unfortunately, many children fail in reading because of school-related factors. Such factors include use of teachers who do not understand the child and the child's problem; use of teachers who are not well trained to teach reading; the child's frequent absence from school due to illness, moving, and truancy; the child's absence from school during the beginning stages of reading. Often, a study of the child's school history will reveal such early school experiences.

Cultural Differences

Many reports indicate that children who live in an environment that is culturally different from the mainstream of American culture tend to have low reading attainment. These children are given a variety of labels, such as *disadvantaged children, inner-city children, poor children,* and *minority group children.* The Coleman report, a study of the relationship between cultural differences and academic achievement, found that the differential achievement of students was due to factors outside the school program rather than to factors controlled by the school system (Coleman, 1966). That is, the child's environment, not the school, was the factor that differentiated these students.

Indeed, many studies of the reading achievement of the

culturally different student population indicate that the educational gap tends to widen as the students get older. By secondary school age, the disadvantaged have reading levels that are two to three years below the norm for their age group (Dyer, 1968).

Language Problems

There are two types of language problem that seem to interfere with learning to read. One kind of language problem is referred to as a *language disorder*. This problem is discussed in the section on psychological correlates, and it refers to the language of children who are not developing normal language patterns despite the fact that they live in a standard English-language environment.

The second type of language problem is found among children who have an environmentally based language difficulty. Their problem is called a *language difference*, that is, they develop language in a normal fashion but their language reflects the environment in which they live. Children who live in the inner city or in a rural area have dialect differences—such as Black English or an Appalachian dialect. Children who live in an environment in which a foreign language prevails may have a bilingual problem. In both cases, the language spoken in their native environment differs from the language of the school. This difference appears to be a serious problem that interferes with learning to read.

Some children are handicapped with both kinds of language problem. Not only do they have an environmentally caused language difference, but they also have a psychological language disorder.

Emotional and Social Problems

Children who are failing in reading often have accompanying emotional and social problems. Because children with reading difficulties are usually studied a few years after the problem begins, it is hard to tell which is the primary problem—the reading problem or the emotional problem.

Harris and Sipay (1975) distinguish several types of emotional problems that are contributing causes of reading disabilities. They include the following: (a) conscious refusal to learn, (b) overt hostility, (c) negative conditioning to reading, (d) displacement hostility, (e) resistance to pressure, (f) clinging or dependency, (g) quick discouragement, (h) belief that success is dangerous, (i) extreme distractibility or restlessness, (j) absorption in a private world.

As the child approaches the adolescent years, the emotional problems tend to increase. Teachers report that by the time pupils with severe reading problems enter the secondary school, many have accompanying personality problems.

Psychological Correlates

Many studies have been undertaken to determine psychological differences between good and poor readers. As with the physical and emotional factors, the results of these psychological studies are not consistent. However, a few differentiation functions are commonly noted, including auditory perception, sound blending, auditory closure, speed of visual perception, visualization or visual memory, and language deficits—inability to express thoughts and concepts.

Auditory Perception

Auditory perception is the ability to organize the sensory data received through the ears, and problems with it are more highly related to reading difficulties than are auditory acuity problems. This correlate includes the ability to discriminate and differentiate speech sounds as well as the ability to blend sounds (Bond & Tinker, 1967). It also includes the functions of auditory closure and auditory memory. Children with auditory discrimination problems may not be able to differentiate between the words *chin* and *shin* or the pair of words *pin* and *pen*. The child with a blending problem may not be able to blend the sounds *m—a—n* into the word *man*.

Auditory perception difficulties are frequent among atypical learners. Studies have shown that both slow learners and disabled learners have difficulty with this correlate of reading (Bateman & Wetherell, 1965; Gillespie & Johnson, 1974; Sabatino, 1973; Wiseman, 1965). Children with a deficit in auditory perception often have difficulty learning phonics skills.

Sound Blending

Children who have a disability in sound blending at the first-grade level appear to have more difficulty learning to read than do those without such a disability. Elkins (1972) states that sound-blending disabilities are found more frequently among poor readers than among good readers at the first- and second-grade level, but that it is not an important factor at grades three, four, and above. In other words, sound blending may be a factor in learning to read, especially when reading is taught by a phonics method, but it may not be a factor at the more advanced stages of reading.

Auditory Closure

Auditory closure is the ability to grasp a word when only part of the word is presented. A child must utilize closure to recognize the incomplete word. Auditory closure is needed, for example, to grasp a telephone conversation when there are background noises interfering with and blurring some of the sounds. According to Elkins (1972), this ability shows up more in the third grade than in the first grade and appears to be correlated with success in reading.

Speed of Visual Perception

Some studies have reported visual perceptual speed (the ability to perceive visual stimuli rapidly) to be a factor related to reading. Through his analytic studies, Thurstone (1960) was the first to isolate visual perceptual speed as one of the primary mental abilities. It is reasonable to expect that in the advanced stages of reading, success involves rapid perception of the visual symbols. Goins (1958) found that speed of perception enhances learning to read.

Visualization or Visual Memory

Visual memory has long been associated with reading ability. Hinshelwood (1917) stated that a lesion in the memory center in the left angular gyrus in the left hemisphere produces word blindness. Recently, studies by Kass (1966), Macione (1969), and others have shown that those who do poorly in the early stages of reading instruction have poorer sequential visual memory than good readers of the same grade level. Visual sequential memory seems not to be a factor, however, with children 9 and 10 years of age who are at a more advanced stage of reading.

Language Disorders: Inability to Express Thoughts and Concepts

Language disorders refer to a lack of normal speech and language development despite the fact that the child has been reared in a standard middle-class language environment and has had normal speech and language opportunities and stimulation. A language disorder must be differentiated from the language difference problem, which was discussed in the previous section on "Environmental Correlates." The child's language disorder could appear in one or more of the following categories: deficits of articulation, delayed speech, syntax or word order problems, or a limited vocabulary.

Interrelationship of Correlates of Reading Failure

Diagnosis and treatment would be much easier if a single factor could be determined to be the only cause of the reading problem. For most slow and disabled learners who are failing in reading, a combination of factors appears to be related to the reading problem.

It is difficult if not impossible for the teacher to change, remove, or ameliorate certain of these factors, particularly those classified as physical and environmental correlates. The psychological correlates, however, can often be affected by the teacher. Thus, many of the teaching techniques suggested in this book emphasize remediation of the psychological correlates. This is particularly evident in the discussion of components of reading readiness and of readiness activities in Chapter 2.

Implications of the Correlates of Reading Failure

Research findings do not consistently relate any of the correlates under discussion directly to reading failure. This inconsistency may be due to the fact that reading disabilities cannot be isolated from the instructional factor. The studies on the physical and psychological characteristics of children with reading problems must be related to the methods of teaching these children if any one of these factors can be ascribed as a correlate. The phenomenon of "Aptitude-Instructional-Interaction" must be taken into account: to find a relationship between the aptitude or characteristic of the individual and his learning achievement, it is necessary to describe the aptitude in relation to the instructional interaction.

This approach seems logical, since difficulties in reading have been corrected when a remedial method has been found that matches the abilities or disabilities of the child or that compensates for the deficit discovered. For example, some children who have a deficit in visual memory have been able to learn to read by a method that emphasizes the writing of words and sentences from memory. The Fernald method (discussed in Chapter 6) is such a program. This method trains visual memory while teaching the reading of words and sentences. In these children, reading difficulties cannot be ascribed to a visual memory deficit alone, but rather to a failure to teach reading by a method that develops visual memory.

Some children with marked visual defects have been found to be retarded in reading when taught by a sight method. When these same children are taught by a phonics method, they may not develop difficulties in reading. In these cases, it is not the visual defect that causes the disability but the use of inappropriate methods for the particular child. This is probably why some researchers find a relationship between visual defects and reading difficulties, while others do not.

It is likewise true that if a child has a hearing defect and is taught by a phonics method, he or she has a good chance of having difficulty learning to read. Such a child would probably progress faster if taught by a sight method.

If one were to generalize from these studies, one could say the following:

1. Some children with visual memory problems can learn to read through a memory training program in reading similar to Fernald's kinesthetic method. This involves

direct training of defective visual memory in a reading task.

2. Some children with visual deficits can learn best through a phonics method. Phonics is an auditory, compensatory method to aid visual recognition.
3. For hearing-handicapped children, the "look-and-say" or sight method may be the most beneficial. The sight method is direct and may be compensatory for these children, providing they do not have other problems.
4. Children with directional orientation problems exhibiting reversal errors in reading and writing require a direct approach rather than a compensatory one. Writing letters, words, and sentences, particularly from memory, helps remove reversal errors.
5. Children with sound-blending disabilities are best taught by direct training of blending and phonics.

Research findings do not indicate any direct causal relation between these correlates and reading failure. The instructional factor must be taken into account. In other words, properly designed and applied instruction may be able to compensate for any of the correlates that would otherwise interfere with the child's ability to learn to read.

Instructional adaptations can ameliorate or compensate, at least partially, for the learning problems of even slow-learning or learning-disabled children. A more detailed discussion of the research on reading in slow and disabled learners appears in Chapter 9.

Cases of Slow and Disabled Learners with Reading Problems

Children can be retarded in reading for various reasons and in varying degrees. In the previous discussion of the correlates of reading retardation, it was pointed out that these correlates cannot be isolated from the instructional factors. It follows that regardless of the factors that may have retarded reading, there may be a teaching method that can counteract the factors. This section concentrates on variations in reading ability and the kinds of children that need special remediation. Several representative case studies of slow and disabled learners are presented.

Variations in Reading Ability

A twelve-year-old slow learning child with an IQ of 75 will have a mental age of approximately 9-0. An average nine-year-old child is usually in the fourth grade and is reading at the fourth-grade level. Suppose this child is reading at the third-grade level; would he or she be considered a child with a reading disability requiring remediation? Likewise, will the nine-year-old child of average intelligence be considered to have a reading disability if he or she reads at the third-grade level? Both of these children are reading one year below their grade expectancy based on mental age.

Suppose these two children read at the second-grade level or even at the first-grade level. Would they be considered disabled in reading?

In most instances, the determination of a disability is arbitrary and dependent on the criteria that are established. Since humans are characterized by variability, we can expect a certain range of variability to be average or normal. If the average weight of a woman is 120 pounds, we do not consider a woman who weighs 100 pounds or 130 pounds to be abnormal. But we do consider extremes, especially in those who have some endocrine disorder like cretinism, to be abnormal. Similarly, we would consider a dwarf of four feet, five inches, or a man with gigantism who is six feet, ten inches tall to be abnormal. Most persons who deviate markedly in height have a biological or biochemical abnormality that retards their growth or that increases it abnormally.

Likewise, we can tolerate a certain degree of variation in reading ability in a grade, but when the retardation is extreme enough to require special attention, it should be considered deviant.

For the purpose of this book we will define the child with a specific reading disability as one who (a) has had ordinary exposure to reading instruction and has not learned, (b) has the potential for reading at a higher level if subjected to a special method of teaching reading, and (c) is sensorially relatively intact, that is, not blind or deaf.

An Operational Definition

Any definition needs an operational explanation, and the above definition is no exception. The following can help operationalize the definition.

1. Ordinary instruction in school implies that the child has been exposed to school from the age of 6 or 7, and after several years in the classroom where other children have learned to read, the child has failed to learn. In contrast, there is the child who has not attended school up to the age of 8 or 9, who, after being admitted to school at that age, is found to be a nonreader. When exposed to ordinary reading instruction, this child will probably learn to read very well. He or she will not necessarily need special methods since the developmental methods used in the schools will very likely be adequate. Some children, because of home conditions or personality clashes with the teacher, refuse or fail to learn to read in the

first grade and become hostile and negativistic toward school. These children do not necessarily need special methods of instruction but a change of environment. They need an environment that assures success and furnishes proper reinforcement for learning.

2.   It is necessary to determine a child's potential for learning to read. If a child is obviously mentally retarded with a mental age level below age 6, it is likely, but not definite, that he or she will have difficulty learning to read. A practical guide for estimating potential is (a) the mental age and (b) arithmetic computation. Mental age correlates at .50 to .60 with reading achievement. It is one of the few measures that has some reliable relationship to reading achievement. Arithmetic computation is another indication of potential since it indicates what the child has learned in a school subject unrelated to reading. A child who has not attended school or one who has not learned because of severe emotional problems or personality conflict with the teacher would be retarded in both reading and arithmetic.

Inability to learn to read has been called *word blindness, alexia,* or *dyslexia.* These terms denote some cortical deficiency that renders the individual incapable of learning to read. Educators, however, prefer a descriptive term such as *reading disability* because it does not imply knowledge of a causal or etiological factor.

The Concept of Discrepancies

A general guide for determining whether a child has a reading disability and requires specialized techniques of remediation is to determine the degree of discrepancy between intelligence and achievement that is tolerable. A one-and-one-half- to two-year discrepancy for children under grade four might be acceptable. For example, a child whose mental age is 8–0 and whose arithmetic computation achievement is at the third-grade level, but who reads at the middle of the first grade would be considered to have a one-and-one-half-year discrepancy.

The concept of discrepancy applies to mentally superior, mentally normal, and mentally retarded children. Figures 1.4, 1.5, and 1.6 present cases of slow and disabled learners with and without reading disabilities.

Some Illustrative Cases

Tim

Tim (Figure 1.4) is a fourth-grade boy whose age is 10 years, 8 months. He has an IQ of 100 and a mental age of 10–8. In arithmetic computation he is in the fourth grade. In reading and spelling Tim is in high first or beginning second grade. The average child with an IQ of 100 and a mental age of 10–0 is usually in the fifth grade in reading. Tim's reading ability is three years below his mental capacity and two-and-one-half years below his arithmetic achievement. He is, therefore, considered to have a severe reading disability. The arithmetic computation grade indicates that in a subject unrelated to reading he has made considerable progress. It appears from the educational profile that his disability is specific to reading. Tim's reading scores show that he is only slightly higher in word recognition and word discrimination than he is in oral and silent reading.

Sandra

The profile shown in Figure 1.5 is that of Sandra, who is placed in the third grade although she is eleven years old. Her mental age is 7–8, giving her an IQ of 70. Her arithmetic is at the second-grade level, and on spelling and reading tests she scores at the second-grade level. Children of 7 years, 8 months are expected to be in the second grade. Therefore, although for her chronological age Sandra is retarded in reading, she is not considered to have a reading disability because her mental capacity and other achievements do not predict more than second-grade reading achievement.

Figure 1.4   Educational Profile of Tim

Grade	C.A.	M.A.	Arithmetic	Spelling	Oral reading	Word reading	Silent reading	Word discrimination
8	13-6							
7	12-6							
6	11-6							
5	10-6							
4	9-6							
3	8-6							
2	7-6							
1	6-6							

Barbara

Shown in Figure 1.6 is the profile of a twelve-year-old girl,
Barbara, with an IQ of 75 and a mental age of 9–0 on the
Stanford-Binet. She has been promoted to the fourth grade
because she is capable of fourth-grade arithmetic. Her reading and spelling are consistently first-grade level. Although
Barbara is borderline in intelligence, she is considered to have
a reading disability because her mental age and her arithmetic
warrant fourth-grade achievement. Her reading ability is
two-and-one-half years below her other capacities.

Frank Smith

The hardship an adult nonreader suffers is revealed in the case
of Frank Smith, a thirty-six-year-old man of average intelligence who sought help at a university learning disabilities
clinic. Employed as a journeyman painter and supporting his
wife and four children comfortably, Mr. Smith had to learn
to cope with many daily situations that required reading skills.
He was unable to read the color labels on paint cans; he
could not decipher street and road signs; he could not find
street addresses or use a city map. He had learned to manage
by compensating for his inability to read. He visually memo-
rized the color codes on the paint cans to determine the color;
he tried to limit his work to a specific area of the city because he could not read street signs. When sent into an

Educational Profile of Sandra   Figure 1.5

Grade	C.A.	M.A.	Arithmetic	Spelling	Oral reading	Word reading	Silent reading	Word discrimination
8	13-6							
7	12-6							
6	11-6							
5	10-6							
4	9-6							
3	8-6							
2	7-6							
1	6-6							

unfamiliar area, he would ask a fellow worker who could provide directions to accompany him, or he would request help from residents of the area to help him reach his destination. He watched television to keep abreast of current affairs, and his wife read and answered correspondence for him. However, inevitably the day came when advancement was no longer possible if he did not learn to read. Moreover, his children were rapidly acquiring the reading skills that he did not possess. His handicap was a continual threat for him and finally led him to search for help. It is remarkable that after so many years of failure and frustration he still had the interest and motivation to attempt once again the formidable task of learning to read.

In this case, intensive diagnosis and teaching put Mr. Smith on the road to reading.

Illiterates in the Army—World War II

Adults with reading disabilities were seen by the senior author during World War II, when the army admitted what it called illiterates and set up special training programs for them. Many of these men were undiagnosed slow learners or disabled learners during their school careers and they went into the army unable to read the directions, signs, and other notices required of military personnel. Consequently, the United States Army had to set up special training units to teach men how to read and write. In most cases, this was accomplished in an eight-week period in camps. The army trained approximately one-third of a million men in this way.

Figure 1.6   Educational Profile of Barbara

Grade	C.A.	M.A.	Arithmetic	Spelling	Oral reading	Word reading	Silent reading	Word discrimination
8	13-6							
7	12-6							
6	11-6							
5	10-6							
4	9-6							
3	8-6							
2	7-6							
1	6-6							

This book is designed to help teachers and prospective teachers teach reading to slow and disabled learners. Many specific examples of teaching techniques are included in appropriate chapters. Chapter 1 has presented an overview of the problem of teaching reading to slow and disabled learners. Chapter 2 deals with the problem of preparing children for reading.

Methods of teaching reading are presented in Chapters 3 through 6. The methods chapters are divided as follows: the developmental reading methods and materials used with normal learners are described in Chapter 3, adaptations of these developmental methods for use with atypical learners at the beginning stages of reading are presented in Chapter 4, adaptations of developmental methods for use with students at the later stages of reading are described in Chapter 5, and specialized remedial reading techniques are presented in Chapter 6.

Evaluation of reading is discussed in Chapters 7 and 8. Informal assessment procedures such as teacher-made tests are described in Chapter 7; formal assessment procedures, such as standardized tests, are presented in Chapter 8.

In Chapter 9 reading research is discussed, with emphasis on reading research dealing with slow and disabled learners.

Summary

Slow and disabled learners have difficulty learning to read by ordinary methods of instruction. This chapter has dealt with the characteristics of children who are slow learners and those who are disabled learners.

Reading problems often occur with children who are slow or disabled learners. In this book the term slow-learning children includes children who are borderline (IQ of 85 to 68), mildly retarded (IQ of 67 to 52), and moderately retarded (IQ of 51 to 36). Disabled learners are children whose learning patterns deviate from the norm to such a degree that it is difficult for them to acquire academic skills such as reading through ordinary classroom instruction.

The disabled learner may be classified on the basis of neurological dysfunction, uneven growth patterns, difficulty in academic and learning tasks, discrepancy between potential and achievement, and through the exclusion of other primary disabilities. Learning-disabled children are discussed in terms of physical, psychological, language, social, and emotional characteristics. Illustrative case studies of slow and disabled learners with and without reading problems have been presented.

Despite the fact that much information comes to us from nonprint media, reading remains an essential skill for every individual.

Children who have a slow rate of learning, children who have a lag in maturation, and children who have an atypical manner of learning need help acquiring the skills that will enable them to benefit from reading instruction. This set of skills is often referred to as *reading readiness*. This chapter (a) discusses the concept of reading readiness, (b) examines the components of reading readiness, (c) presents tests of readiness abilities, and (d) suggests selected activities for building reading readiness skills.

The Concept of Reading Readiness

The term *readiness* refers to a state of development that is needed before a skill can be learned. For example, readiness for walking requires a certain level of development of the nervous system, adequate muscle strength, and the development of certain motor skills. Until an infant has these abilities, attempts to teach walking would be premature and unsuccessful. In a very different area of learning, an individual must have certain mathematical skills and knowledge before he or she can profit from a course in calculus. The term *reading readiness* refers to the collection of integrated abilities, traits, and skills that the child needs in order to learn the complex process called reading.

While reading readiness skills may be picked up in an incidental fashion by the normal learner and reinforced within the regular kindergarten curriculum, slow and disabled learners require special attention in terms of both diagnosis and teaching. Some schools have developed programs to identify "high-risk" youngsters at the preschool age. Three-, four-, and five-year-olds who evidence potential learning problems can be discovered through screening and assessment techniques. Special teaching programs are needed to help youngsters who are likely to fail to acquire the prerequisite skills and abilities for reading.

Research and observation suggest that many factors contribute to reading readiness. Important components of reading readiness are (a) mental maturity, (b) visual abilities, (c) auditory abilities, (d) speech and language development, (e) thinking skills, (f) physical fitness and motor development, (g) social and emotional development, and (h) interest and motivation.

In a sense, these factors comprise a systems network in that they interact and interrelate with each other. For example, thinking skills are closely related to visual functions, auditory functions, and language.

Figure 2.1 presents these factors as a system, all of whose components are needed by the child to assure success in reading. Slow or disabled learners are likely to be deficient in several of these components.

While researchers have found these factors to be highly correlated with learning to read, a single factor cannot be assumed to be the cause of reading failure. Causation and correlation signify different relationships. Statistical data might show a high correlation between the appearance of storks and an increase in the birth rate; such a correlation, however, does not imply a causal relationship between the two. The acquisition of a prerequisite skill does not assure that the child will learn to read; it means only that the child is better able to benefit from reading instruction.

A Systems Network of Components of Reading Readiness   Figure 2.1

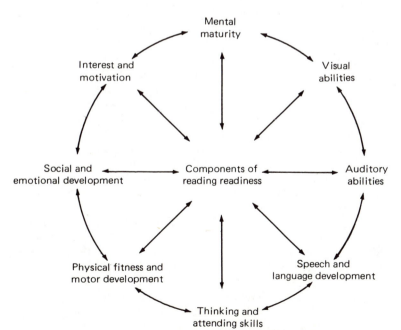

This section examines the components of reading readiness; the next section offers suggestions for teaching readiness skills.

Mental Maturity

Mental maturity refers to the overall intellectual development of the child, and thus is related to all the other readiness components. Although it cannot be determined when an individual child should begin to learn to read, it is unlikely that children with low intelligence can learn to read by the time they reach the chronological age of 6. A mental age of 6–6 is often considered to be the minimal mental age required for learning to read. Whatever mental age is used as the norm for determining readiness for reading, there will always be exceptions to the rule.

Any norm should, of course, be taken as a suggestion for a group and is not necessarily applicable to an individual child. For example, Davidson (1931) taught children with a mental age of 4–0 to read. Durkin (1966) identified and studied young children who learned to read before they entered school; she found that on the average, they possessed superior intelligence as well as other characteristics and experiences that engendered early reading. The decision about when to teach the child to read should not be based on a single predictor such as mental age (Gillespie & Johnson, 1974).

Educability of Intelligence

There are two opposing views concerning the *educability of intelligence,* or the acceleration of the mental maturation in a child through home and school training. The first, known as the heredity viewpoint, hypothesizes that training cannot develop mental maturity faster than the child develops naturally. The proponents of this point of view believe that it is best to delay reading instruction until the child achieves sufficient mental maturity to begin reading. On the other hand, proponents of the environmental viewpoint believe that the factors in intelligence that are required for reading are at least partly the product of early home and school training. In their view, it is best to establish a stimulating environment that will accelerate mental growth. If this is done and mental maturity can be obtained earlier, then the teaching of reading can begin earlier.

Studies on the inheritance of mental deficiency led Goddard (1916) to conclude that mental deficiency is inherited in about 80 percent of cases and that training would not alleviate mental deficiency. In more recent years, Goddard's view, which had been widely accepted, has been strikingly challenged.

Skeels and Dye (1939) reported on an experiment in Iowa in which thirteen children less than 3 years of age were removed from an orphanage and committed to an institution for mental defectives. These infants were placed, only one to a ward, with adolescent mentally retarded girls, who gave them attention and training. These children had an average IQ of 64 on the *Kuhlmann Test of Mental Development,* with initial IQs ranging from 35 to 89. A contrast group of twelve children remained in the orphanage. This group had an initial IQ of 87.6. Two years later both groups of children were tested. The researchers reported that the babies who had received a great deal of attention and stimulation from the retarded girls in the institution increased their IQ scores by 27.5 points, while those who remained in the orphanage in an unstimulating environment experienced a decrease of 26.2 points in their IQ scores. This experiment, which challenged the common belief in the constancy of the IQ, was criticized severely.

In follow-up studies of these children, Skeels (1942) found three years later that the experimental children had retained their accelerated rate of development in foster homes, while the orphanage children retained their decreased intellectual performance.

Skeels followed up these subjects twenty-one years later (Skeels, 1966). All of the twenty-five subjects were located. He found that the thirteen children in the experimental group were all self-supporting. Not one of them was in an institution. Of the twelve in the contrast group, one had died and four were wards of institutions. In education, the experimental group had completed a median of twelfth grade. Four subjects had college education. The contrast group completed a median of third grade.

Kirk conducted an experiment on "the effects of pre-school education on the mental and social development of young, mentally retarded children." In this experiment, two preschools for the mentally retarded were organized—one in the community and the other in an institution. Descriptions of the experiment were published by Kirk in 1958 and 1965. The results of the experiment are shown in Figures 2.2 and 2.3.

Figure 2.2 presents test-retest differences in intelligence quotients (IQs) and social quotients (SQs) for a four-year period, comparing the IQ and SQ changes of the two groups of children.

The top bars represent changes seen in fifteen institutionalized children who received intensive preschool training from the ages of 4 to 6 and then attended either the regular institution school or public city schools. The first bar represents changes in IQ score on the *Stanford-Binet* test, the second on the *Kuhlmann Tests of Mental Development,* and the third on the *Vineland Social Maturity Scale.*

The lower (shaded) bars show the comparable changes in the test scores of the contrast group of children who received no preschool education but attended the institution school after the age of 6.

Comparing the two groups, we can readily see that the children who received the two years of preschool education increased in both mental and social development and retained the increase to the age of 8; those who did not receive pre-school education dropped in both IQ and SQ.

Test results are not the final criteria of the effects of training. In this particular experiment, six of the fifteen experimental children progressed so rapidly that they were paroled to family life. None of the contrast group was paroled from the institution during this period. One boy in the experimental group had been committed to the institution by the courts when he was two and one-half years old upon the recommendation of two physicians and one psychologist. The courts declared him to be feebleminded with a convulsive disorder. When the boy was admitted to the preschool at the age of 4, he was not talking intelligibly and had an abnormal EEG; however, he had no further convulsions. On various tests he achieved an IQ score of 50 to 64. During the first year and one-half of training his IQ increased so dramatically

Figure 2.2   IQ and SQ Change Scores of Institutionalized Retarded Children as a Function of Preschool Experience

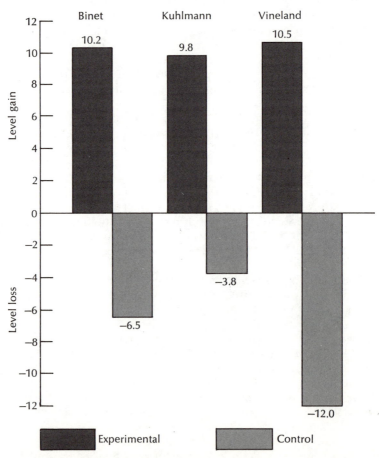

Source: Kirk, Samuel A., *Educating Exceptional Children,* Boston, Houghton Mifflin Company, 1972, p. 180.

that he was no longer eligible for retention in the institution. He was therefore paroled and later adopted by an upper middle-class family. Although he had some difficulty learning to read in the first grade and was allowed to repeat the fourth grade, he continued to progress under rather intensive remedial education. His EEG at the age of 8 was still abnormal. At age 23 this young man graduated from college with above-average grades and assumed a teaching position.

In another experiment with retarded children in the community, one group of children received preschool training, while their twins and siblings served as a contrast group, receiving no preschool education but entering school at the usual age of 6 (Kirk, 1958, 1965).

Figure 2.3 shows comparisons of these children from psychosocially deprived homes under three different circumstances.

The first bar in Figure 2.3 represents the progress of four children who were removed from inadequate homes by the social agency, placed in foster homes, and sent to the special preschool. By age 8, this group made marked gains.

The second bar represents the progress of a group of twelve children who remained in their own homes but attended the experimental preschool. These children made substantial

Average Change in Levels of Development as a Function of Preschool and Foster Home Experience   Figure 2.3

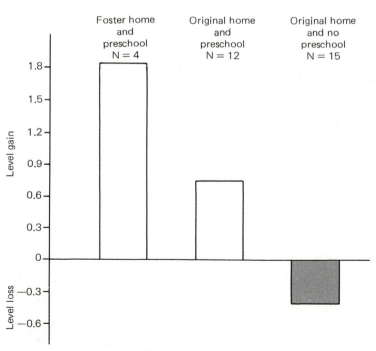

Source: **Kirk, Samuel A., "The Education of Intelligence,"** *The Slow Learning Child,* 20 (July 1973): 67–83.

progress in test results and in ratings by three independent raters.

The last bar represents ratings of the fifteen siblings and twins who comprised the contrast group. These children lived in their own homes and did not attend the preschool, but entered school at the age of 6. The test results at the age of 8 show a decrease in their rate of development.

The most extensive experiment done on the effects of preschool education was organized by Heber, Barber, Harrington, Hoffman, and Fallander (1972) of the University of Wisconsin. Heber hypothesized that intervention in the experiment that Kirk conducted was too late, as it started at the age of 4, and that such intervention should begin at birth. He selected newborn black children from high-risk families whose mothers had IQs of less than 70. At 3 months of age, the children were taken to a day school for an all-day program. This all-day program continued until the children entered public school at the age of 6. A similar group of high-risk babies received no such intervention but were tested periodically. Both groups of children were examined with psychometric tests and rating scales throughout the experiment.

Figure 2.4 shows the results of intelligence tests for both groups over a period of six years. The top graph represents the mean IQ of the experimental group from twelve months to seventy months of age. The lower graph represents the mean

Figure 2.4   Mean IQ Performance with Increasing Age for the Experimental and Control Groups

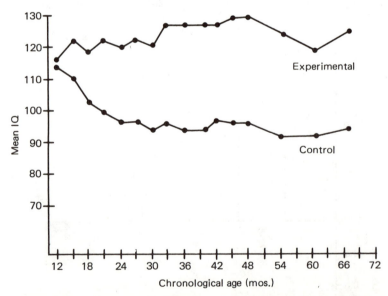

Source: Heber, R. et al., "Rehabilitation of Families at RISK for Mental Retardation," *Rehabilitation Research and Training Center in Mental Retardation: Progress Report,* Madison, Wisconsin, University of Wisconsin, 1972.

IQ of the control group. It will be noted that there is little difference between the two groups at age 12 months, but after that differences appear. The experimental children tested at the superior level throughout. On the other hand, the IQs of the control children tended to drop as the children's age increased, so that by the time they were 70 months old they had a mean IQ of about 92. There were approximately 30 points difference in IQ between those who had received attention and stimulation at an early age and those who had not.

Heber gave many other tests and found approximately the same growth curves, namely, that the experimental group was substantially ahead of the control group after age 2.

The conclusion derived from all these studies is that for children from disadvantaged or psychosocially deprived homes, preschool intervention is necessary to increase intellectual development or mental maturity. Neglect of children results in decreased levels of functioning. These findings may not apply to children from more adequate homes where more interest is shown and more stimulating experience is given.

What does such research suggest about the controversy over the relative importance of heredity and environment? If we accept the hypothesis that heredity accounts for 80 percent of the variance in intelligence, we can assume that we can raise or lower the IQ by 30 points through environmental intervention. If we accept the notion that we are born with what the geneticist Dobzhansky (1955) calls *the norm of reaction* (for example, one child may be born with a potential IQ range of 75 to 110), we can assume that intensive and appropriate education at an early age can account for 20 to 30 point increases in IQ. Hence the findings presented above are within the realm of theoretical possibility.

Preparing the child for reading is preparing the child for intellectual development. The factors tested by intelligence tests include language, reasoning, memory, and so on, which are actually the factors constituting reading readiness.

It is interesting to note that Alfred Binet, the originator of the intelligence test, was one of the first to use the phrase "the educability of intelligence." In 1909 he opened classes in France for mentally retarded children in an attempt to train their attention and reasoning abilities.

Binet rejected the notion that "when one is stupid, one is stupid for a long time" (Kirk & Lord, 1974).

Measuring Mental Maturity

Mental maturity refers to an individual's overall intelligence level. Typically, mental maturity is measured with an intelligence test, which is a test of several mental abilities such as reasoning, vocabulary, spatial relationships, language skills, number ability, quantitative thinking, and memory. Intelligence tests report on the child's IQ, or rate of intellectual growth, and the mental age (MA), or present level of mental growth. Information about intelligence tests can be found in Chapter 8.

The Relation of Measured Intelligence to Reading Achievement

Intelligence tests give information about the child's rate of mental development and the level of mental maturity. Although the tests do not lead the examiner to a specific educational program, they do help determine placement.

IQ. The IQ is a figure giving the rate of mental growth. A child of eight whose mental age is 4–0 is considered to be developing at one-half the normal rate. In such a child, the ratio of mental age to chronological age is $4/8 = .50$. This is multiplied by 100 to express an intelligence quotient. Thus a child who grows mentally one-half a year each year would have an IQ of 50, while a child who grows three-fourths of a year each year would have an IQ of 75, and a child who grows one year each year would have an IQ of 100. Ordinarily a deviation IQ is used. This is considered statistically more valid than a ratio IQ. Some intelligence tests give the score only in IQs. The *Wechsler Intelligence Scale* gives the score only in deviation IQs for the test as a whole, while the *Stanford-Binet* gives a mental age from which a deviation IQ is derived.

Mental Age. The *mental age* is a figure that represents the level at which a child is functioning, regardless of chronological age. A child of ten whose mental age is 10–0 is said to be performing on the intelligence test like the average ten-year-old child. Eleven-year-old Rosemary scored a mental age of 8–0; it is therefore assumed that she is functioning mentally like the average eight-year-old child.

Mental Age and Reading. Many educators believe that a minimum mental age between 6–0 and 6–6 is necessary for a child to learn to read. This recommended minimum age is based on the findings of classic studies done in the 1930s of youngsters in city and suburban public school classrooms with average enrollments of thirty to thirty-five (Gates, 1937). It is important to remember, however, that certain factors can modify the necessary minimum mental age, such as the difficulty of the material, the pace of instruction, the specific methods used, the amount of individualized help, and the child's specific abilities. For example, a child with a mental age of 5–0 may learn to read under certain conditions not present in the original studies, while a child with a mental age of 7–0 may have difficulty learning to read.

The child with a learning disability may have an overall IQ in the average or above-average range, and his or her learning deficits may be masked or averaged out because some abilities are high while others are low. The overall IQ may be deceiving, and one must examine subtest areas to determine needed readiness skills.

The correlation between intelligence test scores and reading achievement in the first grade is substantial. In one large-scale reading study, the correlations ranged from .42 to .56, with a median of .50 (Bond & Dykstra, 1967). Such correlations are interpreted by Harris and Sipay (1975) as meaning that reading success can be predicted on the basis of intelligence test scores for a *group* of children, but for an individual child reading scores cannot be predicted with much accuracy on the basis of IQ.

Table 2.1 shows estimated mental ages for various IQs and chronological ages (CAs). To use the table, find the intersection of IQ and chronological age. This indicates the child's mental age (MA).

The figures in Table 2.1 are derived from the following formula:

$$\text{MA (in months)} = \frac{\text{CA (in months)} \times \text{IQ}}{100}$$

Since the chronological age is expressed in years and months (e.g., 10 years, 11 months), it should be converted to months before the mathematical calculations are begun. For example, Mary has a chronological age of 10–11 and an IQ of 90. Ten years and 11 months equal 131 months. 131 months × .90 = 118 months = 9–10, or 9 years, 10 months (mental age).

Table 2.1 Mental Maturity for Reading: The Relationship Between Ratio IQ, Chronological Age, and Mental Age

Chrono-logical Age	IQ Score							
	60	70	80	90	100	110	120	130
	Corresponding mental age							
5–0	3–0	3–5	4–0	4–5	5–0	5–5	6–0	6–5
5–6	3–3	3–9	4–4	5–0	5–6	6–1	6–6	7–2
6–0	3–6	4–2	4–8	5–4	6–0	6–6	7–2	7–8
6–6	3–9	4–6	5–2	5–9	6–6	7–2	7–8	8–5
7–0	4–2	4–9	5–6	6–3	7–0	7–7	8–4	9–1
7–6	4–5	5–3	6–0	6–8	7–6	8–3	9–0	9–8
8–0	4–8	5–6	6–4	7–2	8–0	8–8	9–6	10–4
8–6	5–1	6–0	6–9	7–7	8–6	9–4	10–2	11–5
9–0	5–4	6–3	7–2	8–1	9–0	9–9	10–8	11–7

According to Table 2.1, if Robert, whose chronological age is 7–0, has an IQ of 80, his mental age is 5–6. If we assume that a mental age of at least 6–0 is desirable for beginning reading, Robert does not have sufficient mental maturity to learn to read.

A child aged 5–6 will have a mental age of 3–9 if the IQ is 70; 4–4 if the IQ is 80; and 7–2 if the IQ is 130. The facts to notice from such a table are that a child aged 6–6 would have a mental age of 4–6 if the IQ is 70, and may have difficulty learning to read, whereas a child of the same age with an IQ of 100 would have a mental age of 6–6 and would very likely learn to read unless there were a specific disability inhibiting learning.

It should be emphasized that the mental age of a child, except in the extremes, does not accurately determine the child's learning ability, and a high mental age does not assure the child's ability to learn to read. A child with a mental age of 7 or 8 or 9 who is still a nonreader is considered to have a reading disability, since there is a discrepancy between potential for learning to read according to the mental age, and reading achievement. As indicated in Chapter 9, the reading grade expectancy is usually determined from a mental age. However, the mental age correlates at about only .50 with reading and therefore is not perfect. For this reason, other tests have been used to try to establish the readiness of a child for reading. Such tests are called *reading readiness tests.* In general, readiness tests have not correlated with reading much better than mental age.

Visual Abilities

There are two areas of visual abilities that are of concern in a discussion of reading readiness. One is *peripheral visual functions,* the condition of the eye; the other ability deals with *central visual functions,* the various functions of perception, association, and memory.

Peripheral Visual Functions

Vision is the sensory pathway through which printed words are transmitted to the brain for interpretation. Poor visual acuity might impair a child's ability to see clearly. Any dysfunction of the eyes such as defective visual acuity might cause difficulty in learning to read unless the child compensates for the defect. In addition to acuity, the child must be able to coordinate the two eyes, including following the line of print from left to right and fusing into one the images of words seen by both eyes. It is important to detect any defects of either visual acuity or eye muscle imbalance in binocular vision through a visual screening examination and through teacher observation. Significant symptoms that indicate possible visual difficulties include: (a) facial contortions and forward thrust of the head, (b) facial contortions and tilting of the head, (c) facial contortions and tension during close work, and (d) forward thrust of the head and holding the book close to the face (Spache, 1973). The remediation of visual acuity and eye muscle imbalance is typically done by ophthalmologists and optometrists, although there might be some orthoptic training as well. Although the research is not clear with respect to the relationship between visual difficulties and learning to read, it is always advisable to correct eye defects.

Central Visual Functions

Many children whose eyes are apparently normal have disorders in their central visual functions, that is, in interpreting, remembering, and recognizing what is seen. There are many components of the central visual functions, including: visual discrimination, visual reception, visual association, visual closure, and visual memory. If the child is able to see and there is nothing wrong with the child's eyes, we then examine the various components of the central visual functions.

Visual Discrimination. *Visual discrimination* refers to the ability to visually discriminate likenesses and differences in objects, geometric shapes, pictures, letters, and words. To learn to read, a child must be able to visually discriminate the difference between *m* and *n* or *house* and *horse.* Visual discrimination also includes directional orientation. In reading, a child must learn to discriminate between *on* and *no, pot* and *top, was* and *saw.* During the growing process, a child learns to visually discriminate differences in his or her environment and learns to make the fine visual discriminations needed in reading. If the child has difficulty discriminating fine visual differences, it is necessary that this ability be developed during the initial phases of reading instruction.

Visual Reception. *Visual reception* refers to the ability to understand the significance of what one sees. Some children find it difficult to translate visual symbols into meaning or to grasp the meaning of pictures. Remediation is directed toward helping these children attach meaning to words and other written symbols and to interpret gestures, facial expressions, body posture, and pictorial presentations and drawings of objects or actions. In primers, sentences are reinforced with pictures that are interpreted by the child. Hence it is necessary for the child to understand and interpret pictures.

Visual Association. *Visual association* refers to the child's ability to relate two or more things that have been presented visually. In making the relationship, the child also uses much of what is referred to as thinking skills (reasoning, critical thinking, problem solving).

Visual Closure. *Visual closure* refers to the ability to identify a common object from an incomplete visual presentation. When reading, the competent reader uses visual closure because he or she needs to see only part of a word to recognize or interpret the whole word or sentence. Ability in visual closure will supply the gestalt or wholeness to the word.

Visual Memory. *Visual memory* refers to the ability to remember what is seen. In order to read, the child must retain a visual memory of letters and words.

Auditory Abilities

Auditory abilities include *peripheral auditory functions* and *central auditory functions.* These functions include sub-abilities such as auditory discrimination, auditory reception, auditory association, auditory closure, sound blending, and auditory memory.

Peripheral Auditory Functions

Auditory acuity is the ability to hear sounds and words of varying pitch and loudness. Youngsters who have a degree of hearing loss will miss much that goes on around them. They may miss some of the language and communication in their environment; they may miss parts of words or they may not hear certain environmental sounds such as cars, bells, dogs. Signs of difficulty in hearing acuity include inattentiveness, frequent requests to have statements repeated, forgetting or misunderstanding simple directions, turning up the volume while watching television or listening to a radio or stereo. An audiometric examination or hearing test is needed to check the child's auditory acuity.

Central Auditory Functions

Many youngsters who do not have a hearing loss do have difficulty with their central auditory functions. They have difficulty listening or interpreting what is heard although there is nothing wrong with their hearing mechanism. The several components of the central auditory functions are described below:

Auditory Discrimination. *Auditory discrimination* refers to difficulty differentiating similar sounds (a doorbell and a telephone ring, or similar words such as *pin* and *pen*). It is necessary for a child to discriminate between words and sounds if he or she is to learn to read by the oral methods used in beginning reading. If the child is deaf, he or she learns to read by a visual method at a much slower rate than do hearing children.

Auditory Reception. Children with difficulty in auditory reception have difficulty deriving meaning from spoken language and other auditory symbols. This ability is interrelated with the language abilities, and remedial techniques for auditory reception overlap with those of language development, particularly receptive language. Disabilities in this area are sometimes called *receptive aphasia* or *listening disabilities.*

Auditory Association. This is the ability to relate concepts presented orally. Children with a deficit in this area need help organizing and integrating ideas received through the auditory channel. Since such information is usually verbal, this area overlaps with language skills, especially the comprehension of language.

Auditory Closure. Some children are deficient in the ability to recognize and use common units of auditory experience when only parts of those units are presented or heard. These children must be helped to identify what is heard in this experience and to fill in the missing parts of what is partially heard.

Sound Blending. The ability to synthesize isolated sounds into words is essential for learning to read. Children who hear and can pronounce isolated sounds (such as *c—a—t*) but cannot synthesize these sounds into the word *cat* are likely to have difficulty learning to read unless they are taught by a visual whole-word method not dependent on phonics.

Auditory Memory. Some children have difficulty remembering what is heard long enough to repeat it immediately. Children who have a deficiency in short-term auditory memory may also have difficulty imitating words and sentences. Learning to talk depends in part on the child's ability to imitate words and sentences in the environment. Failure in this area may cause delayed speech.

Speech and Language Development

Since reading is a language activity, speech and language are obvious prerequisites for learning to read. Indeed, if reading is considered a language process, then a reading disability can be considered a language disorder.

Speech is the ability to articulate or pronounce clearly the sounds of our language system and to use appropriate voice and rhythm patterns. The seven-year-old child who substitutes the *f* sound for the *th* sound, saying "fank you," has a speech problem. Faulty speech may cause a child to confuse sounds that are associated with the printed letter.

Language refers to the ability to use and understand words and sentences. The child who has a limited vocabulary for his or her age or who formulates inappropriate sentence patterns has a language disorder. For example, four-year-old Mark says "Table sit me," meaning, "I want to sit at the table"; Alice, three-and-one-half years old, has acquired no language skills at all.

Both speech disorders and language disorders are to some degree related to reading problems. The incidence of speech and language problems is higher among the mentally retarded, slow-learning, and learning-disabled population than among normal children. Furthermore, youngsters with severe reading problems are frequently deficient in underlying oral language skills (Scheifelbusch, Copeland, & Smith, 1967; Vogel, 1974, 1975). An important element in preparing children for reading, therefore, is training in speech and language skills. Recent work in the field of psycholinguistics has renewed our awareness that reading is a language activity and that language competence is a prerequisite to reading success.

Thinking Skills

The cluster of skills needed for reading is collectively referred to here as *thinking skills*. Thinking skills (or cognitive skills) are a collection of mental abilities that enable one to know, be aware, conceptualize, use abstractions, reason, judge, criticize, and be creative. It is difficult to discuss thinking skills apart from the other correlates of reading readiness because the growth of cognitive ability cannot be separated from the basic growth of the individual. Thinking skills are part of auditory and visual perception, language ability, memory, as well as areas of motor and social learning. Nonetheless, a cluster of thinking skills is a prerequisite for learning to read.

Attending

Attending refers to the ability to concentrate on a task for a prolonged period. Attentional abilities are essential for the child to receive necessary information and complete certain activities. Many atypical learners exhibit characteristics of distractibility, impulsivity, and a lack of perseverance and patience. Attentional deficits are viewed as the most critical defect of learning-disabled children by Dykman and associates (1971; Ross, 1976), and faulty attention should not be overlooked as a correlate of reading failure.

In a review of research on attentional problems of children with learning disorders, Keogh and Margolis (1976) identify three separate but interrelated phases of attention. They are: (1) coming to attention, (2) decision making, and (3) sustaining attention over time. The initial phase, *coming to attention*, refers to the regulation of activity to provide a "set" for learning. The hyperactivity found in learning-disabled children may inhibit their ability to come to attention. The next stage, *decision making*, relates to problem solving. Impulsive children may be fast decision makers, but they make many errors, blurting out answers, jumping to conclusions, and guessing wildly. Such children have to learn to slow down, to become more reflective, and to monitor their answers. The last phase, *maintaining attention,* refers to diligence, or the ability to continue to give attention to a task once it is begun. Slow and disabled learners are easily distracted. They shift their attention rapidly and therefore often fail to finish an assignment. In fact, Ross (1976) believes that the ability to sustain selective attention is the one cognitive function with which most learning disabled children have difficulty, and which indeed might serve to define learning disability. Keogh and Margolis (1976) suggest that diagnosis should attempt to specify the phase of attention with which the child has difficulty and provide remediation techniques specifically for that attentional deficit.

Concepts

Concepts are symbols that stand for a class of objects or events with common properties. The word *chair* does not stand for a particular chair, such as a kitchen chair, folding chair, or rocking chair, but for an essence that is common to all of these chairs. Concept development is important to word meaning and therefore to reading comprehension. Slow and disabled learners may lack essential concepts that are related to the material they are reading. Some children may have little difficulty with concrete symbols (such as *dog* or *running*) but they may not understand more abstract symbols (such as *loyalty, between, after, fairness, yet, result*). Children who lack concepts need educational experiences that will help them build the needed concepts.

Organization and Classification Abilities

Children must learn to associate and relate information. Each new piece of learning and information must be related to what the child already knows or it will be forgotten quickly. Some of the specific skills needed for this were discussed earlier under "Visual Association" and "Auditory Association."

Physical Fitness and Motor Development

Learning is an active process and requires that the child be alert, have energy, and be able to concentrate. The child who is listless or tires easily may have an underlying medical problem. For this reason, good physical health is a primary condition of reading readiness.

Adequate motor development is viewed as a prerequisite of reading achievement by a number of researchers and theorists (Ayres, 1973; Cratty, 1973; Getman, 1965; Kephart, 1971). According to such writers, motor learning is the foundation for cognitive learning; without adequate motor development the child is not ready to acquire cognitive skills such as reading. The motor problem is often noticed in gross motor activities: walking, running, jumping, hopping, skipping. Such difficulties require numerous opportunities to experience these activities in order to develop adequate gross motor movements. The child also needs fine motor skills: eye-hand coordination, using the two hands, cutting, pasting, tracing, writing. Reading readiness programs may include both gross motor and fine motor activities.

Social and Emotional Development

Children differ as greatly in their social and emotional maturity as in their mental maturity. Some children are independent, stable, and enthusiastic as they come to reading; others are babyish, immature, and lacking in self-help skills and confidence. All of this appears to have an impact on their success in reading. There is a greater incidence of social and emotional problems among poor readers than among good readers (Gillespie & Johnson, 1974).

Harris and Sipay (1975) perceive three aspects of social and emotional maturity that are significant for reading readiness: (1) emotional stability (control of volatility and temper tantrums), (2) self-reliance (the desire and ability to help oneself), and (3) social adjustment (the ability to participate actively and cooperatively in group activities).

Prerequisites for learning to read are self-confidence and self-esteem, which come as a result of many successful experiences and adult approval. Youngsters who are slow or disabled learners are likely to know that they cannot do things well by themselves and that their attempts to do things in many areas have disappointed their parents. As a consequence, they may have feelings of inadequacy and may exhibit social and emotional immaturity. This may be revealed as overdependence, intolerance, aggressiveness, unhappiness, shyness, or temper tantrums.

Interest and Motivation

Learning to read requires hard work and effort, and the child must therefore be interested and motivated to learn this task. (Molly was a first-grade child who showed little desire to learn to read. When questioned by the teacher about her lack of interest, Molly explained that she was not concerned about learning to read because she was planning to get married anyway.) One of the essential elements of learning to read, then, is the desire to acquire this skill. The amount of effort a child exerts will be determined largely by the extent of his or her interest and motivation. Because reading is a difficult task requiring concentration and work, the child who does not have a strong inclination to learn will not put forth sufficient effort. It is important that children who are slow or disabled learners have sufficient readiness skills before they are expected to learn to read. When such children are exposed to reading instruction before the prerequisite skills are developed, they become easily discouraged by their failures and soon begin to dislike reading and attempts to teach reading. Once the child is ready for reading, however, interest and motivation become important considerations. The most important factor in interest and motivation is the success factor, which in itself is a powerful social reinforcer. Teaching materials and methods of instruction that allow for success at every step in the learning process are essentials in developing interest and motivation.

Tests for Assessing Readiness

Several kinds of measures can be used to assess the child's readiness for reading. This section discusses the use of (a) intelligence tests, (b) reading readiness tests, and (c) tests of specific mental functions.

Using Intelligence Tests to Assess Readiness

General intelligence tests give global scores: a mental age and an IQ. Unless the subtests are analyzed, these global scores do not point out a child's major abilities and disabilities. Tests of specific mental functioning (instead of general intelligence tests) are needed to show whether there are imbalances in mental abilities. Abilities and disabilities are measured by intraindividual tests, which measure specific kinds of functions. Certain mental functions may be superior, some average, others very much below normal. Awareness of these imbalances or intraindividual differences within a child can be useful in planning readiness activities for the slow or disabled learner. For example, Louise performed well on spatial relations and quantitative items on an intelligence test, but she did poorly on vocabulary and other verbal items.

Although abilities of an individual are correlated, some children have specific disabilities that inhibit their learning to read. For example, Mary, age 6 years and 9 months, can test at the 7-year level in understanding language, at the 6½-year level in expressing language, and at the 7-year level in reasoning ability. Her test results range from 6 years to 7 or 8 years. An average of all the tests could be age 6 years and 9 months, with an IQ of 100. Another child, Sally, of the same age, tests at the 4-year level in memory, at the 5-year level in visual understanding of pictures, at the 9-year level in quantitative thinking, and at the 7-year level in understanding language. When we average these and other test results, this child could also have a mental age of 6–9 and an IQ of 100. Yet these children are different. Mary has learned to read like other children. Sally is having difficulty learning to read. To differentiate the Marys and the Sallys so as to adapt instruction to each of them, reading readiness tests and other intraindividual tests have been devised.

Reading Readiness Tests

A number of tests are designed specifically to assess readiness for reading. Reading readiness tests are generally given to all children at the end of the kindergarten year or at the beginning of first grade before the formal reading curriculum is begun. Sometimes placement in first-grade reading groups is based on results of these tests.

Reading readiness tests measure general factors of mental functioning that are closely related to reading. Most of these tests are designed as group tests. Factors that they measure include visual discrimination, vocabulary, number ability, sentence comprehension, knowledge of the names of the letters of the alphabet, and so on. Commonly used reading readiness tests include:

Gates-MacGinitie Readiness Skills Test
Metropolitan Readiness Tests
Harrison-Stroud Reading Readiness Profiles
Macmillan Reading Readiness Test
Monroe Reading Aptitude Test

Descriptive data about these tests are included in Appendix C.

Tests of Specific Mental Functions

Some formal tests are useful in assessing specific mental functions that are prerequisites to learning to read. Such tests help determine if the child has a deficit in one of the components of reading readiness. Some of these tests are batteries that contain subtests of various components:

SRA Primary Mental Abilities Test is useful for measuring the following mental functions: verbal meaning, number facility, reasoning, perceptual speed, and spatial relations.

The Detroit Tests of Learning Aptitude consist of a number of subtests that are designed to assess specific underlying mental functions. This test is both an intelligence test and a test of special abilities.

The Illinois Test of Psycholinguistic Abilities (ITPA) is designed to measure discrete mental functions. Twelve specific mental abilities are measured with the *ITPA*. To interpret the scores, the subtests on the *ITPA* can be reclassified in the following ways: levels of organization (representational and automatic), channels of communication (auditory-vocal and visual-motor), and psycholinguistic processes (reception, association, expression).

Search is designed to locate five- and six-year-old children who are vulnerable to learning failure. It contains subtests of visual and auditory perception, as well as intermodal tests and body image tests.

Some tests measure only specific functions. Tests designed to measure auditory factors as specific reading readiness functions include:

Wepman Auditory Discrimination Test
Screening Test of Auditory Perception
Goldman-Fristoe-Woodcock Test of Auditory Discrimination

Tests that measure visual factors include:
The Marianne Frostig Developmental Test of Visual Perception. This test measures five areas of visual perception: eye-motor coordination, figure-ground, constancy of shape, position in space, and spatial relationships.
The Developmental Test of Visual-Motor Integration (Beery-Buktenica) is another test that assesses difficulties in visual perception. All of these tests are described in Appendix C.

Activities for Building Reading Readiness Skills

Under normal conditions, most children proceed uniformly in all developmental functions. The stimulation of parents and siblings at home and the activities in any preschool tend to enhance the development of language, visual and auditory perception, and the other components listed in the systems network described earlier in this chapter.

Special instruction and emphasis on any of these components may be required if the child shows special disabilities in some functions.

Figure 2.5 presents the profile of a four-year-old boy who was assigned to a preschool class for trainable mentally retarded children. He was diagnosed as a possible mongoloid (Down's syndrome) because (a) he had a chromosomal translocation found in cases of Down's syndrome, (b) he did not talk at the age of 4, and (c) his tested IQ was below 50.

It will be noted from the profile that this four-year-old boy tested at the six-year level in visual reception and visual association; at the five-year level in manual expression and visual closure. In other words, he was significantly above his chronological age on these tests. On the other hand, he scored significantly below his chronological age in auditory reception and auditory association. He obtained no scores on verbal expression, grammatical closure, and other auditory abilities.

Although this child cannot be considered mentally retarded,

it is obvious that he will have difficulty learning to read unless his auditory and verbal abilities are developed before he begins reading instruction. Such a child will require systematic and intensive training to develop auditory and verbal language abilities.

Principles for Teaching Readiness Activities

Children who are slow in development and children with specific disabilities need special programs. The programs that are designed for these children include special procedures not needed with an average child. To develop such programs, the following steps are necessary:

1. *The child's strengths and weaknesses should be diagnosed.* An analysis of the child's abilities and disabilities should be made. This analysis could be an aid in program planning.

2. *The instructional program should allow for systematic instruction based on a task analysis.*

Figure 2.5   A Case of Chromosomal Translocation Diagnosed as Trainable Mongoloid

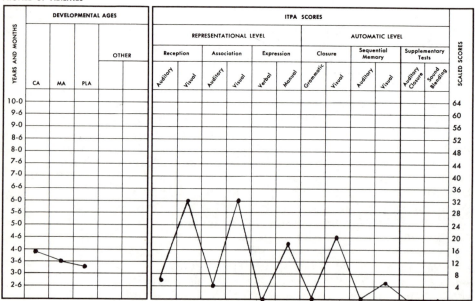

Source: Samuel A. Kirk, "The Education of Intelligence," *The Slow-Learning Child*, 20 (July, 1973).

3. *The program should provide for success experience at
every step or stage in the instructional process.* If materials
and methods are based on the principles of minimal change,
success is more readily attained.

53
Activities for
Building
Reading
Readiness
Skills

4. *Remedial teaching should be integrative.* Although testing or observations of children tend to be discrete (i.e., one
function, such as auditory discrimination, is observed in isolation), effective teaching is integrative. This implies that a
function like auditory discrimination is not trained in isolation, but rather it is trained in relation to other functions.
In teaching auditory discrimination, it is more effective to
relate it to the child's attention span, meaning of words and
sentences, and to his or her verbal repertoire than to give
drills on discrimination of nonsense sounds. Relating the skill
to the child's life situation assures some rehearsal and transfer to situations outside the instructional period.

5. *The child's assets or abilities should be used to train the
disabilities.* For the child in Figure 2.5, the visual receptive
ability was superior to the auditory receptive ability. In a life
situation this means that the child understands the picture of
a bridge, for example, but does not understand the word
bridge presented orally. To teach him or her to understand
the word *bridge,* the picture and word should be presented
simultaneously to help the child understand the word without
the presentation of the picture. Similarly, if a child does not
understand the oral direction "wiggle your finger," or "raise
your hand," then a game such as Simon Says could be used.
In this game, the teacher provides the visual clue of wiggling
a finger or raising a hand while simultaneously giving the
auditory direction.

6. *The child's areas of deficit should be trained.* If a child
does not understand what is seen but understands what is
heard, time should be devoted to ameliorate the visual deficit.
Only when a deficit cannot be ameliorated do we disregard it
and compensate for it through the assets. If a child is totally
deaf, we compensate for the deficit by teaching the deaf child
through vision and other senses. But if the child is hard-of-
hearing, we give auditory training to develop the ability or to
minimize the deficit. Fortunately, the human organism is
flexible, and defects can be ameliorated or compensated for.

7. *Abilities should be developed functionally.* It is preferable to develop abilities in a natural, everyday situation rather
than in an artificial setting. If a child has a deficit in visual
discrimination, it is advisable to train the child in the discrimination of letters and words rather than in the discrimination of geometric figures. If a child has difficulty in visual
sequential memory, it is preferable to train visual sequential
memory with words and sentences rather than with objects or

geometric figures. One should always ask whether the activity is transferable to a life situation. If a child is delayed in talking, faster progress will be made if the lessons provide functional words and sentences that are used in the home and at school.

8. *Materials should be analyzed to determine their usefulness.* There are many materials sold commercially whose claims of usefulness are exaggerated. It is essential that a teacher determine objectives for a particular child and select the specific materials that will be helpful in attaining those objectives. A set of materials that is useful for one child could be useless for another.

9. *Multisensory approaches should be used appropriately.* In general, the simultaneous use of more than one sense field serves to intensify learning. Multisensory approaches in teaching are common and useful. On the other hand, indiscriminate bombardment of multisensory stimulation *may* be more confusing than helpful. Sometimes a unimodal presentation is more beneficial. The decision about when to use multisensory approaches or when to use a unimodal presentation is contingent upon the child's stage of development and the circumstances.

10. *Feedback during teaching sessions should be utilized.* Feedback consists of three elements: (a) what the teacher receives from the child in answer to a question, (b) what the child receives from the teacher when the teacher is confirming or correcting the pupil's response, and (c) what the child receives from his or her own body in terms of motor or vocal responses.

11. *All activities should be presented gradually.* Of prime importance in teaching is the transition from simple materials to more complex materials. This transition should take place in all activities so that the child will succeed at every stage of development. The following game illustrates the advantages of such a procedure. The teacher asks the children if they would like to play Lotto. When they consent, each child is given a card on which are pictures of nine familiar objects, as shown in Figure 2.6. Under each picture is written the name of the object, which the children do not recognize.

(*a*) The teacher cuts a card into nine smaller cards and presents them one at a time. When the picture of a shoe with the word *shoe* printed under it is shown, each child looks at his or her card and places a marker on the picture of the shoe. This continues until markers are placed on all of the pictures. The children's and some of the teacher's cards are presented in Figure 2.6.

(*b*) In the above procedure, the children match their pictures with the teacher's pictures without noting the word beneath them. In a second procedure, shown in Figure 2.7, the teacher increases the difficulty of the game. The teacher presents his or her cards, which show the words without the pictures, and the children are required to match the teacher's words with their own words, at the same time associating the word *shoe* with the picture of the shoe.

(*c*) After the first two procedures have been performed for several days, the teacher gives the children cards with the same nine words on them but without pictures, as shown in Figure 2.8. The teacher's cards consist of single pictures without words. The children are required to identify the picture of a shoe, to find the word *shoe* among their own cards, and then to place a marker on the appropriate word.

The game described above demonstrates one method of gradation. At first, the materials used are simple enough to guarantee success. Gradually, the materials are made more complex but always within the learning capacity of the

Lotto Game, First Procedure   Figure 2.6

CHILD'S CARD

TEACHER'S CARDS

Source: Samuel A. Kirk. *Teaching Reading to Slow-Learning Children.* Copyright © 1968, 1940 by Samuel A. Kirk. Reprinted by permission of Houghton Mifflin Company.

children. Activities should be presented to slow and disabled learners in this way to stimulate learning and an interest in school.

Developing Speech and Language

There is no uniformity among theorists on how language develops in a child. Some linguists believe that language acquisition is "controlled by a biologically determined set of factors and not by intentional training" (Lenneberg, 1964, p. 106). Behaviorists believe that language is developed through training (stimulus, response, and reinforcement). The Piaget theorists explain the acquisition of language in terms of stages at different periods. A practical point of view would allege that the biological structure of human beings is necessary for the acquisition of language, but that it develops by imitation

Figure 2.7   Lotto Game, Second Procedure

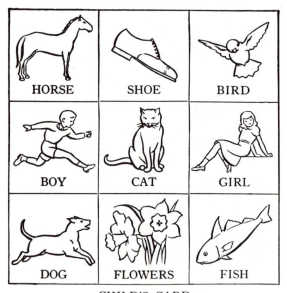

CHILD'S CARD

TEACHER'S CARDS

and reinforcement, and that its complexity increases by stages at different periods of a child's life. To learn to run, the child must first walk, and to learn to walk, the child must first stand. So it is with language development.

Our major concern is to develop the child's maximum language ability within biological limits. Karnes (1975) has developed Early Language Activities for Children as young as one and one-half to three years of age. In addition to activities, she presents some excellent techniques for stimulating language development. These techniques are presented below:

1. *Demonstrate what you want the child to do.* It is not enough to tell the child what you want done. To ensure understanding and success in participating in the activity, show the child what you want him to do before he tries it. For example, if you want him to roll the ball, say, "Roll the ball." Then, roll the ball and while you are doing so, comment, "I roll the ball. Now, you roll the ball." If the child doesn't understand what you want him to do,

Lotto Game, Third Procedure   Figure 2.8

HORSE	SHOE	BIRD
BOY	CAT	GIRL
DOG	FLOWERS	FISH

CHILD'S CARD

TEACHER'S CARDS

Source: Samuel A. Kirk. *Teaching Reading to Slow-Learning Children.* Copyright © 1968, 1940 by Samuel A. Kirk. Reprinted by permission of Houghton Mifflin Company.

repeat the demonstration enthusiastically. Convey to the child that you have faith in his ability to do what you want him to do.

2. *Tell the child what he is doing.* Weeks and months before the child is able to talk in words, phrases, or sentences, he is building a repertoire of knowledge from seeing and hearing you and others talk about what is happening. For this reason, it is imperative that you talk about what is going on. "You're playing with a truck. It's a big truck," or "It's time to eat. Here's your soup. The soup is hot."

3. *Encourage the child to talk.* When the child attempts or begins to talk, encourage him by showing excitement and genuine enthusiasm about his efforts. Do not pressure him to talk, but encourage him and reward him for doing so. If an adult becomes overly concerned when a child lags in language development and tries to force him to talk, the child's reaction will more likely be resistance to talking than an increased interest in the production of expressive language.

4. *Give the child something to talk about.* The environment can become monotonous to a child as well as to an adult. Introduce something exciting such as a new toy you made or purchased for him, a bright, fragrant flower you picked from the garden, a pair of adult shoes he can put on and walk about in. When the child has something to talk about and is ready to talk, he will talk.

5. *Pay attention to the child when he talks.* All of us want attention and so does the child. The best reward you can give him for talking is your attention. When he talks, stop what you are doing and listen, especially if he is a child who has difficulty expressing himself verbally. Look at the child when he speaks; merely responding to what he says may not convey to him that you are really listening. Your response should be compatible with what he is saying; attempt to sustain a dialogue; do not offer only a methodical "yes" or "uh-huh."

6. *Reflect back what the child says.* Hearing extensions of his own words helps the child expand his own language system. When the child says, "pretty," enlarge upon this observation, "Yes, it's a pretty leaf. The leaf is pretty."

7. *Note the activities the child enjoys most and repeat them often.* The adult soon learns which activities a child enjoys most and are likely to encourage his verbal response. He may ask to hear the same story over and over again; read or tell it to him as many times as he wishes. Ask him questions to elicit his verbal responses. Reward his spontaneous verbal expressions with a smile, a hug, or a pat to let him know how pleased you are.

8. *Give the child a chance to talk.* Be patient and wait for him to talk. Don't rush in and do his talking for him. Adults often find it difficult to wait for a handicapped child to struggle to find the word he needs to express himself. It is easy to supply the word for him, but the child doesn't learn to talk if an adult always talks for him.

9. *Don't correct the child every time he makes a verbal error.* Be happy that the child is talking and don't drill him on how to say a word correctly. If an adult is constantly correcting him, he may stop trying to communicate verbally because the rewards for doing so are minimal.

10. *Physically get down on the child's level.* If you want the child
to talk to you, sit with him, get down on the floor with him, or
create a similar setting that lends itself to face-to-face interaction.
When you give him your individual attention, he knows that you
care about him and what he says and does. Play with him at his
level of development, taking cues from his behavior. Play what he
wants to play, and take every opportunity to encourage him to talk.

11. *Let the child know you enjoy his company.* The child soon
learns whether or not you like to be with him. When he knows
you truly like him, he will try harder to please you. If he knows
you enjoy hearing him talk, he will try his best to do so. Smiles,
laughter, a hug now and then assure him that he is an important
person you like to be with.

12. *Be flexible.* You may have decided what you want to do, but
the child may not respond to the activity as you had hoped. Try
something else. See what he wants to do. Take advantage of spontaneous events—an airplane flying low in the sky, a blue jay
perching on a nearby branch, a fire engine going by, a puddle on
the sidewalk. Learning materials to stimulate language development are everywhere. (Karnes, 1975, pp. 10–12)

Additional suggestions for developing speech and language
are:

13. *Provide activities for listening and speaking.* In addition
to sounds, one of the more sophisticated language skills the
child must learn as a prerequisite to reading is the concept of
a word as a component unit of a sentence. In written language words are independent units divided by white space,
but not in spoken language, where there are no physical breaks
between words. Sawyer (1975) suggests that a word perception test be used to determine if children recognize units of
words. In this test, the examiner utters a sentence and the
child is to place a series of blocks in a row, one for each word
in the sentence. The test is presented by beginning with a
three-word sentence and moving gradually to six-word sentences. Children who experience great difficulty with this task
are probably not yet ready to deal with language units smaller
than sentences and might better profit from activities in
listening and speaking.

14. *Show the children an interesting picture that they are to
describe and interpret.* At first children will tend to describe
the picture in words or short sentences. The teacher should
help them express their ideas in longer sentences and in logical
sequence. In this way, more complicated language usage is
developed.

15. *Read and tell children stories.* Storytelling provides
good training in language development. The children may
also tell stories to the class or retell the story that the teacher
has read. Thus, language usage is developed and additional
vocabulary training is given.

16. *Introduce games with speaking parts.* Such games are
interesting to children and are valuable in developing

language ability. The games may be arranged by the teacher as part of the classroom activities.

17. *Encourage children to tell the class about interesting situations they have experienced at home.* They may tell about their dog, their cat, or the newborn baby. This activity may be introduced simply by having the children bring something from home and show it. Later, encourage the children to tell about the item brought (show and tell). Finally, have the child relate an incident without holding an object.

18. *Make toy telephones in the classroom.* The children can carry on conversations over these telephones.

19. *Use dramatization with learned parts as a valuable prereading activity.* Dramatization also aids in the training of memory for sentences.

20. *Increase the child's vocabulary by the introduction of new words in many of the activities listed above.* Teachers should remember that free expression and spontaneous speech are not sufficient to increase vocabulary, but new words should be added continually through activities such as those listed above.

21. *Have the child follow verbal directions.* Tell the child, "Draw a blue line at the top of your paper; draw a red circle at the bottom of your paper; draw a green square in the middle of your paper, connect the square and circle with an orange line." These directions can be taped and the child can use earphones to listen to the tape.

22. *Have the child listen to a story and retell it as accurately as possible.* Start with a very short story and gradually increase the length. Use visual clues to aid the child, such as pictures, flannel board characters, and so on.

23. *Show the children a picture, remove it, and ask one of the children to describe the picture from memory.* Other children can fill in what the first child missed. The teacher should help the class formulate a longer sentence, which the child repeats.

24. *Help the children learn directions for games and activities* (such as making something). Have the children follow directions given by other children.

25. *Memorize poems and songs.* This training is good for developing the memory for sentences and ideas. This training may be included in dramatization or music activities.

26. *Help the child develop memory for sentences.* Exercises that involve repetition of sentences of increasing complexity aid in developing this skill. A puppet can be used to present this activity in an informal manner and the activity can be incorporated into other classroom activities. For example, if the child comes to the teacher saying, "Gimme pencil," the

teacher might say, "Mrs. Jones, will you please give me a pencil?" Have the child repeat the whole sentence. Later the teacher may say, "Mrs. Jones, will you please give me a pencil because my lead has broken," or "because I want to draw." In this way the child will learn to repeat and will come to use longer and more complicated sentences.

Developing Visual Functions

The activities listed below are suggestions for developing central visual abilities. Although they are grouped under visual discrimination, visual reception, and so forth, an activity that includes a number of these visual functions is preferable to an activity that develops only one. These activities should be presented in the form of interesting games.

Visual Discrimination

1. Select a series of animal pictures and present the child with the pictures of four cats and one dog. Ask the child to circle the picture of the animal that is different. In addition to animals and known objects, geometric designs and letters may be used to train children to detect differences in visual symbols.

2. Point out likenesses and differences in objects in the room. Ask the children to discuss the similarities and differences between the desks and chairs, for example. (The desks may be similar in shape but of different size, or one may be movable and the others not.) Comparable pictures of different plants and animals should be shown to let the children detect similarities and differences. Discussing these comparisons involves training of the language function and memory for sentences and ideas.

3. Have the children collect objects. They can collect leaves, for example, and sort them, putting together those that look alike. Animals, pictures, flowers, and pictures of vegetables from seed catalogs can also be used.

4. Matching letters and words and playing with letters and words can be useful in training visual discrimination. Visual discrimination of letters and words has a high correlation with reading achievement.

5. Drawing activities and work in industrial arts and crafts also furnish valuable prereading exercises for the development of visual discrimination.

6. Have the children duplicate designs made by the teacher. Use colored blocks, pegboards, and so on. Later, make drawings of the designs and have the children duplicate the designs from the drawings.

7.   Have the children trace designs, shapes, letters. Use a variety of media—the blackboard, stencils, ditto sheets, and so on.

Visual Reception

8.   Teach the children to recognize and differentiate various shapes and simple objects even when in different sizes, colors, and positions (form perception). Go beyond squares, circles, and triangles to faces, arrows, letters, and words.

9.   Provide experiences in shopping, traveling, visiting places and people of interest. Organize field trips to give the child knowledge and experience.

10.   Help the children observe and talk about what is seen. Play games to see who can see the most objects in a store window or on a table.

11.   Teach the children to understand symbols and pictures. Help them recognize and discriminate color, size, shapes, pictures of people, foods, furniture, clothing, toys, and so on.

Visual Association

12.   Have the children verbalize and point to comparable parts of an object and its picture. Describe each. Ask leading questions and give verbal and graphic clues.

13.   Help the children learn to identify opposite concepts presented in visual form by beginning with tangible characteristics (big-little) and progressing to more abstract ideas that may have to be verbalized (happy-sad).

14.   Use pictorial analogies. For example, show a picture of a dog and one of a bone: find the picture to go with *cat, mouse,* or *bowl of milk.*

15.   Have the children classify concepts into "sets" by finding pictures or objects that fit specific categories, beginning with a single class (for example, *food*).

16.   Brainstorming. Find as many different meanings, as many attributes, as many relationships, as many associated visual images for a picture as possible.

Visual Closure

17.   Take one of two duplicated pictures and cut it into various shapes. Have the children reconstruct the cut-up pictures and make them correspond with the uncut or model picture. Carefully selected jigsaw puzzles may also be used.

18.   Present a visual stimulus (word, letter, picture, color) for a few seconds and have the child select the same item from among several choices.

19.   Present closure experiences in which the child must integrate all parts presented. Let the child put together commercial form-boards and jigsaw puzzles of gradually increasing difficulty, both with and without completed models. Also put together numbers, letters, faces, and so on.

20.   Use a tachistoscopic presentation of words and pictures to develop speed of perception. Gradually decrease the time of exposure.

Visual Memory

21.   Place several objects on a table and hide them all with a screen while you cover some of them with a box or remove one or more objects. Remove the screen and ask the children to tell what objects are covered or gone. Increasing the number of objects on the table or the number of objects removed makes the task more difficult.

22.   Show the children a simple pattern, either a geometric design or a simple picture. Remove the picture and ask the children to draw from memory what they have seen. If they do not draw all the details, show them the picture again, ask what they have missed, and allow them to complete the picture or design. The complexity of the picture or pattern may be increased gradually.

23.   Show the children a picture and then remove it. Ask them to enumerate the items in the picture.

24.   Tack a length of yarn on a bulletin board. Tell the children you are going to hang clothes on a clothesline. Place flannel cutouts of clothes on the yarn clothesline. Remove the clothes and ask the children to hang up the clothes in the same order.

25.   Develop memory for things seen by having the children describe what they remember, places they have been, and people they have seen, color of clothing, location of furniture.

26.   Teach techniques for immediate recall: use rehearsal, grouping, verbalization, motor responses.

Developing Auditory Functions

Auditory Discrimination

1.   Give a series of words that start with the same initial sound, along with one word that does not, such as *table, tail, ball, telephone.* Have the child identify the word that does not start with the same sound.

2.   Give a series of words that rhyme, together with one word that does not, such as *cat, rat, fat, foot;* or *hit, bin, sit, bit.* The children should tell the teacher what word does not rhyme.

3. Blindfold a child and ask him or her to tell from what direction a sound is coming, what child in the class made a certain noise, or what animal the child is attempting to imitate.

4. Tap on the desk, glass, on paper, on the blackboard, and on other objects in the room while the children are looking the other way. The children should name the object that was tapped. Make noises with other objects (such as tearing a sheet of paper, closing a book, zipping a zipper, using chalk on the blackboard, and so on) and have the children identify what they hear.

Auditory Reception

5. If the child does not recognize sounds in the environment, sound a buzzer and have the child clap or raise a hand when the sound is heard.

6. If the child does not have a listening attitude, use tangible reinforcers. Ask the child to guess correctly when an object is described.

7. For the child who has difficulty attaching meaning to words, present motor experiences simultaneously with the auditory stimulus, but emphasize the meaning of the auditory.

8. If the child does not understand consecutive speech, the teacher should be aware of complicating factors such as length of sentences used, sentence structure, rate of speech, and word emphasis.

Auditory Association

9. Help the child hold two or more concepts in mind by considering them in relation to each other. Have the child name objects that satisfy two specific requirements: for example, things that are both round and hard.

10. For the child who has difficulty identifying and verbalizing first-order relationships (two verbal concepts), demonstrate opposites (e.g., big-little) using tangible objects. Have the child find similarities in two concepts.

11. Help children identify and verbalize second-order relationships. Use activities with analogies: for example, "grass is green" tells the color of grass. Then find a second concept. "Grass is green; the sky is _____."

12. Have children classify concepts. Have them find common attributes from "sets" of objects: for example, find clothing among objects that include both clothing and nonclothing.

13. Some children have difficulty evaluating alternative solutions to a problem. Brainstorm to stretch the child's recognition of a variety of solutions or meanings: for example, how many meanings are there to the word *saw?*

Auditory Closure

65
Activities for
Building
Reading
Readiness
Skills

14. Help children develop the habit of rehearsal. Have them listen to material and say it to themselves before they say it out loud.

15. Give the partial word or phrase and ask the child to complete it. "Bread and bu_____." "Write with chalk on the black_____."

Auditory Sound Blending

16. For children who have difficulty with sound blending, teach them to blend words with only two sounds; then proceed to three- or four-sound words. Increase the duration at which the sounds are pronounced to facilitate learning (see "Methods of Teaching Phonics" in Chapter 5).

17. Make tapes of word sounds and have the children formulate the words: for example, *m-a-n; s-a-d*. The children can play a game of guessing the words from the sounds.

Auditory Memory

18. Help the child recognize relationships of order: *next to, after, middle, below, last, first.*

19. Use rehearsal. Teach the child to rehearse (repeat to self) the first part of the stimulus while the rest is being presented.

20. Have the child find identifying characteristics. For example, the difference in the spelling of *meet* and *meat* can be remembered because the one we eat has *eat* in it.

21. Tap on the desk with a pencil and ask the child how many times you have tapped. Ask the child to repeat rhythm patterns made by tapping.

22. Teach the children jingles and nursery rhymes within their comprehension.

Instructional Materials

There are many instructional materials and methods currently available. A few of the more extensive ones follow:

Karnes, M. B. *The Karnes Early Language Activities.* Gem Materials Enterprises, 1975. P.O. Box 2339, Station A, Champaign, Ill., 61801
This is a kit of fifty activities for each of motor, auditory, visual, and verbal areas suitable for children from 1½ to 3 years of age. They are designed with behavioral objectives for each activity and a record card to check when the child has achieved that objective.

Karnes, M. B. *Goal, Language Development.* Milton Bradley Co., 1972. Springfield, Mass., 01101

This kit, which is similar to the one described above, presents many activities for children between the ages of 3 and 6, including activities for all of the functions tested by the *ITPA*.

Karnes, M. B. *Goal, Level II, Language Development.* Milton Bradley Co., 1972. Springfield, Mass., 01101 This kit is designed for pupils in grades 2 and above, especially for slow learners, retarded children, and children with learning disabilities in language.

Karnes, M. B. *Goal, Mathematical Concepts.* Milton Bradley Co., 1972. Springfield, Mass., 01101

Karnes, M. B. *Early Childhood Enrichment Series: Development of Perceptual Skills. Development of Language Skills. Development of Number Skills. Development of Reading Readiness.* Milton Bradley Co., 1970. Springfield, Mass., 01101

Minskoff, E., Wiseman, D., and Minskoff, J. *The MWM Program for Language Abilities.* Educational Performance Associates, 1972. Ridgefield, N.J., 07657 This kit of materials includes detailed lesson plans for the remedial teacher on the development of *ITPA* functions. A task analysis of the functions has been made and remedial procedures for each are presented in a step-by-step program.

Dunn, L. M., and Smith, J. O. *The Peabody Language Development Kits.* American Guidance Service, 1966. Circle Pines, Minn., 55014 This series consists of six kits, each for a different level of ability, for children ages 3 to 8 years. Although designed primarily for classroom use, the activities can be used for smaller groups. The manual gives step-by-step directions for the teacher. Many of the activities promote development in visual-motor areas, but in general the activities are weighted in the direction of auditory-vocal experiences.

Bush, W. J. and Giles, M. T. *Aids to Psycholinguistic Teaching.* Charles E. Merrill, 1969. Columbus, Ohio, 43216 This book describes materials and activities for each of the subtest functions of the ITPA. The activities are grouped according to the grade level for which they are appropriate, from first to sixth grade. For the remedial teacher who is looking for materials and procedures for ameliorating disabilities found on the ITPA, this book will furnish numerous suggestions.

Frostig, M. *The Frostig Program for the Development of Visual Perception.* Follett Publishing Co., 1962. Chicago, Ill., 60611 This is a remedial program of 359 exercises that teaches visual-motor coordination, figure-ground perception, perceptual constancy, perception of space, and perception of spatial relations.

Engelmann, S. *Distar Language I and II*. Science Research Associates, 1969. Chicago, Ill., 60611
This program consists of highly structured materials designed to teach basic language concepts, build vocabulary, and teach communication I (preschool level) and II (primary level).

Summary

Readiness refers to a state of development that is needed before a skill can be learned. Reading readiness is the collection of integrated abilities, traits, and skills a child needs in order to learn the complex process called reading.

Components of reading readiness include: mental maturity, visual and auditory abilities, speech and language development, thinking skills, physical fitness and motor development, social and emotional development, and interest and motivation.

Research has demonstrated that with developmentally delayed children, especially those from psychosocially deprived homes, mental maturity can be accelerated.

The mental age required for beginning reading is around 6–6 for the majority of children, but the only way to know when any particular child is ready is to try to teach reading when that child appears to be ready to learn, regardless of mental age.

The visual abilities related to reading readiness include peripheral visual functions and central visual abilities, that is, visual discrimination, visual reception, visual association, visual closure, and visual memory. The auditory abilities related to reading readiness include peripheral auditory functions and central auditory functions, that is, auditory discrimination, auditory reception, auditory association, auditory closure, sound blending, and auditory memory.

Speech and language disorders are often found among slow and disabled learners. Since reading is a language activity, it is obvious that language and speech are prerequisites for learning to read.

Thinking skills include a variety of cognitive abilities that are needed for reading. Skills particularly needed for learning to read are the ability to attend, to develop concepts, and to organize and classify ideas.

Some theorists feel that physical fitness and motor development are key readiness attributes. Social and emotional maturity are important readiness factors. And, of course, learning any task requires that the individual be motivated to learn that task.

Several principles for teaching readiness activities were presented in this chapter. Activities for developing speech and language and visual and auditory abilities were discussed.

3 Developmental Reading Methods and Materials

Chapters 3 through 6 deal with methods and materials for teaching reading to slow and disabled learners. Chapter 3 reviews developmental methods and materials used in the regular classroom. Chapter 4 presents adaptations of developmental reading methods and materials for the slow and disabled learner at the beginning stages of reading, while Chapter 5 discusses adaptations of developmental methods for the advanced stages. Chapter 6 presents special methods for the atypical learner, sometimes referred to as remedial methods.

Developmental reading refers to the patterns and sequence of normal reading growth and development, and to the methods and materials used in the regular classroom for children who are learning to read at a normal and expected pace. A parallel term *developmental psychology* is widely used in reference to normal child-growth patterns. The teacher who desires to help children with reading problems must have a thorough knowledge of developmental reading. Once an understanding of how the normal child grows and develops in reading is achieved, modifications of developmental methods can be made for the deviant learner. In addition, the teacher of slow and disabled learners must be competent in the special or remedial methods that have been developed over the years to help atypical learners acquire the skill of reading.

There have been more effort, research, and debate in the area of teaching reading than in any other area of the school curriculum. Despite this effort, research into methods of teaching reading has failed to prove that one method is vastly superior to another. Most children learn to read using many methods and a variety of materials. What seems to work well in one school, classroom, or locality does not seem to work as well in another. Sometimes what seems to work in one year with one class is a disappointment the following year. Most important, what is successful with one child may fail with another. Some research studies on reading methods and materials are reviewed in Chapter 9.

The concern of this book is teaching reading to atypical learners. This does not mean, however, that methods and materials that have been developed over the years to teach reading to average or normal learners are not useful with atypical learners. In fact, many of these developmental materials and methods are useful in a modified form. Moreover, research has *not* shown that certain methods should be used exclusively with one type of exceptionality (such as mentally retarded youngsters), while another should be used with another type of exceptionality (such as children identified as learning-disabled or dyslexic). Each classification of exceptionality comprises a heterogeneous group of learners—individuals who need different methods and materials. It is important that teachers who work with atypical learners be familiar with many materials and have competencies in using a wide range of methods to teach reading and in making adaptations for the diverse individuals who are identified as slow and disabled learners.

During the early days of education in the United States, an alphabet method of teaching reading was utilized. Children first learned the alphabet and then learned to read by spelling words. The children would name the letters *c—a—t* and then pronounce the word *cat*. This was a slow and laborious process and was soon discontinued in favor of the phonics method, which was an improvement over the alphabet method. Through the use of phonics, children learned the sound (rather than the name) of the letter. They were able then to decode words and thus they learned to read. Later, educators discovered that children could learn words as wholes without learning either the alphabet or phonics. It was also observed that during the initial stages of reading, children could learn even simple phrases and sentences without knowing phonic elements or individual words (Smith, 1965).

Developmental Stages in the Reading Process

Despite all the research on reading, the controversies about the best method of teaching reading, whether it is the phonics method, the experience method, the linguistic method, or some other approach, have not abated. From generation to generation, different methods are favored.

It is possible that the controversies arise because the various experts are dealing with a different part of the problem, namely, each child's particular stage of development in the reading process.

In 1940, Kirk (1940) applied the theories and stages of development proposed by the biologist Coghill (1929) to the process of reading. Kirk stated that a reading instructional method is successful only insofar as it takes into account and provides for the developmental steps in the reading process. Studies in biology and psychology indicate that the general process of human development follows three stages, namely:

(1) mass action, (2) differentiation, and (3) integration. Applied to the reading process, these developmental stages become: (1) reading wholes, (2) learning details, and (3) reading without awareness of details. These three stages of reading development are used as a framework by a number of reading authorities (Smith, 1974).

Stage I: Reading Wholes	Stage II: Learning Details	Stage III: Reading Without Awareness of Details

Stage I: Reading Wholes

In the first stage, children rely heavily on memory and configuration clues. They are presented with a short written passage usually based on their own experience and dictation. Memory of what they have said and what has been repeated by the teacher helps them to "read" the sentences as wholes. The child gets a visual picture of each sentence and is aided in recall by the gross differences between them. Outlining the configuration of the sentence may aid considerably at this stage. For example, the sentence

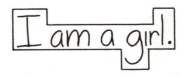

looks quite different from

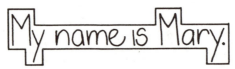

In other words, children's first impression is of whole sentences or of a short story, which they remember. They are only vaguely aware of the blocks and gaps between words. They do not necessarily recognize, discriminate, or perceive the separate words or letters in the passage.

After whole sentences or paragraphs are recognized in this manner, children are gradually led into the second stage of reading by directing their attention to the details of the sentences and words.

Stage II: Learning Details

Although the method of utilizing vague impressions is valuable in beginning reading, children cannot progress in reading merely by seeing vague phrases and sentences and making some differentiation between them.

To progress in reading, the child must discriminate the individual words within the sentence. Perceiving individual words requires the perception of the different elements in each word.

Initial Phase

During the initial phase of Stage II (word discrimination), attention is called to the separate words that make up the sentence by having children see each word as a whole. Again, configurational clues often help emphasize the gross differences between words. To use the example given above: at this stage each word would be separated into its own configurational outline and the details of the word stressed. The sentences would now appear as a collection of individual words:

It is true that many superior and average children need little instruction in learning the details, since during the process of reading sentences they learn to discriminate between different words. Many atypical children, however, require aid, and teachers of primary reading attempt to guide them by having them use a specific method as they go from wholes to details.

Secondary Phase

Learning to discriminate the word *dog* from the word *beautiful* is simple enough, but to learn the discrimination between the word *dog* and the word *boy* is more difficult, since the configuration of the words is the same. Therefore, in the second phase of Stage II (attention to individual elements), the child must learn the different components of each word.

The child must recognize that *d* is different from *b*, that the *o* in both words is similar, and that the *y* is different from the *g*. In other words, learning to differentiate between words that are very similar in configuration requires a discrimination of the individual parts or elements of the words. This does not mean that children must be taught the various letters or different sounds in each word at this stage, but that they must be able to make these discriminations perceptually even though they may not know the names of the individual letters or sounds.

The concept of learning wholes and then learning details becomes clearer if we take an example from adult behavior. If adults were shown two similar leaves, their first impression would be of the leaves as wholes, rather than of the characteristics differentiating them. When they were shown the leaves again, they might be able to differentiate or to recognize that the first leaf is from a red oak tree and the second from a white oak tree. Being told the names of the leaves might help the individual discriminate between them. To facilitate differentiation, the individual might further be told, "This is identified as a red oak leaf because it has certain characteristics that differ from those of the white oak leaf."

In other words, adults perceive wholes on the first impression and gradually discern details as they become better acquainted with the object.

Retarded children and children with perceptual problems often have difficulty making fine discriminations. Details must be pointed out to them through word study and phonic analysis. A number of reading difficulties that appear later in a child's life might be avoided if more attention were given to details during this stage of the reading process. Phonics, or synthetic methods of instruction (detailed in Chapter 5) emphasize this approach.

After a period, detailed analysis of word elements (at least in familiar words) is no longer needed and would serve only to slow down the child's reading rate and comprehension. The child is now ready to integrate these skills and move to the third and final stage of the reading process.

Stage III: Reading Without Awareness of Details

The purpose of reading is to comprehend thought units without being aware of the details on the printed page. This process is known as *cue reduction*. For example, a person learning to drive a car is at first conscious of many things, such as the brake, the steering mechanism, the rearview mirror, and so on. With more practice, consciousness of such details becomes short-circuited and driving is done automatically. This process of cue reduction operates similarly in reading. It makes for efficient and rapid readers—but *only* if at an earlier stage, differentiation of details has been mastered.

Since advanced readers read without awareness of details, some teachers feel that Stage II of the reading process is unnecessary and that details need not be taught. Consequently, they stress the "whole word" method of teaching reading throughout the training period. Some children learn to read despite this method, since they are capable of learning details without specific instruction. Other children develop reading disabilities because their teacher allows them to omit an essential process in reading. Awareness of details is a crucial element in learning to read. It is imperative that the teacher instruct the children in details of sentences and words and then use methods that will help the child read without attending to, or being aware of, the details. In this way the child will achieve the goal of reading—namely, comprehending thought units and ideas without being conscious of the process.

According to the three-stage model of reading (reading wholes, learning details, and reading without awareness of details), the alphabet and phonics methods emphasize Stage II rather than Stage I at the beginning of reading instruction. The three-stage model, however, suggests that only after the child has had experience in perceiving objects, pictures, and words as wholes should direct instruction be given in observing details through the use of phonics and word analysis. Larger thought units can be introduced later so that the child, through the process of cue reduction, can read without noting the details of words or sentences, yet can fall back on them if necessary. It should be noted, however, that some reading authorities believe that teaching reading should begin with the teaching of phonics.

Teachers of atypical learners have a more difficult task than teachers of normal children, since slow and disabled learners are likely to be deficient in making inferences, in learning by themselves, and in using cue reduction. The teacher, therefore, must be alert to detect the stage at which the child is reading and must intensify the instruction to aid the slow learner in some of the steps that the average child learns without instruction. Teachers who recognize the three stages of reading can formulate a method to fit the process of reading at each particular stage.

Methods of Reading Instruction

"Meaning Emphasis" versus "Code Emphasis"

According to Chall (1967), methods of teaching reading fall generally into two main groups, reflecting differences in the instructional approach used. The first group is based on the "meaning emphasis" approach, while the second is based on the "code emphasis" approach (Cawley, Goodstein, & Burrow, 1972; Harris & Sipay, 1975). In the former group, stress is placed on the immediate acquisition of meaning through learning whole words, sentences, and paragraphs at sight. Phonic instruction is introduced later. Included in this group are most of the basal reading series that emphasize story content.

The code-emphasis approach, on the other hand, stresses the early introduction of the sound-symbol system and the principles of phonics, with individualized instruction emphasized. With this approach, story content is minimized, particularly in the early stages of instruction. The rationale for this approach is that most primers and first-grade readers contain vocabulary used by four- and five-year-old children, and that the emphasis should be on perception and discrimination rather than on meaning, which is not a problem in the early stages.

In general, code-emphasis approaches place greater stress on word recognition skills and less on meaning. As indicated earlier, the code-breaking phase of the reading process is intermediate between Stage I (the vague awareness of whole words) and Stage III (reading without awareness of details). Insufficient or inappropriate instruction during this crucial intermediate phase may spell the difference between success and failure in reading, especially for slow or disabled learners.

Several methods of teaching reading combine elements of both the meaning- and code-emphasis approaches. Below, methods that stress meaning will be treated first, and then those that emphasize the breaking of the code will be discussed. Methods in both of these categories are essentially visual-auditory approaches to reading instruction.

Meaning-Emphasis Approaches

Several methods of reading instruction are primarily meaning-emphasis approaches. The basal reader, individualized reading, and language-experience methods are presented in this section.

Conventional Basal Readers

The conventional basal reading approach is the one most commonly used in the schools today. One reason for its popularity is the convenience provided the teacher in materials of instruction accompanied by a detailed manual describing their intended purpose and use. Flash cards, workbooks, film strips, and so on, that synchronize with the readers are frequently available for a total teaching approach.

In this approach, initial emphasis is on the development of a minimum sight vocabulary. Context and picture clues are relied on, with comprehension of meaning being the major goal.

Basal readers do have an important role to play in the reading curriculum of slow and disabled learners, but they must be used with discretion. The availability of a teacher's manual, offering a kind of prepackaged lesson plan, along with brilliantly illustrated texts and workbooks does make the basal reader route an attractive one. Generally, however, the methods and materials are designed to meet the reading needs and rates of the average child.

To use a basal reader effectively with a slow or disabled learner, a great deal of supplementary material must be individually prescribed and provided. Mastery of each step in the reading curriculum must be assured before any child is allowed to continue page after page in a primer or workbook. The criterion of success is not the number of pages covered, but rather how well the child has mastered the reading task at hand.

In a basal reading series, new words, new reading tasks, comprehension skills, and methods of word attack are presented in a sequence and at a pace established by the author of the series. Teachers of deviant learners cannot be caught in the bind of dispensing this material as presented; instead, they must use it as a guide, they must become diagnostic teachers. Cawley and associates (1972) state that "diagnostic teaching must give assurance that each child has attained criteria on a given task before being confronted with an additional task that contains prerequisites from the original activity" (p. 204).

Suggestions given in the teacher's manual for drill, for experimentation, and for supplementary activities can be valuable aids to the resourceful teacher to enhance and ensure overlearning experiences for slow and disabled learners.

The teacher cannot rely solely on scores attained on periodic standardized reading achievement tests or those accompanying basal reading series to determine a slow-learning child's reading level or capacity. For the slow learner, the disabled learner, and the mentally retarded child particularly, ongoing diagnostic teaching (teach-test-reteach, if necessary) is a must if the child is to learn to read to maximum potential.

Individualized Reading

The individualized reading method permits each child to read material of his or her own choosing (self-selection) and to progress at his or her own rate (self-pacing). Emphasis is on comprehending the meaning of words and sentences from the beginning—before word analysis is begun.

A wide variety of reading materials of different levels of difficulty is made available to the children. Each child selects a book, magazine, or newspaper that he or she wishes to read independently, asking the teacher for help only if and as it is needed or as often as the teacher has time to confer with the pupil. During the "conference," the teacher may ask the child to read parts of the story orally to check on comprehension. The individual work is often supplemented with some group activities, utilizing basal readers and workbooks that provide needed practice on specific reading skills.

This method is advocated for gifted children and is useful with average children; however, it is of questionable value with slow-learning, retarded, or learning-disabled children.

Too much is left to self-learning. There is little or no systematic check on whether basic steps in the reading process have been mastered or if and where any breakdown in the process has occurred.

Each child selects any printed material he or she wishes to read and asks the teacher for assistance only if and when needed. Atypical learners may assume the posture of a reader, gain some meaning from the illustrations and the few words they can recognize, answer key comprehension questions on the passage, and yet be grossly deficient in word attack skills, word analysis, sound blending, and so on. In the beginning reading process, specific decoding errors undetected for even a brief period of time may transform a potential reader into a potential failure.

Only after a slow or disabled learner has mastered the fundamentals of reading and has successfully reached Stage III (reading without awareness of details) would the individualized instruction method be appropriate.

Language-Experience Method

The language-experience method of teaching reading utilizes the child's experiences and vocabulary. Since words familiar to the child are used in this method, it becomes meaningful and therefore facilitates learning. Oral composition, spelling, handwriting, and reading are functionally integrated.

In the language-experience approach, the children's first reading materials consist of chart stories dictated by the youngsters about their own experiences and recorded by the teacher. For example, after a field trip to a farm, the teacher may ask the class or an individual child, "Where did we go yesterday?" The children's responses would be accepted, discussed, and refined to "We went to the farm." Further questions from the teacher would elicit such responses as "We saw a dog. We saw a cow. We saw a horse." These sentences would be written on the board as the children relate their experiences.

> We went to the farm.
>
> We saw a dog.
>
> We saw a cow.
>
> We saw a horse.

Each line and word of the story are pointed out by the teacher while the children learn to repeat the story as a whole from memory. Clearly, this represents Stage I of the reading process—reading wholes. Next, the children learn to differentiate the parts of the story in response to the teacher's specific questions regarding content or meaning. After the children can read each sentence meaningfully, they are asked to match or identify single words. While editing the stories, the teacher shows the children the connection between sounds and letters. Attention is thus called to Stage II—learning details.

Integration, or reading without awareness of details (Stage III) follows as the child learns to reconstruct the story and read whole thought units without being aware of the process. Because the experience or chart story method allows for each stage of the reading process, it is highly appropriate and a very popular method for introducing reading to slow or disabled learners.

Jordan (1963, pp. 21–27) compares the language-experience approach with basal readers as to their adaptability for use with children identified as retarded, and who may be expected to display the following learning-relevant behaviors more often than other groups display them. Jordan's revision of her 1963 comparison follows:

Experience Approach	*Basal Readers*
1. *The rate of learning is slow.*	
Any number of chart stories can be developed at any level, allowing the children to move at their own pace.	Basal series are paced for the mentally average child and can be slowed only by re-reading or by use of supplementary materials.
2. *Retention is poor, requiring overlearning and frequent review.*	
Chart stories by and about the children should hold their interest through more re-readings.	Review must consist in re-reading the same text.
New stories can be developed with only minor changes for fresh review material.	Retardates often lack background for the predominantly middle-class reader stories; lose interest quickly.
3. *Language abilities are deficient.*	
Children can dictate the chart stories only in words in their speaking vocabularies.	Reader vocabularies are drawn from samples from normal children.
Chart stories use known concepts. Children do not write about ideas perceived only vaguely.	Readers assume a conceptual development average in number and complexity.
Sentence structure can be controlled to the children's needs by skillful elicitation of the chart stories.	Sentence structure is restricted by the small sight vocabulary or level of development of word recognition skills.
4. *Learning tends to be concrete, with lessened ability to handle the abstract.*	
The first goal of the experience method is to tie meaning to the abstract symbol.	Sight or letter-sound relationship are the first learnings, both abstract and only tenuously related to past language experiences.

Experience Approach	*Basal Readers*
The children's background experiences are directly related to the chart stories.	The experience background of the children may be quite irrelevant to the reader story.

5. *Past failure proneness lowers tolerance for additional frustration.*

Success can be assured by control of content. There is opportunity for success in both creating and reproducing the stories.	Readers move too fast to allow the retardate consistent success. Limited understanding of the stories adds further frustration.

6. *The attention span tends to be short.*

The ego-centric nature of the beginning reader should make it easier to focus his attention on stories having a direct relevance to himself.	Stories are about abstract characters engaged in often unfamiliar activities. The retardate would have difficulty in identifying closely with them.
Reading is made functional from the start; it is used to answer questions and convey information.	Acquisition of sight vocabulary may not be seen as functional by the learner; the communicative nature of the reading process may never be recognized.
Frustration proneness militates against attention to tasks, reduction of frustration aids concentration.	Lack of success breeds frustration, which in turn reduces the desire to concentrate and pay attention.

7. *Imagination and creativity are weak, leading to perseverative behaviors and resistance to change.*

Children create as well as reproduce the story, and can receive recognition for both kinds of activity.	Reading is apt to be perceived as responding to printed symbols, to what others have written.
Meaningful activities combat perseveration. Meaning is developed from the first.	Rote learning encourages perseverative behavior; without safeguards both sight vocabulary and letter sound relationships lend themselves to rote-memorizations.

8. *There is relatively less spontaneous learning, making it necessary to include more common learnings in the curriculum.*

The learnings necessary for each class can be incorporated into the chart stories.	Basal readers assume a normal social development and mastery of common social learnings.

9. *Transfer and generalization occur less often and less spontaneously.*

The extreme flexibility of the chart reading materials makes coordination of reading with other lessons easy.	The lessons and the stories' subjects are fixed and not adaptable to the interests of a given group.

A method of instruction that capitalizes on the learning strengths of retarded and slow-learning or learning-disabled children while counteracting their learning difficulties holds great promise of success. For this reason, teaching familiarity with the language-experience approach to beginning reading instruction should be a focal point in training programs for prospective teachers of special children.

The language-experience approach, advocated by Lee and Allen (1963) and by Allen (1968, 1976), treats reading as a part of language and thought. The native language of the child is used to build the competence required for reading printed materials. Language is treated as a human experience for writing and is reconstructed through reading.

The language-experience method views reading as an integrated extension of the facets of the language arts. Reading skills are interrelated with the development of the skills of listening, speaking, and writing.

In the Allen system, there is no predetermined, rigid control over vocabulary, syntax, or content, and the teacher uses as raw material the reading matter that the child composes to develop reading skills. This approach to reading has a vitality, immediacy, and creativity that have proven useful both in the beginning-to-read stage with young children and in corrective work with older pupils. Although the child's interest is high, this approach is initially very dependent on the visual modality and visual memory for words. The emphasis is on reading material that grows out of the child's experiences, written in the child's natural language.

For a fuller treatment of Allen's ideas, the student is referred to *Language Experiences in Communication* (Allen, 1976).

Code-Emphasis Approaches

Code-emphasis approaches to reading include phonics methods, linguistic methods, the initial teaching alphabet (i/t/a), and programmed instruction.

Phonics Methods

Most phonics methods teach children to associate speech sounds with letters or groups of letters to help them pronounce unfamiliar words. The teaching of phonics is started earlier and is more structured than it is in basal reading programs.

Chall refers to those phonics methods that teach letters representing certain sounds first that are then blended to form words as "synthetic" methods (1967). Some phonics programs do not expose children to words or sentences until they have mastered a considerable knowledge of phonics. The presentation varies from program to program, some beginning with short vowels, some with long vowels, and others with consonants.

Phonics systems range from complete reading programs such as the *Open Court Reading Series* or Lippincott's *Basic Reading Program* to the partial or supplementary programs of Hay-Wingo, the Writing Road to Reading, the Hegge-Kirk-Kirk Remedial Reading Drills, and Distar. (Several of these methods are described in Chapters 5 and 6). Some systems stress phonics in conjunction with practice in sight and meaningful reading. Other systems emphasize separate phonics instruction and depend upon existing published reading materials for practice in the other skill areas.

Phonics training, if used judiciously and properly, has a definite place in the teaching of reading to slow and disabled learners. When properly taught, phonics is not confusing to these children, but rather becomes a helpful tool in the decoding process, especially when emphasis is not placed on the learning of phonics rules.

Unless the child has a specific problem in learning and retaining sight words, phonics should be introduced after a basic sight vocabulary of fifty to one hundred words has been acquired and attention can be focused on word components. Instruction in phonics should be integrated with the basal reader or the language-experience approach at this point in beginning reading instruction.

Since phonics training plays such an important role in teaching reading to slow and disabled learners, specific suggestions for its use are given in Chapter 5. A sample phonics page is shown in Figure 3.1.

Many prospective teachers did not receive phonics training in their elementary school days, or they may have forgotten this instruction. A phonics self-quiz, together with common phonics generalizations, is given in Appendix A.

Linguistic Methods

Findings from the field of linguistics have given us a better understanding of the reading process. One recent trend in reading instruction is based on a linguistic approach. While there is no single linguistic method, this approach relates beginning reading to the child's previously learned oral language. The linguistic approach differs from the conventional basal reader approach in that breaking the written language code is emphasized rather than meaning. It also differs from phonics approaches in that sound or phoneme elements are not presented in isolation.

Early linguistic instruction places primary emphasis on breaking the code before comprehension is introduced. For this reason, the use of context and picture clues in the reading material is discouraged in some linguistic series. Bloomfield and Barnhart (1961) and Fries (1963), early advocates of the linguistic approach, maintain that meaning comes naturally to the child after the code is broken. They believe that children are mature users of language who already understand oral language. To learn to read, children must learn only how to decipher the written form of language.

In linguistic reading materials, words are read as wholes, beginning with words that have a regular spelling pattern. Words are carefully selected so that only one sound for one letter is used consistently. Sounding and blending exercises are not included in the linguistic approach. According to proponents of the linguistic approach, children should be able to discover for themselves the relationship between sounds and letters. For example, the child is shown the words *man, fan, ran, can*. The child is to discover that these words differ only in a single sound and a single letter. The child then generalizes about the sound or phoneme difference and the letter representing that sound.

With linguistic methods, initial emphasis is on words and letters, with letter-sound combinations stressed before any meaningful reading takes place. This approach begins at the

Sample Phonics Page   Figure 3.1

Source: **Louis Krane.** *Phonics Is Fun,* Book 1. © 1970, Modern Curriculum Press, Cleveland, Ohio, p. 28. Used by permission.

second stage of the reading process, because it focuses on details in the printed word before the mass or wholistic stage has been mastered.

Normal children would learn from this drill phase rather quickly and would carry over their new skills to reading, comprehending sentences and paragraphs they are now able to decode. It would be difficult, however, to maintain the atypical learner's interest and motivation to learn when the first exposure to reading is emphasis on letters and sounds with little or no immediate purposeful feedback.

The linguistic approach assumes that children are able to discover for themselves the relationship between sounds and letters. This assumption may not hold for retarded, slow-learning, or learning-disabled children, who have difficulty generalizing. They need direct instruction in each step of the process so that no intermediate steps are overlooked or taken for granted.

The following is a list of some linguistic series:

Let's Read. C. L. Barnhart, Inc., 1963. P.O. Box 359, Bronxville, N.Y., 10708
Miami Linguistic Readers. D. C. Heath & Co., 1965. Lexington, Mass., 02173
Merrill Linguistic Reading Program. Charles E. Merrill Publishing Co., 1975. Columbus, Ohio, 43216
The Linguistic Readers. Harper & Row, 1966. New York, N.Y., 10022
SRA Reading Skills. Science Research Associates, 1970. Chicago, Ill., 60611
The Benziger Readers. Benziger, Bruce & Glencoe, 1971. 8701 Wilshire Blvd., Beverly Hills, Calif., 90211

A sample of linguistic reading materials is shown in Figure 3.2.

Initial Teaching Alphabet (i/t/a)

The *initial teaching alphabet* (i/t/a) approach is a method for beginning reading instruction. Forty-four characters are employed in the i/t/a orthography, each symbol representing one speech sound in the English language. The i/t/a alphabet includes twenty-four of the familiar letters, dropping *q* and *x*. Twenty additional characters are added to achieve greater correspondence between the written and spoken forms of a word. Only lower-case letters are used in i/t/a; a larger type size of the lower-case form indicates capital letters (Sceats, 1967).

In i/t/a, a word is spelled the way it is pronounced. For example, *baby* is *baeby; thought* is *thout; could* is *cood;* and *any* is *eny.* The initial teaching alphabet is used only in beginning reading instruction. After the child achieves some proficiency in the use of this system, the i/t/a characters are gradually phased out of the reading materials and the child is transferred to traditional orthography (t/o), the conventional alphabet and spelling. When using i/t/a, the child is encouraged to sound out the word, then write the sounds on paper. For a great number of words in t/o, this principle applies; however, the child must also learn a certain number of rules and apply them to irregularly spelled words in the language.

The i/t/a system has been used with varying degrees of success with atypical children. The method cannot be modified too extensively but can be combined with other techniques to make it more appropriate for slow and disabled learners.

An inherent difficulty is the eventual transfer from i/t/a orthography to regular print or traditional orthography. Because of poor transfer and generalization ability, some slow and disabled learners may experience difficulty making this transition. It is difficult for them to learn two methods of doing something and they must in effect unlearn the sound-symbol association previously learned in order to make the transition to regular print.

A sample i/t/a page is shown in Figure 3.3.

Programmed Instruction

A rather recent innovation in reading instruction and one growing in popularity is programmed instruction. The student is actively involved in the learning process, continuously responding while working with material broken down into

Sample Linguistics Page   Figure 3.2

				22	23

lim	slim	cab	scab	lug	slug	A Split Slat
kim	skim	lab	slab	mug	smug	
wim	swim	tab	stab	nug	snug	Stan had a sled. Sal had a pan.
						Stan slid. Sal slid.
	cot	Scot	cum	scum		Jim had a big red sled.
	lot	slot	lum	slum		Jim sat on it. It slid. It sped.
	pot	spot	wum	swum		It hit a snag. A slat split.
						Did Jim skin a leg?
	Stan	stun	stud			Yes, Jim did. Sad Jim skin-a-leg!
	span	spun	spud			Jim got up. Sal had Jim sit in a pan.
						Stan slid Jim in it. Jim sped.
spin	span	stab	stem	stub		Jim did not hit a snag.
spit	spat	stag	step	stud		Jim sped on.
split	spat	Stan	step	stun		
spit	slat	scan	stop	spun		

Source: From *Let's Read,* Part 4. Clarence L. Barnhart, Inc., Bronxville, New York. Used by permission.

small, sequential steps. Repeated practice, self-pacing, and immediate feedback are essential elements of good programmed material.

These elements in programmed instruction can help sharpen the focus of goals and methods for teaching slow and disabled learners. These teaching principles hold the promise of being both effective and efficient in overcoming the learning problems characteristic of atypical learners.

Programmed instruction materials include:

The Fitzhugh Plus Program. Allied Education Council, 1965. Galien, Mich., 49113
Student-consumable workbooks in five levels covering perceptual learning and understanding, spatial organization, language and numbers.

Figure 3.3   Sample i/t/a Page

fiend a wæ

wuns ſhær woſ a littl œld wɷman.

uſher peepl wɷd sæ,

"ie cannot dɷ it. ſhær iſ nœ wæ."

but not ſhe littl œld wɷman!

ſhee wɷd sæ, "ſhiŋk! fiend a wæ!"

wun dæ ſhe littl œld wɷman sed,

"ie wɷd liek sum fiſh tɷ eet.

ie will wauk intɷ toun and get sum."

Source: From the book, *Find a Way,* Book 4, *Easy-to-Read i/t/a Program,* revised by Albert J. Mazurkiewicz and Harold J. Tanzer. Copyright © 1966 by Initial Teaching Alphabet Publications, Inc.

Sullivan Programmed Materials. McGraw-Hill Book Co., 1965. New York, N.Y., 10020
Series of twenty-three storybooks and accompanying programmed workbooks for pupils. Teachers guides.

Programmed Reading. Globe Book Co., 1970. New York, N.Y., 10010
A single book composed of fifteen units. Designed primarily to take the pupil from his present level of achievement to a higher one. Appropriate for fourth- or fifth-grade readers.

Summary

Underlying this book's approach to teaching reading is a theory of three developmental stages of learning: Stage I, reading wholes; Stage II, learning details; and Stage III, reading without awareness of details.

Two major approaches to beginning reading instruction are the meaning-emphasis approach and the code-emphasis approach. The meaning-emphasis approach stresses teaching the child to understand the content of the story. The code-emphasis approach stresses word recognition.

Meaning-emphasis approaches include:

1. Basal reader—the most commonly used tool for teaching reading in our schools today. It is an organized sequential system of materials for teaching a variety of reading skills.
2. Individualized reading—a method that allows the student to select his or her own materials and to progress at his or her own rate.
3. Language experience—a story method based on the child's experience and language pattern. In this approach, the child reads materials that he or she has created.

Code-emphasis approaches include:

1. Phonics—A method emphasizing the sound-symbol relationships of letters as a means of teaching word recognition.
2. Linguistic method—an approach emphasizing words with a consonant-vowel-consonant combination (c-v-c). Children learn the whole word and discover by themselves the generalizations concerning the relationship between sounds and letters.
3. Initial teaching alphabet (i/t/a)—a method utilizing an alphabet of forty-four symbols that represent the basic sounds of the English language.

4. Programmed instruction—a systematic presentation of learning materials broken down into small sequential steps. Repeated practice, self-pacing, and immediate feedback are basic principles of programmed instruction.

The developmental methods discussed in this chapter represent those used with normal children. Adaptations of these materials for the atypical learner will be discussed in the next two chapters.

Adaptation of Methods and Materials for Atypical Learners: Early Stages of Reading

4

Both this chapter and Chapter 5 discuss ways of adapting developmental methods of teaching reading to meet the needs of the atypical learner. This chapter deals with the beginning stages of reading; Chapter 5 focuses on the later stages of reading.

One outcome of the cross-categorical or noncategorical movement in special education is an emphasis on the commonalities rather than the differences among the various categories of exceptional children. The message from this noncategorical framework is that there is not a specific approach for teaching reading to the mentally retarded, another for slow-learning children, and yet another for the learning-disabled. Instead, diagnostic and teaching methods cut across the categories of exceptionality. Furthermore, the noncategorical position suggests that more important than the category of exceptionality are such factors as the child's abilities and disabilities in learning, present developmental levels in a variety of functions, and attitudes toward learning. In short, there is much overlap in the ways of teaching reading to children who are identified as mentally retarded, slow learners, learning-disabled, and other categories of exceptional children (Bateman, 1971; Dunn, 1971; Gallagher, 1971; Hallahan & Kauffman, 1976; Meyen, 1971; Quay, 1971).

Levels of Reading Performance for Atypical Learners

Slow-learning and mentally retarded children vary in degree of retardation. Disabled learners also exhibit differences in abilities, and some can reach only a limited reading level. Retarded children with varying degrees of intelligence reach differing levels of performance in reading and should not be pressed to go further than their capabilities warrant. Children with severe learning disabilities may have difficulty achieving high reading performance. Nevertheless, certain reading functions are needed and can be set as realistic goals. It is helpful to think of three levels of performance: (1) reading for protection, (2) reading for information or instruction, and (3) reading for pleasure. It should be pointed out that we really have no way of knowing what the ceiling is for each child. Therefore, it is necessary to keep the door open for further achievement.

Reading for Protection

Some children can learn to read only simple words and phrases. If a child is moderately retarded, it would be frustrating to both child and teacher to try to achieve more than this. For such a child, the aim of reading instruction should be to teach him or her to read certain signs for information and self-protection.

Learning to read words and phrases such as the following is essential for the moderately retarded child:

BE CAREFUL	DOCTOR	GENTLEMEN
WALK	ENTRANCE	NO TRESPASS-
INFLAMMABLE	BUS STATION	ING
DANGER	OUT	LADIES
UP	DOWN	POISON
IN	PRIVATE	WET PAINT
MEN	BOYS	WOMEN
EXIT	STOP	GIRLS
EXPLOSIVES	REST ROOMS	SLOW
DYNAMITE	HELP WANTED	SCHOOL
FIRE	KEEP OFF	FIRE ESCAPE
GO	RAILROAD CROSSING	KEEP OUT

Reading for Information or Instruction

Most borderline and mildly retarded children can learn to read for information or instruction. They should be able to learn to look up names in a telephone book, to read official signs and warnings, to read timetables, directions, and some sections of the newspaper.

Reading for Pleasure

Many retarded children at the upper level of retardation as well as slow and disabled learners can learn to read for pleasure. The teacher should help these children attain this goal.

Specific Directions for Instruction in the Initial Stages of Reading

89
Specific
Directions for
Instruction in
the Initial
Stages of
Reading

The teaching of beginning reading to a nine- or ten-year-old child who has failed to learn to read during his or her previous school career is a different problem from the teaching of beginning reading to a six-year-old mentally normal child who has not been faced with school failures. By the time the failing child is ready to learn to read, he or she has already become discouraged, and in many cases has developed defense mechanisms toward school work. To teach such a child to read, the teacher must: (a) reestablish the child's self-confidence, (b) introduce a great deal more repetition than is ordinarily employed with normal children, (c) introduce a greater variety of presentations, and (d) prolong the period of training for each stage of reading. Assessment of the child should lead to selection of a method of instruction and of materials appropriate to the child's abilities and disabilities.

After the child has been given prereading experiences in the manner outlined in Chapter 2, the teacher should determine whether the child is ready to read and whether he or she can profit from instruction in reading. This may be determined by the child's mental level and ability to learn via incidental reading materials presented during the prereading period.

Two methods used simultaneously in teaching beginning reading are discussed below.

The Incidental Method

The incidental method of teaching reading refers to the presentation of words and phrases related to the immediate experiences of the child. With slow learners, mentally retarded, and learning-disabled children, the incidental method can be used to help determine readiness for reading at the close of the prereading period and later as a supplement to a systematic reading method. The incidental method alone will not teach slow and disabled learners to read. It should be used only as an aid to a more systematic method.

During the course of prereading activities, the teacher should occasionally introduce written words and phrases connected with the child's activity at the moment. When teachers discover that some children are beginning to learn these words and are capable of reading them, they know that the children are about ready to learn to read, regardless of their mental age.

During the beginning reading stage and even thereafter, a great deal of learning can be absorbed by incidental reading of signs, labels, bulletin boards, and other materials described below.

1. *Bulletin boards.* A bulletin board could be utilized for incidental reading. Children's names and simple directions for

their participation in activities can be written on the bulletin board. For example, if Tom, Bill, and Mary are selected to perform a particular task, the teacher writes the names *Tom, Bill,* and *Mary* and their duties on the bulletin board. In this way, the children will learn to recognize their names and possibly some words and phrases. At a later stage the bulletin board may be used to display new items and directions for various activities.

2.   *Labels.* Labels may be used during the prereading period as well as during beginning reading. The word *chair* can be printed and hung on a chair. Likewise, the table, door, desk, and so forth may be used to give the children a concrete example of the symbol. Removing the labels and allowing the children to replace them on the proper objects is another game that can be used for incidental learning.

3.   *Pictures.* Pictures of animals or children, labeled appropriately, may be hung on the walls. Pictures serve a valuable purpose in incidental reading and may be used with words, phrases, or sentences.

4.   *Assignments.* During beginning reading, certain assignments may be given the children outside of the reading period. If the children are about to engage in handwork, the teacher may discuss what each child is going to do and may write on the board the directions, such as, "Sally will set the table," or "John will draw a picture."

5.   *Greetings.* Greetings and other statements by the teacher may occasionally be written on the board in place of the oral expression. When the children come into the classroom in the morning, the teacher may write on the board, "Good morning" and ask the children whether any of them knows what was written. It can be expanded later with "Good morning, boys," "Good morning, girls," and "Good morning, children."

6.   *Rules.* Certain rules of health, cooperation, or of classroom activities may be discussed and then printed on cards to be posted around the room. "We brush our teeth," "Our hands are clean," "We are quiet in class," and similar statements may be used for incidental reading. These cards should be changed as frequently as the children learn them. This approach is useful during the latter part of the prereading period and during the beginning reading period.

The Language-Experience Method

Reading should be taught to slow-learning, mentally retarded, and learning-disabled children in accordance with the conventional language-experience method described in Chapter 3, but greater variation and more repetition should be used. A systematic plan will be discussed to aid the teacher in the use

91
Specific
Directions for
Instruction in
the Initial
Stages of
Reading

of this method. Teachers must remember that all children do not react alike, and they should use the method that will work best with each child. For example, Miss Jackson was confronted with the following situation when she attempted to introduce a paragraph of chart reading to Peter, a boy who had attended school for a number of years and still had not learned to read. When Peter, age 10, whose mental age was 6–0, saw the chart, he retorted, "That's baby stuff. I had that in the first grade. I want to read books like the older boys."

In such cases it is defeating for teachers to present material in the usual sequence. Instead, they should vary the beginning reading materials so that pupils do not recognize them as first-grade materials.

The typical sequence of six steps in the language-experience method is described below. However, the teacher may have to vary the sequence to suit the needs and abilities of certain slow and disabled learners.

Step 1. The teacher should first be sure that the children are ready to read. They must be sufficiently mature mentally; they should have acquired a vocabulary and other abilities listed in Chapter 2. The most important requirement is that the children have a need and desire to read.

Step 2. On the basis of their immediate experiences, the children should be stimulated to tell a story. For example, if they had been to a circus the previous day, they might describe their experiences. As the children relate their experiences the teacher writes the sentences on the board in this way:

We went to the circus.

We saw a lion.

We saw a monkey.

We saw a clown.

Printing rather than cursive writing is used since it is easier, more uniform, and more like the printed materials. The children then read the sentences. These may be left on the board until the next day, when the children may be asked to reread the sentences before formulating others about a different experience.

In formulating these paragraphs, the teacher should keep in mind a number of principles: (a) the stories should contain short sentences; (b) the sentences should be derived from the children's immediate experiences; (c) the paragraphs should contain only three or four sentences at the beginning of training, with a gradual increase in the length of each sentence and of the paragraph; and (d) words should be introduced that will later appear in the book to be used for reading instruction.

Step 3. On the following day, the paragraph that had been written on the board should be copied onto a chart. The children should then be asked to read the story from the chart. In this way the children read the same material in a different setting. The charts are read aloud by several or all of the children. At this stage of the reading process, the children are reading the chart paragraphs partly from memory and partly on the basis of the configuration of each sentence and the paragraph. They see vague wholes, rather than words or letters in words. They are perceiving wholes and are in the first stage of the reading process.

Step 4. On succeeding days, new paragraphs should be written on the board. These paragraphs should utilize the immediate experiences of the children and should contain relatively few new words. These stories should also be put on charts. The chart materials may be made up in the form of a large book so that the children can read continuously as they turn the pages of stories that they have experienced and that they have helped construct.

Step 5. The first four steps in beginning reading are usually sufficient to teach normal children a sight vocabulary. Many teachers of normal children utilize the method presented above for the first six to twelve weeks of the first grade and then introduce preprimers and primers. Many more presentations, however, should be given children who are retarded, slow, or disabled learners. Teachers of such children must continue the introductory reading experiences and go beyond the point where they would stop for normal children.

The following devices and methods of presenting the same materials are recommended so that words and sentences may be repeated in a variety of settings:

(a) *The moving-picture method.* This method can either take the place of the chart method or supplement it. Some children object to chart reading because it is "baby stuff" and because they have had it in past years. The moving-picture method presents reading materials in a novel and interesting fashion. To use the moving-picture method, a large box should be constructed, about the size of reading charts, with a roller at each end. A roll of reading materials may be placed on one roller and the end attached to the second roller. A crank is attached to the second roller, and the teacher or a child can turn the crank until the first story appears. The children can then read the story, turn the crank, and read the next one. This presentation is highly motivating because it has the appearance of a show. It is effective because it presents chart and board reading materials in a different setting.

One teacher utilized the moving-picture method as follows: She asked Donald if he had a pet at home. Under repeated questioning, Donald related the following story:

93
Specific
Directions for
Instruction in
the Initial
Stages of
Reading

> I have a dog.
>
> His name is Jip.
>
> He can play.
>
> He can run.
>
> He can jump.

The teacher wrote this story on the board and had the children read it; she then wrote it on a chart with a light pencil. Donald filled out the penciled marks of the teacher so that he would be able to see the writing at a distance. He used a black crayon to color the letters that formed the words and pasted a picture of a dog at the top of the page. Another child in the class, Sally, gave the following story:

> I have a little brother.
>
> His name is Tom.
>
> He can play.
>
> He can run.
>
> He can jump.

This story was written on a chart by the teacher, and Sally was asked to fill out the words. Other children in the class wrote or helped write stories of their own. The charts were then pasted on a long piece of heavy paper and were placed over one of the rolls of the moving-picture box. One child turned the crank until the first paragraph appeared. The teacher then asked, "Whose story is that?" Donald, the boy who helped write this story and who had pasted a picture of a dog on it, read the story. Sally also read her story and the other children read theirs. Later, the children read one another's stories.

Preparing charts for a "moving-picture" reel gives children greater familiarity with words and sentences since they must trace the words and sentences, color them, or mark them as they wish before they are placed on the reel. These activities become interesting and purposeful for the child.

(b) *Duplicating the stories.* This is done for the purpose of further repetition, which facilitates fixation of words and phrases. Stories that were used on charts and in the moving picture may be duplicated by the teacher and given to the children for reading purposes. In this way, the same material is presented in a new setting.

As a further incentive to reading the duplicated sheets, the children may use them to make books. Each child makes his or her own book of stories. Children may read and illustrate these books by drawing or pasting pictures on the duplicated sheets. Binding the books and keeping them as a permanent record to read at various times or to take home and read to their parents also stimulate the children's reading interest.

Since preprimers and primers may not be interesting to older retarded children, many duplicated booklets will have to be given to them during their period of beginning reading. In addition to duplicating the stories that the children have read on the board, on charts, or in the moving picture, the teacher may make up stories that are interesting to the children and are within their range of abilities. In this way, the negative attitude of older children toward preprimers and primers can be eliminated. At the same time, much reading material may be presented.

(c) *Overhead projector or slide projector.* With the use of the overhead projector, the teacher may print on slides the stories that have been read from the charts or the moving-picture box. These slides may be placed in an overhead projector and shown on a white wall. This presentation, because of its novelty, motivates the children to reread the materials. This technique helps many distractible children pay attention to the reading materials. Whenever children begin to show disinterest in chart reading or in duplicated stories, the teacher should immediately vary the method of presentation. Visual projectors are one alternative method of presenting reading materials in a way that maintains attention and interest.

Step 6. After the children have acquired a sight vocabulary through reading stories of their own experiences, the teacher should help them become aware of details by teaching them how to learn to recognize individual words. This is the second stage in the reading process and may be facilitated by a variety of methods. Some of these devices and methods follow:

(a) When the children read a story from the board or from the moving-picture box or the duplicated sheets, the teacher may ask them to point out individual words. In this way, the children are introduced to learning the individual words in a story.

(b) The chart or duplicated stories may be cut into sentences and the children asked to reconstruct the story by placing the sentences in the correct order. In this way the children begin to learn differences in larger units. After they have reconstructed a number of charts and a number of cut-up duplicated sheets at their desks, they may go on to a second step in learning details.

(c) An effective method of teaching the children to make differentiations among words is to cut the chart into sentences and then to cut the sentences into words. A rack should be built so that the children can take a series of words and reconstruct a sentence from them. At first it may be necessary for the child to have a model of the original sentence for

reference. Later, reconstructing the sentence without the
original model should be encouraged.

95
The Beginning
Reading Period:
Duration and
Materials

The methods given above are more intense and introduce
more repetition than those usually used with the normal child.
With normal children it is sufficient to ask them to find a
specific word on a chart. With the slow or disabled learner,
however, the teacher must introduce a great variety of presentations, utilizing the same materials repeatedly in many
settings.

The language-experience method is flexible enough to meet
the needs of the slow and the disabled learner. As the sight
vocabulary builds up through the development of experience
charts, a firm foundation is being established for later learning
in word analysis and phonics. The child is also gaining an
appreciation of reading for what it really is—"talk written
down."

The Beginning Reading Period:
Duration and Materials

For children who learn in a normal fashion, the chart-reading
period is usually planned for the first six to twelve weeks of
the first grade. During this period many charts and stories are
read. The children will have acquired a sight vocabulary of
one hundred or more words before preprimers and primers
are given to them.

For the slow or disabled learner, the beginning reading
period requires more than six to twelve weeks. If the teacher
of such children spends at least one semester to one year with
beginning reading materials before introducing books, the
time is well spent. During this time, the child gains self-
confidence in reading. A prolonged chart-reading period may
also be helpful for the child with a maturational lag. After
a substantial chart-reading period, the children find that books
are not too difficult for them. In this way, discouragement
may be avoided.

Basal Readers

Because most basal readers have been designed for average
children, they frequently need modification for use with slow
or deviant learners. The introduction of new vocabulary is
often too rapid and frequently there is not enough repetition
of known words to assure mastery or overlearning.

To this end, duplicated stories that utilize words occurring
in first readers or simple books may be used, but over a much
longer period than they are used with normal children. The
teacher may write stories that include preprimer and primer

vocabulary but that have a more mature outlook and are presented in a different setting. Some children enjoy reading preprimers and primers. In such cases it is permissible to introduce a preprimer or primer after the child has acquired some sight vocabulary. In introducing books and reading materials for exceptional children, the teacher should keep in mind the following points:

1. Continue chart reading, moving-picture reading, and the use of cut-up charts and sentences, duplicated stories, and the overhead projector even after book reading has begun. The words used in these stories should include the unfamiliar words that are going to be presented in the book material in order to make book reading easier and more pleasurable.

2. Stress accuracy rather than speed with slow and disabled learners. These children tend to continue to repeat their mistakes. It is better, therefore, to teach them the correct response first rather than to correct errors later.

3. When book reading has been introduced, find a variety of books of simple materials. Allow the children to read many of these books. Even with normal children it is good practice to have them read several preprimers and primers before introducing the first-grade reader. With atypical learners, many such simple books should be read.

Many publishers of primary books are supplementing the regular basal readers with additional reading material at the same grade level for children who need more repetition of the same vocabulary. *The Codebook Series* (1975) published by Lippincott Company is a teacher-directed working text activity for children who are experiencing difficulty moving ahead in reading. This series can be used as an independent program or it can be used for class or individual remediation.

Rand, McNally & Company has devised a *Curriculum Motivation Series* (1972) designed for less able readers that provides supplementary material to parallel or to follow the basic reading program. In Macmillan Company's *Solo Books* (1975), basal readers are supplemented by optional readers.

Ginn & Company's *Reading 720 Series* (1976) supplements a strong reading skills development program with a variety of additional experiences in the language arts. These booster activities include games, manipulative activities, read-along recordings, and decoding sound filmstrips.

When supplementary materials like these have the same vocabulary as the reader, many more repetitions are given. These supplementary aids may be substituted for some of the stories that the teacher would otherwise have to write for the children. It should be remembered, however, that no book can be as meaningful as a story based on the child's immediate experience. Consequently, supplementary readers should not wholly replace "made-up stories" in a class of atypical children.

Table 4.1 220 Basic Word Sight Vocabulary

Preprimer	Primer	First	Second	Third
1. the	45. when	89. many	133. know	177. don't
2. of	46. who	90. before	134. while	178. does
3. and	47. will	91. must	135. last	179. got
4. to	48. more	92. through	136. might	180. united
5. a	49. no	93. back	137. us	181. left
6. in	50. if	94. years	138. great	182. number
7. that	51. out	95. where	139. old	183. course
8. is	52. so	96. much	140. year	184. war
9. was	53. said	97. your	141. off	185. until
10. he	54. what	98. may	142. come	186. always
11. for	55. up	99. well	143. since	187. away
12. it	56. its	100. down	144. against	188. something
13. with	57. about	101. should	145. go	189. fact
14. as	58. into	102. because	146. came	190. through
15. his	59. than	103. each	147. right	191. water
16. on	60. them	104. just	148. used	192. less
17. be	61. can	105. those	149. take	193. public
18. at	62. only	106. people	150. three	194. put
19. by	63. other	107. Mr.	151. states	195. thing
20. I	64. new	108. how	152. himself	196. almost
21. this	65. some	109. too	153. few	197. hand
22. had	66. could	110. little	154. house	198. enough
23. not	67. time	111. state	155. use	199. far
24. are	68. these	112. good	156. during	200. took
25. but	69. two	113. very	157. without	201. head
26. from	70. may	114. make	158. again	202. yet
27. or	71. then	115. would	159. place	203. government
28. have	72. do	116. still	160. American	204. system
29. an	73. first	117. own	161. around	205. better
30. they	74. any	118. see	162. however	206. set
31. which	75. my	119. men	163. home	207. told
32. one	76. now	120. work	164. small	208. nothing
33. you	77. such	121. long	165. found	209. night
34. were	78. like	122. get	166. Mrs.	210. end
35. her	79. our	123. here	167. thought	211. why
36. all	80. over	124. between	168. went	212. called
37. she	81. man	125. both	169. say	213. didn't
38. there	82. me	126. life	170. part	214. eyes
39. would	83. even	127. being	171. once	215. find
40. their	84. most	128. under	172. general	216. going
41. we	85. made	129. never	173. high	217. look
42. him	86. after	130. day	174. upon	218. asked
43. been	87. also	131. same	175. school	219. later
44. has	88. did	132. another	176. every	220. knew

Source: **Dale D. Johnson, "The Dolch List Reexamined,"** *The Reading Teacher* 24 (February, 1971), pp. 455–456. The 220 most frequent words in the Kucera-Francis corpus.

The Basic Vocabulary

Teachers of slow and disabled learners often ask, "What words should be introduced and made a part of the child's sight vocabulary?" One of the most influential sight word lists used in the past thirty years has been the Dolch Basic Sight Word List (Dolch, 1948, p. 99). This list was compiled in the mid-1930s from studies of frequency of use done in the 1920s. Johnson (1971) recommended that this list be updated, since the frequently used words have changed over the past forty years. Using the study by Kucera and Francis, *Computational Analysis of Present-Day American English* (1967), Johnson developed an updated 220 Basic Sight Word Vocabulary. This list is shown in Table 4.1 and includes the most frequently used words in the Kucera-Francis corpus. These are words that children should know by sight—that is, without analysis to decode the word. The words are divided into five groups that represent words for the first five reading levels.

Other sight vocabulary lists have been developed. Fry (1957) lists 600 instant words for sight recognition to be used with remedial cases. The Harrison-Jacobson Core Words (Harris & Sipay, 1975, p. 382) is a list of 58 preprimer words, 63 primer words, and 212 first-reader words.

Through an analysis of fourteen vocabulary studies, Hillerich (1974) derived an updated basic reading/writing vocabulary. Of the 240 starter words in the Hillerich list, 190 words appeared on almost all of the vocabulary lists. These words are shown in Table 4.2.

The teacher of atypical learners should be acquainted with the various word lists so that the necessary words will be included in the children's prebook work. Other words may also be used, but unless the child masters by sight the words that appear most frequently in books, reading will become too laborious a process. Mastery of the words used most commonly in primers and first readers helps the child read fluently and with meaning.

Independent Activities for the Beginning Stages of Reading

Slow and disabled learners sometimes learn to read mechanically and without much comprehension. The teacher should constantly help children understand what they are reading. A good method to assure adequate comprehension and to offset any emphasis on mechanics of reading that may have developed in the reading sessions is to provide seatwork activities that direct the child to read for understanding.

Not all reading performance can be accomplished by direct instruction and incidental reading. The child must develop some independence in reading and at the same time engage

Table 4.2 The 190 Starter Words in Order of Frequency of Use (4 original lists)

Midyear Norms, based on individual recognition testing in three school districts:
+ = Grade 1 (N = 186)—eighty-nine words were known by 50 percent or more of pupils.

Grade 2 (N = 208)—all words were known by 50 percent except *through* (47 percent).

Grade 3 (N = 208)—all known by 75 percent, except *through* (71 percent), *every* (61 percent), *were* (50 percent).

+ the	from	+ down	only	last
+ and	+ up	back	much	away
+ a	+ will	just	+ us	each
+ to	+ do	year	+ take	never
+ of	+ said	+ little	name	while
+ in	+ then	+ make	+ here	+ took
+ it	what	who	say	men
+ is	+ like	after	got	next
+ was	her	people	around	may
+ I	+ go	+ come	any	+ Mr.
+ he	+ them	+ no	use	give
+ you	time	because	place	show
+ that	+ if	first	put	once
+ for	+ some	more	+ boy	something
+ on	about	many	water	+ room
they	+ by	know	also	must
+ with	+ him	made	before	didn't
+ have	+ or	thing	+ off	always
+ are	+ can	went	through	+ car
+ had	+ me	+ man	right	told
+ we	+ your	want	ask	why
+ be	+ an	way	most	small
+ one	+ day	+ work	should	children
+ but	their	which	don't	still
+ at	other	+ good	than	head
+ when	very	well	three	left
+ all	could	came	found	white
+ this	+ has	new	these	let
+ she	+ look	+ school	saw	world
+ there	+ get	+ too	find	under
+ not	+ now	been	tell	same
+ his	+ see	think	+ help	kind
as	our	+ home	every	+ keep
were	+ two	+ house	again	+ am
would	+ into	+ play	another	best
+ so	+ did	+ old	+ big	better
+ my	over	long	night	soon
+ out	+ how	+ where	thought	four

Source: "Starter Words" © 1973, Robert L. Hillerich.

in purposeful activities while other children are receiving instruction from the teacher. Some methods for seatwork are presented here.

1. Stories may be made up and traced on charts for moving-picture reading, as mentioned previously. This activity gives the child motor and kinesthetic acquaintance with words. Any reinforcement of words by a kinesthetic cue aids the learning and retention of those words. This activity, therefore, is more than mere busy-work—provided that children know what they are doing and are not simply copying a geometric design.

2. A method of developing word recognition is to duplicate pictures and words and instruct the child to draw a line from the picture to the correct word. Words such as *boy, horse, the, beautiful* may be typed under a picture of a boy. The child may be told to find the word that fits the picture. At a later stage the word *boy* may be presented with words of similar characteristics such as *ball, dog, wing,* and the like. By proceeding from simple to more difficult discriminations, the child's capacity for word discrimination and word recognition is increased.

3. A method similar to the one just described is to write short phrases and sentences under pictures and instruct the child to circle the phrase or sentence that describes the picture. For a picture showing a boy running, the teacher may write several sentences, such as:

The dog is running.

The dog is standing.

The boy is running.

The girl is running.

4. Picture cards with the word and picture on one side and the identifying word on the other side will prove helpful as a supplementary means of teaching word recognition. Children can work independently with the cards, or one child can test another child with these cards. Many games that aid recognition may be played with picture word cards. The children first look at the picture and word, pronounce it to themselves, then turn the card around and try to remember the word without the picture.

A phrase or sentence may also be typed under a picture while the reverse side of the card may show only the phrase or sentence. For example, on a card containing a picture of a dog running, there may be the sentence, *The dog is running.* On the reverse side of the card the same sentence may be written, but without a picture. This permits the child to read the sentence and check the reading by turning the card over and looking at the picture.

101
Independent
Activities for
the Beginning
Stages of
Reading

5. A device similar to the one just described is pasting words, phrases, and sentences written or typed by the teacher on pictures that have been drawn by the children or cut out from magazines. The child may paste the words or sentences on these pictures and make a little booklet of them. In this way word recognition and reading for meaning are facilitated.

6. An interesting device utilizing the sentence completion method may be used: known sentences and stories are duplicated and certain words are omitted. The child may write in the missing word or draw a picture of the missing word. An example of this type of activity is given below:

I am a _____	(The child draws or cuts out a picture of a boy or girl and pastes it in the blank space.)
My name is _____	(The child writes in his or her name.)
I go to _____	(The child pastes a picture of school or writes it in.)

7. Written directions that the child must execute is another useful reading activity. These may be provided in a variety of ways. One way is to write instructions for completing pictures, such as:

Color the apple red.

Color the pencil yellow.

Color the boy's coat blue.

8. Free reading must be provided for the children as soon as they can read. A great variety of easy pamphlets and books should be available in the classroom. Children should be allowed to select any book they want and read it whenever they wish. The teacher must constantly guide the child to read for comprehension by asking questions, setting up goals for reading, and reviewing what has been read. Free reading or individualized instruction will also enable the teacher to observe the interests of the children through their choice of books.

Free reading should be one of the aims of initial instruction. Whenever a child selects a book either to look at the pictures or to read the contents, the teacher should not interrupt the activity. Some teachers insist that a child complete workbook assignments before reading. This attitude indicates that the teacher has lost sight of the end of any assignment for the means.

9.   Independent seatwork activity can also be provided through the use of word games. These games can be used independently in any primary classroom to provide intensive study of phonics and structural skills necessary to ensure successful independent reading. Capitalizing on a child's interest in games, this learning-play activity helps children make associations between sight and sound.

Word cards containing pictures of objects, such as a box, a pen, or a duck, are placed face down in front of the child, who selects a card from the pile and matches it to the key word on the talking picture card according to the initial sound of the word. If two children play the game together, that child "wins" who has the greater number of correctly matched cards. With some adaptations of the rules, these word games can be used with retarded and slow-learning children to provide meaningful seatwork activity.

10.   Many basal readers are accompanied by workbooks that include numerous seatwork activities based on the vocabulary of the reader. If these workbooks are carefully selected and are not too difficult, they can be used with slow and disabled learners for seatwork activities.

In instructing teachers of regular elementary school pupils, McKee (1966) points out:

> If the teacher has the pupil use each exercise only after the skill it is concerned with has been introduced . . . if the teacher makes sure that the pupil understands how to proceed in working on the exercise, if she sees to it that his responses in the exercise are carefully checked, and if she takes time to be sure that he understands why each mistake he makes is a mistake, then workbooks can be quite helpful in relieving weaknesses inherent in group instruction, in providing the pupil with needed practice, in making him aware of his progress, in locating his particular deficiencies and in pointing out where reteaching is in order (pp. 166–167).

Teachers of slow and disabled learners must be particularly conscientious in following McKee's suggestions; otherwise, the use of workbooks is apt to become nothing more than monotonous busy-work for the children.

It is true that seatwork activities instigated by the teacher are better adapted to the experience and ability of the child than are activities suggested by the commercial workbooks. Therefore the teacher should make an effort to prepare for such activities materials that would obtain results superior to those obtained with commercial workbooks. However, the teacher must devote sufficient time and thought to preparing the materials to insure their adequacy. Otherwise, it is preferable to use commercial workbooks in the way McKee recommends.

Mainstreaming Slow and Disabled Learners in the Regular Classroom: Beginning Reading Instruction

103
Mainstreaming
Slow and
Disabled
Learners in
the Regular
Classroom:
Beginning
Reading
Instruction

Special education teachers are generally prepared to teach the initial stages of reading to slow and disabled learners in special education classes. If the special class is homogeneous, the program for reading instruction is given to the whole group, or to subgroups within the larger class. Grouping will depend upon the number of children and their stages of development. If the class is ungraded, the program of initial instruction in reading may be given to the group that requires such training. Similarly, if an exceptional child is placed in the first grade with normal children, it may be well to use a program of teaching as outlined in this chapter. The teacher should intensify, vary, and repeat many stories for the retarded child even though such repetition may not be necessary for the normal or the borderline or disabled learner.

The task of teaching reading to the atypical child becomes more difficult when the child is retained in the regular classroom. This trend, referred to as *mainstreaming,* presents a new and unique problem for the regular grade teacher in terms of reading instruction. Federal law encourages mainstreaming as the "least restrictive alternative" (Public Law 94–142, 1975). The law specifies that to the maximum extent possible, handicapped children are to be educated with non-handicapped children. Many of these children may not have begun to read, but through social promotion and mainstreaming, they are found in second-, third-, fourth-, and even fifth-grade classrooms.

Logically, the teacher should be instructing the child in beginning reading, yet the curriculum of these grades is designed for normal children who can read. Much of the learning in the intermediate grades is dependent upon reading ability. The child who is unable to read is consequently bewildered. When placed in the intermediate grades, the older child who cannot read develops defense mechanisms, a bullying attitude, withdrawal behavior, or other unwholesome compensations. A *behavior problem* has been defined as the discrepancy between a child's capacity to perform and the requirements of the environment. If the environment requires reading ability, as it does in the third, fourth, and fifth grades, and the child is unable to read at all, the stage is being set for a behavior problem.

Many regular classroom teachers ask: "How can I teach the disabled child in my class to read when my curriculum does not provide for initial instruction in reading?" This problem may be attacked by (a) giving the child an opportunity to excel in some nonacademic activity, and (b) teaching the child beginning reading. These objectives may be approached as follows:

1. Give children every opportunity to engage in tasks they can do well. They may be able to draw, dramatize, do handwork, tell about their experiences, and play with other children. They may excel in some classroom activities. Some teachers give the child certain responsibilities in class, such as caring for the pencils, keeping library books in order, handing out and collecting papers, taking care of the garden or watering the flowers, straightening up after class is dismissed, and other similar activities.

The purpose of encouraging an atypical child to do nonacademic work in the class is to help the child establish self-confidence as well as to imbue the normal children in the class with the feeling that the child is their equal in many respects. In this way the exceptional child becomes a part of the group except in some academic activities such as reading. If the teacher succeeds in helping the exceptional child share in many activities with the group, the normal children will soon realize that this child cannot read as well as they can, but that they probably cannot run as fast or care for the plants as efficiently as this child does.

2. Give the atypical learner individual instruction in reading. If the child cannot read and must have the same instruction as a beginner, this pupil should be taught as a beginner. The teacher of a regular second-, third-, fourth-, or even fifth-grade class obviously need not prepare charts based on the child's experience or build a moving-picture box or use an overhead projector for the presentation of simple materials for one or two children in the class who require such instruction. But the teacher can use some of the methods and apply some of the principles that are utilized with exceptional children in a special class.

Many teachers in the elementary grades set aside a part of the day, a "special help period," to aid individual children with their work. In this period teachers may give the slow or disabled learner instruction in beginning reading. They may utilize any of the techniques described in this chapter that may be applicable to the specific child. The following suggestions may aid the teacher who wishes to give instruction in beginning reading to atypical learners in the regular class although the curriculum does not include such an activity:

1. Instead of writing on the board a story that the child relates from past experience, the teacher may write the story for the child on a piece of paper at the pupil's desk and allow the pupil to read it.

2. Instead of placing the written story on a large chart, the teacher may type the story the next day and instruct the child to read it.

3. After many such stories have been typed, the child may compile them into a book and at various times may read these books to the teacher or to others.

105
Mainstreaming
Slow and
Disabled
Learners in
the Regular
Classroom:
Beginning
Reading
Instruction

4. For seatwork activities, the disabled learners may trace or print stories of their own. Occasionally they may ask for help from the teacher or from another pupil.

5. Picture word cards, with a picture on one side and the word or phrase on the other, may help the child learn words and phrases without aid from the teacher. Word games can be used effectively.

6. If a typewriter is available, the atypical learners should be allowed to use it to copy some of their stories or to perform some other exercise that may help them learn to read.

7. Primers or simple pamphlets and books may be used whenever the child has acquired a sight vocabulary sufficient for the task. When these are first introduced, the teacher should devote some time to the child to help provide an adequate start.

8. A supply of high-interest, low-reading-level books should be available in the classroom. Once atypical learners are able to read at a high first- or low second-grade level, their interest in reading can be maintained if they have access to such books. A suggested list of available high-interest, low-vocabulary books is given in Appendix B.

9. In all the child's activities the teacher should aim to develop a sight vocabulary of words most commonly used in primary books. The word lists developed by Dolch, Johnson, Fry, and Hillerich referred to in this chapter should be familiar to the teacher.

10. Children should be given directions in writing so that they may become accustomed to the utilization of reading for a purpose. These directions should be simple and within the children's reading ability.

11. An effective method used by some teachers is to allow an advanced pupil in the class to help the atypical learner. Careful selection of a "tutor" may result in adequate progress. Many teachers are unable to take time from their class duties to give individual instruction to the slow or disabled learner. In such cases, the teacher's instruction must be supplemented with help from another pupil. The teacher should observe the reactions of the pupils in the class toward the retarded or slow-learning child and select the one who is most friendly to help with reading instruction. In many cases other students are happy to have the opportunity to help another child. Sometimes the exceptional child can help the normal child in some other task. Don, who was diagnosed as retarded, put it this way: "My friend helped me in reading and I helped him when he got into a fight."

12. Many school systems today are providing itinerant special teachers or resource teachers to help the regular class teacher with atypical learners. These teachers diagnose and tutor the child and also supply materials and consultant help to the regular teacher.

13.   Cassettes or tapes that accompany stories are very useful. A child can listen to a story on a cassette while reading the story in the book. If earphones are used, the child can engage in this activity without disturbing the rest of the class.

Summary

In teaching reading to slow and disabled learners, materials should be presented to the children in conformity with the psychological process of reading. Children first perceive whole sentences as vague blocks and gaps. To progress in reading they must learn the details of the sentences and the details of the words. Ultimately, by the process of cue reduction, awareness of the details is reduced and the child is capable of reading without being conscious of words or letters.

Because of their relatively inadequate methods of generalization, retarded children as well as borderline and disabled learners must have guidance in learning to read. The systematic experience method, supplemented by incidental reading, is recommended.

The slow and disabled learner must have a variety of beginning reading materials presented repeatedly over a prolonged period and in different settings. The teacher must write stories comprehensible to these children, since readers constructed for normal children are too difficult for atypical learners. If basal readers are used, they should be supplemented with stories duplicated by the teacher, or by adequate commercial supplementary pamphlets, books, workbooks, cassettes, and/or tapes. Seatwork materials designed to aid children in learning details, in word recognition, and in other reading skills should be used.

Instruction in the initial stages of reading may be adapted to slow and disabled learners who are placed with normal children in the regular grades, even though the curriculum of those grades does not provide for instruction in beginning reading. Itinerant and resource teachers in school systems assist slow and disabled learners to read and help regular teachers use special instructional methods for these children.

Adaptation of Methods and Materials for Atypical Learners: Advanced Stages of Reading

5

The teacher's use of the instructions given in the previous chapter will enable slow or disabled learners to read many stories prepared by the teacher as well as a number of simple books corresponding to the primer and first-grade levels.

This chapter focuses on methods of increasing reading efficiency beyond the beginning stages.

Methods of Word Recognition

If children are to read independently, they must be taught a method of recognizing new words. Normal children can usually learn methods of word recognition without prolonged instruction. Children who are mentally retarded as well as borderline or deviant learners require guidance and instruction in learning to recognize new words. Such children are deficient in the ability to make generalizations and inferences, a skill that is required for learning methods of word recognition without aid. Slow and disabled learners can use the same methods of word recognition as normal learners. The teacher, however, must modify the manner in which the material is taught as well as the rate of presentation.

Incidental Methods of Recognizing Words

Children learn to recognize words incidentally during the process of beginning reading. They pick up many sight words if these words are repeated often enough in different contexts. However, mere repetition is not sufficient to teach word recognition. Reading the same story repeatedly does not help the child learn to read the words efficiently. The same words must be presented in different settings and at different times.

Recognizing Words by Some Clue

Children use different methods to recognize words. A child may depend upon some characteristic of the word such as the dot over the i or the shape of the t, or upon the configuration

108
Adaptation of
Methods and
Materials:
Advanced
Stages

of the total word in terms of its form or shape, as pointed out in Chapter 3. Other methods include analyzing the words into visual parts and spelling them.

It may be well to evaluate the methods of word recognition listed above in terms of their applicability to mentally retarded, slow-learning and learning-disabled children. Studies have found that when left to themselves, children use these methods to learn to recognize words. If teachers have emphasized a particular method of word recognition, children naturally tend to use that method. Many children use a variety of methods of word recognition.

When children depend only upon a characteristic in a word, they are likely to make many reading errors since many words have similar characteristics, such as i's, t's, and y's. This method does not teach a slow or disabled learner to recognize words but rather encourages guesswork, which leads the child to make many erroneous responses. Since it is more difficult to correct errors than to teach new words to slow and disabled learners, those methods that do not specifically avoid initial errors are inadequate. The methods listed previously are adequate during beginning reading when relatively few new words from the child's experience are being presented in a story. For recognizing and attacking many new words in reading, however, it is doubtful that these methods will aid the child appreciably.

The spelling method is seldom used with either normal or abnormal learners. Nevertheless, although they have not been taught this method, many atypical learners make use of spelling in an attempt to recognize words. It may be claimed that the spelling method, like the method of depending upon some characteristic of the word or upon the configuration of the word, is followed naturally by children, and that they should therefore be helped in this direction. Yet those versed in the field of reading do not advocate a spelling method of teaching word recognition. Although this method may be picked up by the child, it need not be encouraged or used.

Recognizing Words Through Context Clues

By reading the whole sentence, the child is capable of guessing an unknown word. This is done only when the new word is within the child's vocabulary. The use of context clues for word recognition is probably more difficult for the mentally retarded or learning-disabled child than for the normal child. If such children are deficient in their ability to make inference attempts to recognize words from context clues, they are likely to make a number of wrong guesses. For some atypical learners, the context clues method alone is not a reliable one for teaching word recognition.

In a study of the utilization of context clues, Dunn (1956) found that mentally retarded children were deficient in the use of context clues when compared to normal children of the same mental age. Sheperd (1967) found that better readers among the mentally retarded were superior to poorer readers in their use of context clues.

Recognizing Words Through Phonic Analysis

The phonics method has been widely used in the United States to teach independence in the recognition of new words. Since the value of phonics has been debated for a number of years it might be well to evaluate this method further and to consider its usefulness for slow and atypical learners.

Phonics refers to the method of recognizing new words by relating a sound (phoneme) with the equivalent written symbol (grapheme). This is sometimes referred to as the *grapheme-phoneme* relationship. When the alphabet method of teaching reading was discarded, the phonics method replaced it. Later, however, when it was discovered that children could learn words and sentences without the use of phonics, some school systems discarded the phonics method entirely. Much research has been conducted on the value of phonics in teaching reading to normal children. Some studies have shown that phonics is beneficial, while others have indicated that overemphasis can be detrimental.

Phonics has been assailed on the ground that it is unnecessary, that it makes children word conscious, that it introduces unnatural articulations, and that it teaches children to "bark" at words. On the other hand, several authors who recently evaluated the use of phonics have concluded that a moderate use of phonics is advisable.

Durkin (1972) states:

> Remembering that phonics is merely a means to an end becomes increasingly important because, currently, more and more phonics is being taught earlier and earlier. Whenever this happens there always is the possibility that teachers will begin to view phonics content as an end in itself, forgetting that instruction merits the description 'successful' only when children demonstrate ability to use what has been taught to figure out unknown words. In fact, how well they use phonics with new words is the only meaningful criterion for evaluating any type of instruction (p. 358).

The importance of phonics in teaching reading to disabled learners is pointed out by Money (1966):

> It has been demonstrated by many workers in the field over the last thirty years that the only successful techniques for teaching dyslexics are those firmly founded on a phonetic basis. The logical phonetic structure of English, even if it is not perfect, seems to provide the dyslexic child with a memory reference basis which is more economical than the multitude of arbitrary sound-symbol associations used in nonphonetic methods of teaching reading (p. 196).

110
Adaptation of
Methods and
Materials:
Advanced
Stages

Experts seem to agree that an excess of phonics may be detrimental, but that phonics properly taught is essential to reading.

Chall (1967), summarizing research on phonics approaches to reading instruction, concludes:

> The experimental studies that compared phonic approaches with other approaches to helping disabled readers showed that phonic approaches, if properly designed, achieve good results. Progress may be slower with a phonic emphasis than with other approaches, but the end results are probably more satisfactory (p. 177).

Chall's analysis of these studies indicates that the difficulty of the phonics method used makes a difference in its effectiveness with poor readers. A simplified phonics approach that uses words controlled for spelling regularity is more effective than a phonics emphasis that uses common, irregularly spelled words for practice.

Cawley (1972) concludes that the research is not definitive as to whether slow learners profit from direct concentrated doses of phonics. However, data indicate that synthetic phonics, by which the child is taught separate sound-letter correspondence and is given practice blending the sounds, is as effective for the slow learner as for other pupils, although it takes the slow-learning child somewhat longer to benefit from it.

Methods of Teaching Phonics

Since many college students have forgotten or perhaps never learned phonics rules and generalizations, it may be well to present briefly a system of phonics that may be used with children who are mentally retarded or slow and disabled learners.

When children begin to realize that they require a method of word recognition to make them independent of the teacher, phonics training may be introduced.

General Directions for Teaching Phonics

Many of the arguments against phonics refer to its extreme use, such as in beginning reading, or to its excessive use, which hinders comprehension in reading. Phonics training, if used judiciously and properly, has a place in the teaching of reading to slow and disabled learners. Many teachers, however, have not been trained to teach phonics.

The following guidelines in the teaching of phonics are given to aid the teacher who wishes to utilize this method:

1. Introduce phonics training only after the child has developed an adequate perception of sounds and has come to recognize the significance of the printed word.

2. Give phonics training outside of the regular story reading period and transfer the skills to the story reading situation.

3. Comprehension should not be forgotten during phonics training. Reading is taught as a thought process, whereas phonics introduces the mechanics of reading. If the child first learns to read thought units and has separate phonics lessons that are transferred to the reading period, much of the mechanical reading will be avoided.

4. Be sure the child has learned to blend sounds before presenting the sound-symbol relationships.

5. Emphasize the sounds and words that will appear in the reading lesson.

6. Do not introduce rules for phonics to slow and disabled learners. Rules involve abstract generalizations. Since many of these children may be unable to apply generalizations, they will have difficulty learning and applying the rules. Moreover, there are many exceptions to phonics rules and generalizations. The method of teaching phonics outlined in this chapter avoids the use of generalizations or rules.

7. Remember that the English language does not have consistent sound-symbol spelling patterns, and many words will have to be taught as sight words. If children have also learned context clues, they will be able to recognize many new words in reading, partly through phonic analysis, partly through context clues, and partly from structural analysis.

8. Teach phonics systematically and avoid simultaneous introduction of too many new symbols. Introduction of new material while old material is only partly learned tends to interfere with the retention of the old material. The process by which the introduction of new material tends to inhibit the recall of previously learned material is called *retroactive inhibition*. Overlearning helps counteract the effects of retroactive inhibition.

9. Phonics must be taught carefully lest it confuse the child.

A Specific Method for Teaching Phonics

The method of teaching phonics proposed here is an adaptation of the Hegge-Kirk-Kirk Remedial method (1936) applied to reading disability cases. According to this method, the following suggestions are given:

1. Before phonics is begun, the teacher should introduce ear training so that the child knows that words are composed of sounds. The training of auditory discrimination and

112
Adaptation of
Methods and
Materials:
Advanced
Stages

memory by means of reading games and rhythms helps prepare the child for phonics. It is possible that some slow and disabled learners will not profit from phonics training because they have a deficit in sound-blending ability. In such cases, the teacher's first task is to train the children in sound blending. To do this, the teacher uses two factors: duration and length. *Duration* is the rate at which sounds are presented. The closer they are presented in time, the more readily they will be blended.

(*a*) If the child cannot blend sounds at a half-second interval, ask the child to repeat the word after you, then to repeat it when you say it very slowly. Example: "What is this word: sh (half-second interval) oe?" If the child cannot respond "shoe," ask him or her to say "shoe." Then ask, "What is this? Sh-sh-sh-oe-oe," pronouncing it with each sound prolonged but the two sounds running together. Then try another two-sound word like "m (half-second interval) ee."

(*b*) When the child has learned to blend two sounds with a short interval between sounds, present the sounds at a slower and slower rate until the child can synthesize them into a word when presented at two-second intervals. The reason for teaching the youngster to blend sounds at a two-second interval is that later, when using a phonics system in learning to read, a beginner requires two seconds to recognize a visual letter symbol and recall the sound associated with it. The child must, then, hold one sound in mind for two seconds while translating the next visual symbol into a sound. If the facility of blending sounds at a two-second interval has become automatic, the child can then concentrate on recalling the sounds of phonemes rather than being faced with the dual task of recalling each phoneme while concentrating on blending successive sounds.

Another factor to be considered in training children in sound blending is the word's *length,* or the number of elements presented in a word. Children must learn to blend words of increasing length.

(*a*) First the child should be taught to blend words that have only two sounds, as described above. Then proceed to three- and four-sound words.

(*b*) After the child has achieved auditory synthesis for two-, three-, and four-sound words, he or she must be taught to recognize visual symbols, such as c—a—t, and blend these sounds into words.

Phonics systems may differ in their approaches, but the prerequisite to all of them is adequate sound-blending ability (Kirk and Kirk, 1971, pp. 157–158).

2. After they learn sound blending, the children should be taught the sounds of the consonants and the sound of one vowel, preferably the short sound of *a*. If the children know the word *cat* by sight, they can be shown that it is made up of sounds c—a—t. Then they can be presented with other simple words such as: f—a—t, r—a—t, r—a—n, m—a—n,

and the like. At first the children may have difficulty sounding out the words and blending the sounds into a word, but if the teacher starts at a simple level and gradually increases the complexity, the children will soon learn to use the sounds of the single consonants and the sound of the vowel ă.

A variety of presentations may be utilized. After the teacher has given the short sound of *a*, five or six consonants may be taught and presented in words with the vowel ă. A child may sound out the words and say them, or one child may sound out a word while the class tries to identify it. In this way the children learn sound blending and learn to identify the sounds of some consonants and the short vowel ă.

This method of presentation differs somewhat from most published phonics systems. In the past, two general methods have been used. One method proposes that the initial consonant and the vowel be combined as one sound, such as *ca—t, sa—t*. The other system combines the vowel with the final sound, such as *s—at, c—at*. Slow and disabled learners are often confused by both of these methods. They tend to repeat the consonant with the vowel in other sounds once they have fixated a certain sound combination. To illustrate, if children have learned *c—at, s—at, m—at*, and are presented with *c—ap*, they tend to read it as *c—at—p*. Or if children are presented with *ca—t, ca—p, ca—n*, and are later presented with *co—b, co—p*, and the like, they tend to read them as *ca—o—b, ca—o—p*, and so on. *With deviant learners, it is best to teach the individual sounds, whether or not they are individual letters or groups of letters.* The word *cat* should be sounded as three distinct sounds, *c—a—t*, rather than as two sounds. The word *feed* should be presented as three sounds, namely *f—ee—d*. This method will avoid confusion and perseveration on the part of the slow and disabled learner.

During the reading period, the teacher should not ask children to sound out a word if they have not been taught the sounds. For example, if the child who has learned the sounds of the consonants and the sound of the short vowel *a* is confronted with the word *hit*, the teacher should say "hit" when the child hesitates over the word so that he or she will not be confused. On the other hand, if the child is confronted in reading with the word *fat* and has learned the consonants and the short vowel *a*, the child should be asked to sound it. In this manner, phonics training given in a separate period is transferred to the reading situation.

3. After the child has learned the sounds of most of the consonants and the sound of the short vowel *a*, the sounds of the short vowels *o, u, i*, and *e* should be taught singly. These should be presented very gradually and in connection with sounds and words previously learned. After the child learns ă in combination with sounds and words, the ŏ sound should be introduced in the same manner.

Then the teacher should present words containing either

114
Adaptation of
Methods and
Materials:
Advanced
Stages

ă or ŏ such as *hat, hot, cap, cop, cot, cat,* and the like, so that the child will learn to differentiate the vowels in words. When ŭ is introduced and learned, a review of ă, ŏ, and ŭ should be presented in different words such as *hat, hot, hut.*

Some vowels may cause difficulty. The vowel *e,* for example, occurs more frequently in reading than the other vowels, yet is more difficult for slow and disabled learners to learn. Some exercises in saying ĕ or any other sound that causes difficulty may have to be given by the teacher. It is probable that the sound of ĕ is difficult to learn because it is similar to the sounds of ă and ĭ.

4.   After the vowels and the consonants have been taught, the teacher should introduce sounds made up of several letters. Thus the sound of *ee* in *feed, seed, meet* may be introduced. The child can learn the sound of *ee* as a configuration the same way the sounds of ă and ŏ were learned, without rules. In this way no confusions are introduced. The sound of *ay* in *day* and *ai* in *maid* should also be introduced as configurations and not by rules.

Erroneous methods of phonics instruction are frequently employed in the classroom. One case may be cited. A teacher told the class the symbol *a* was *ay* as in *day,* but that it had four or five different names, just as John (a boy in the class) had three names, John George Smith. She continued that the symbol *a* was ă in *cat,* ā in *day,* and the like, until she had demonstrated the five sounds for the letter *a.* A system of this sort is very confusing to slow and disabled learners since it introduces too many complications.

The system presented in this chapter avoids the confusion. The sound of *a* as in *cat,* is learned only when it sounds ă. When it differs from the sound of ă as in *cat,* it is presented as a new configuration as *ay* in *day,* or *ai* in *maid.* Similarly, *e* is presented only as ĕ in *set.* When it differs from this sound there is a new configuration, as *ee* in *feed* and *ea* in *meat.* The configurations are separated from the other letters thus: *m-ea-t.*

5.   Since retarded, slow-learning, and learning-disabled children must be presented with simple materials, the phonics configurations that are easiest to learn are introduced first. Next come those phonics symbols that appear most frequently. The configuration *ee* in *feed* is probably easier to learn than the sound of ĕ in *set* or the sound of a vowel that is altered because of a final *e.* The simple sounds should be introduced first, and there should be no introduction of sounds that appear infrequently in the primary vocabulary.

6.   The sounds may be varied by the teacher in accordance with the abilities of the children and in conformity with the book that is being used. The teacher should preview the books that the children are reading and select the sounds that they should know for the new words. The sounds may be presented in the following manner:

(*a*) Teach the consonants *b, c* (hard), *d, f, g* (hard), *h, j, l, m, n, p, r, s, t, v, w*, with the vowel *a*, as in *cat*.

(*b*) Teach the sounds of the short vowels, *i, o, u*, and *e* in words with the consonants.

(*c*) Teach sounds such as *oo* (food), *ee* (feed), *ar* (car), *ai* (maid), *ay* (day), *or* (for), *old* (cold), *ea* (meat), *oa* (boat), *ing* (sing), *all* (ball), *er* (her), *ir* (fir), *ur* (fur), *sh* (ship), *ch* (chip), *th* (that), *wh* (when).

(*d*) Combine such sounds as *un, en, in, an, on, ink, ank, unk, ang, ung, and, ound, est, all, ill, ell, ly.*

(*e*) Teach syllabication, suffixes, prefixes, and so forth.

(*f*) The nonphonic or infrequent sounds such as the *a* in *father* or in *was* should not be taught as sounds. Words spelled irregularly should be taught as wholes without attempting phonics.

7. Children should be encouraged to use their phonics knowledge in reading. If children sound out an unfamiliar phonic word it will soon become a part of their sight vocabulary. In this way a method of independent word recognition is being developed.

8. Certain cautions should always be observed in teaching phonics to atypical learners. First, a casual system of teaching phonics is useless. The child should be able to use phonics when needed. Second, emphasis should always be given to comprehension in reading. *Phonics is only a means to an end; it is not an end in itself.* Finally, phonics alone as a method of word recognition is not sufficient for effective reading. In addition to phonics, children should be taught context clues, structural analysis and syllabication, and other methods. With the aid of several methods at the student's disposal, the child can become a more efficient reader.

9. Whatever system is presented, the following guidelines should be kept in mind:

(*a*) Present the materials so that there will be only one response to one symbol, that is, *a* is always *ă*. This is one of the principles used by i/t/a and the Hegge, Kirk, and Kirk Remedial Reading Drills discussed in Chapter 6.

(*b*) Present materials in such a way that there will be only minimal differences among words—such as *fat, rat, mat* (only initial consonant differs), or *pat, pan, pass, pal* (only final consonant differs); then *fat, pan, tap* (both initial and final consonant differ).

(*c*) Overlearn the initial materials so that they will not be forgotten.

(*d*) Use social reinforcement (praise) at each success of the child.

(*e*) Arrange the materials with minimal change so that success will follow each response. Success is a powerful incentive.

A brief phonics quiz and phonics review is provided in Appendix A.

116
Adaptation of
Methods and
Materials:
Advanced
Stages

Methods of Teaching Context Clues

The English language does not have a consistent phonetic spelling pattern. For this reason an additional method of word recognition should be taught. A good supplement to the phonics method is the use of context clues.

Because of their ability to generalize, superior children learn to use context clues without aid from the teacher. Atypical children are weak in the ability to generalize and are therefore deficient in recognizing words by means of context clues. This deficiency can be alleviated somewhat if the teacher gives specific instruction in the use of context clues. When children have learned the sound of *ea* as in *meat* and are confronted with the sentence, "The boy read a book," they will be able to read the word *read* correctly if they have been trained in the use of context clues as well as phonics.

The following exercises and suggestions will help the child utilize context clues:

1.   When the child is reading to the teacher and has difficulty recognizing a word that is nonphonic, the teacher should take that opportunity to apply context clues. By questions and suggestions, the teacher can guide the child to recognize the word without giving direct aid.

2.   Completion sentences about a story aid the development of context clues. The teacher may use exercises such as:

We went to the _____ yesterday.
                             store farm market
I will sing a _____.

There are many variations of the completion sentence. Several words may be written under the blank space and the child asked to select the correct word, underline it, or write it in the space provided. Or a child may be given a set of word cards and asked to paste the correct word in the blank space. This exercise is beneficial with words that are easily confused—such as *was* and *saw*:

The man _____ angry.
I _____ the man.

or *where* and *there*:

_____ are we going?
_____ are many children in school.

3.   If reading is difficult for the children, and the teacher wishes to vary the procedure, the teacher may tell a story, pausing frequently to permit the children to continue the sentence or detect something that has been omitted.

4. Another type of exercise often used is to mix up the parts of a story and have the child rearrange them properly. An example is:

I am _____.	dog
I have a _____.	Mary
His name is _____.	to play
He likes _____.	Jip

If four sentences are too difficult, three could be used to develop this skill.

Teaching Structural Analysis and Syllabication

The term *developmental reading* includes the stages of the reading process encountered by the child learning to read in a normal fashion. Certainly, developmental reading and the sequential stages of reading growth are important concepts that the teacher of atypical children must know. Not all reading authorities agree about the exact order of the steps taken in learning to analyze words. However, the following section lists the steps in a typical sequence (Dolch, 1951):

Steps in Learning to Analyze Words

1. Sounds of single consonants: *s, b, m*
2. Sounds of consonant digraphs: *ch, sh, th*
3. Consonant blends: *bl, br, cl, pl, dr, sm, st, tr, str*
4. Short sounds of vowels: *a, e, i, o, u*
5. Final *e* rule for long vowel sounds
6. Double vowels: *ai, ay, ee, ea, oa*
7. Diphthongs: *oi, oy, ou, ow, eu, ew, oo*
8. Sounds of vowels with *i, ar, er, ir, or, ur*
9. Soft *c* and *g* before *e* and *i*
10. Take off prefixes and suffixes
11. There are as many syllables as vowel sounds
12. Divide syllables between two consonants or in front of one
13. Open syllables, long; closed syllables, short

The first nine steps in the list can be included in phonics, while the last four steps can be considered within the category of structural analysis and syllabication.

Not all slow and disabled learners will be able to complete all the steps in this list. However, the ability to analyze polysyllabic words soon becomes very important.

118
Adaptation of
Methods and
Materials:
Advanced
Stages

Structural Analysis

1. Structural analysis is helpful even with relatively easy
words. When the child compares *jump* with *jumps*, he or she
can observe that the second word is *jump* with an *s* on it.
In linguistic terms, this is referred to as *morphemic analysis*.
Children can be helped to recognize other common endings:
s, ed, es, er, ing.

jump	jumps	jumped	jumper	jumping
walk	walks	walked	walker	walking
kick	kicks	kicked	kicker	kicking

2. Compound words require another type of structural
analysis. The child learns that some words are made up of
two different words:

into	something
snowman	nobody
together	outside
grasshopper	grandfather
butterfly	thanksgiving

3. Still another type of structural analysis is required for
the recognition of root words, prefixes, and suffixes. When
encountering a polysyllabic word, the child is aided if he or
she can detect a root word, prefix, or suffix. This kind of
analysis is particularly important when working with difficult
vocabulary in the content subjects such as social studies and
science. A root word is the main part of the word; a prefix,
the first part; a suffix, the ending. For example:

re	*turn*	*able*
(prefix)	*(root)*	*(suffix)*

The five prefixes most commonly included in the elementary
school program are:

dis-   en-   in-   re-   un-

Other common prefixes with their meanings are:

ab- (from)	*dis-* (apart)	*pre-* (before)
ad- (to)	*en-* (in)	*pro-* (in front of)
be- (by)	*ex-* (out)	*re-* (back)
com- (with)	*in-* (into)	*sub-* (under)
de- (from)	*in-* (not)	*un-* (not)

Common suffixes appropriate for the elementary level are:

-er, -est, -ful, -ish, -less, -by, -y, -ing, -ed

Eight other common suffixes are:

-ion, -ian, -ity, -ical, -ic, -ital, -ious, -ate

Slow and disabled learners often find it difficult to learn the vocabulary in science and social study lessons. An effective way to help the pupils learn these words is to list the words on the blackboard and then point out root words, prefixes, or suffixes that they may already know.

Syllables

A syllable is a unit of speech containing only one vowel sound. Children can learn long words when they are divided into syllables. Many slow and disabled learners will have great difficulty learning and applying the syllable generalizations. Many syllable and accent rules are quite complicated and can become quite confusing for the deviant learner.

Karlin (1971) suggests three steps for teaching syllables that may be helpful with the exceptional learner. This work should only be undertaken with those pupils who have a good foundation in phonics:

1. *Help children hear syllables in spoken words.* How many syllables are in the following words? (Say them but do not write them. The child should tap for each syllable.)

can	Bob	*sit*
Mary	*candy*	*nation*
*tele*phone	Roberta	*removing*

2. *Write words that have been practiced auditorially.* Have children underline vowel sounds.
3. *Give children practice in dividing words.*

   For the teacher's use, a few rules for syllables are listed below. Many slow and disabled learners will be unable to learn these rules and should not be expected to:

1. Divide word into syllables between two consonants: sum-mer, win-dow.
2. Usually divide between the root word and affixes: dis-count, help-ful.
3. A single consonant between two single vowels can go with either syllable.

120
Adaptation of
Methods and
Materials:
Advanced
Stages

The Significance of Oral and Silent Reading

In recent years the schools have minimized and neglected oral reading for normal children. The justification is that since silent reading is more rapid than oral reading, and since adults read silently, children should be taught to read silently. Also, oral reading has been found to conflict with efficient silent reading. For these reasons, silent reading has surged forward even in the lower grades. First-grade children are required to read silently as soon as they can, sometimes too soon. Few authors, however, have advocated the elimination of oral reading in the initial stages of reading.

Actually, it is difficult for children to read silently without first learning to read orally. Oral language is the tool with which the child comes to school. The aim of the school is to teach the child to apply this tool to reading. Reading, consequently, begins through the use of visual-auditory symbols, rather than visual symbols and meanings—the adult reading method. Inaudible reading, a stage that is commonly mistaken for silent reading, is in fact the first stage in the development of silent reading. The child uses the same throat and oral musculature as in oral reading but does not use the voice. This is exhibited by the great frequency of lip reading among beginning readers and particularly retarded children. Therefore, it may be concluded that comprehension of the thought from the printed page through the visual sense comes only after prolonged practice and through a short-circuiting process that begins with oral reading, and progresses first to inaudible reading, then less vocal movement, less lip movement, and finally little or no vocal movement.

Furthermore, slow-learning or learning-disabled children should continue oral reading longer and at a higher grade level than is usually allowed with the average learner. The reasons for this are the following:

1.   Studies of eye movements in oral and silent reading found that during the initial stages of reading there are more fixations per line in silent reading than in oral reading. Betts (1936) reported that there were 16.0 fixations in oral reading and 18.6 fixations in silent reading in grade 1. This indicates that during the initial stages, oral reading is more efficient than silent reading. In grade 2, however, the fixation pauses per line decrease in silent reading and are fewer than in oral reading. Betts (1936) reported that there were 12.0 fixations per line in oral reading in grade 2, and only 10.7 fixations per line in silent reading. These data indicate that oral reading is essential during beginning reading but that silent reading later becomes more efficient, as measured by fixation pauses.

2.   Oral reading is a logical first step in learning to read. The child learns the meaning of words first through the auditory sense. When children begin to read, then, they must

associate the sight of the word with the sound of the word that they already know and then make the connection from sight to meaning.

Strang (1969) stresses the need for oral reading in the primary grades:

> Where the basic sight vocabulary and word recognition skills are acquired, oral reading is essential as a basis for diagnosis. As the child reads aloud, the teacher notices proficiency and progress as well as errors and difficulties. The latter might go uncorrected in an individualized silent reading program. Classmates, too, learn from other pupils' self-correction of errors in oral reading (p. 67).

Some investigators recommend that oral reading activities for slow learning children be used for diagnostic purposes only (Cawley, Goodstein, & Burrow, 1972). Another encourages oral reading as long as the mentally retarded child is learning to read (Slaughter, 1964). Oral recital of words seems to help children retain them. Slaughter states that for some retarded children and in some situations, oral reading never wholly loses its usefulness: "For example, the young retarded woman as she reads a recipe may say as she reads, 'two cups of flour'; and as she measures the flour she may say, 'one cup, two cups'; and she is less apt to use a wrong amount than if she had read silently and said nothing" (1964, pp. 93–94).

3. In the teaching of atypical learners, accuracy rather than speed should be emphasized. When the child reads aloud to the teacher, reading accuracy is tested. The teacher will know what errors the child is making and can correct these errors before they become fixated into permanent habits.

4. Through oral reading, the atypical child can learn better pronunciation and enunciation and may learn a better use of the English language. Oral reading also helps the child group words into thought units that he or she may not have used in the environment.

5. Oral reading will also give the teacher insight into whether children comprehend what they read. By observing intonation and the grouping of words in reading, the teacher can tell how well the child understands the content. Oral reading then becomes a diagnostic method as well as a teaching method.

The above comments on the use of oral reading with mentally retarded and learning-disabled children are aimed to offset the great emphasis being placed on silent reading with normal children in beginning reading. Many teachers of atypical children now emphasize silent reading. As a consequence, many of these teachers have been unable to produce any reading in some children. It is not known how many normal children become reading disability cases because the first-grade teacher stressed silent reading before the child had learned oral reading sufficiently or before the child was ready for silent reading.

122
Adaptation of
Methods and
Materials:
Advanced
Stages

In this connection, Dolch (1931) states, "The simple fact seems to be that anyone becomes a silent reader just as soon as the mental process of comprehension goes too fast for the pronouncing to keep up with it" (p. 163). In discussing the causes of lip reading, Dolch further states:

> Persons of low intelligence, for one thing, read slowly because their mental processes are slow. Therefore, retarded persons may read with lip movements all their lives. They may practice until pronouncing is no longer necessary, but there will always be time at their slow comprehension rate for incidental pronouncing, and the overflow of nervous energy will tend to produce it (1931, p. 164).

Aberrant learners may need the verbal input obtained in oral reading to strengthen their understanding of the material.

Stone (1936) also advises against the elimination of lip reading in the first grade. He believes that it is unwise to suppress the tendency to vocalize in reading during the early stage, and that the elimination of lip movement in the first grade should not be a specific objective.

The opinions of Dolch and Stone indicate that these authors recognize that although the aim is silent reading, this aim will have to be attained through oral reading during the beginning stages. This point should be emphasized even more with mentally retarded and slow-learning children. *Suppressing oral reading and articulation at the beginning of reading may be suppressing the ability to read.* Therefore it is safe to state that a longer period of oral reading should be stressed with mentally retarded children. The child's lip reading is the natural result of early attempts to read and should not be suppressed at the outset by artificial directions such as "Read with your eyes, not your mouth," and the like. As atypical learners progress in oral reading, they should acquire the ability to do silent reading—and they should be encouraged.

The Function of Interest in Increasing Efficiency

Experiments with schoolchildren have shown that learning takes place more rapidly and efficiently if the reading matter is meaningful and interesting to the child. In addition to the emphasis on repetition and developing a method of word recognition, the degree of interest in materials presented to a child should be considered.

If children have attended school for several years and have been confronted with primers and first readers and have failed to learn, they sometimes resent having these books again. Classmates have gone beyond primer reading, while they have not even mastered the primer. Because of their feeling of inferiority in this respect they attempt to justify their disinterest by calling such books baby books. In Chapter 4 it was emphasized that much repetition of simple material should be given at first without the use of primers. This may apply only to children who have faced failure for a number of years.

Very few studies have been reported on the interests of mentally retarded children or slow or disabled learners in the selection of reading materials. Gates (1930) studied the reading interests of normal and mentally retarded children. He concluded that materials that are interesting to normal children are also interesting to mentally retarded children and vice versa; materials that were uninteresting to mentally retarded children were uninteresting to normal children. He found that the elements in children's reading material that contribute most to interest are:

Surprise. Unexpected and unforeseen events, happenings, conclusions, and outcomes.
Liveliness. Action, movement, and "something doing."
Animalness. Stories describing animals, their acts, characteristics, and experiences.
Conversation. Stories that include dialogue.
Humor. Stories that are humorous from the child's point of view. Many incidents that are humorous to the adult are not funny to children.
Plot.
Suitability. Stories that come within the children's range of experience.
Difficulty. Stories that are not too difficult in vocabulary and meaning.

In a study done thirty years later, comparing the story preferences of American and Finnish children, Gaier and Collier (1960) found that children age 9 or 10 preferred stories about travel, tales of exciting, dangerous pursuit and escape, and stories about social situations involving subterfuge and escape, surprise, or humor and comical enjoyment. Animal stories were still favorites.

It would seem that children's reading interests have not changed too much over the years. If books with these themes are provided for children, their natural interest should encourage them to read.

With atypical learners, especially those who have experienced failure, one of the most important factors in creating interest is *success in reading.* If the teacher presents material that the child can read successfully, interest will be greatly accelerated. Materials may have the elements of surprise, liveliness, humor, and so on, but if they are beyond the child's ability, he or she will not become interested in them. Materials selected should be within the children's ability but should not be so simplified that they will learn nothing from reading or that they will become bored. *The materials should be easy enough for the child to read and sufficiently difficult to require effort and promote learning.* A list of high-interest, low-vocabulary books is given in Appendix B.

124
Adaptation of
Methods and
Materials:
Advanced
Stages

Methods of Improving Comprehension

The aim of reading is to understand and evaluate what has been read. Too much stress on phonics, context clues, structural analysis, or oral reading without due emphasis on comprehension violates the main aim of teaching reading. The teacher should keep in mind that many of the devices suggested for increasing the efficiency of reading are only means to an end. Reading should foster an attitude of interest in and understanding of the material, not merely word recognition and pronunciation.

Children must go through several stages in order to derive meaning from the printed page. They must recognize words and symbols before they can "get the thought" of these symbols. Furthermore, there can be no critical evaluation of reading materials until one "gets the thought" from the printed symbols.

How well a slow or disabled learner evaluates reading material is of course partly dependent upon the individual's intelligence level. The mentally retarded may not reach the achievements of normal children in the critical evaluation of reading materials.

Comprehension is a broad concept; several ways of viewing comprehension have been suggested by reading experts.

One widely used classification of comprehension skills is based on four levels of reading:

1. Literal comprehension: Reading to understand specifically what the author says; getting the literal, primary meaning.
2. Interpretation: Reading to probe to greater depths of meaning; understanding what the author meant.
3. Critical reading: Evaluating what is read and passing personal judgment; evaluating what the author says.
4. Creative reading: Using the reading material as a starting point of inquiry; going beyond the implications derived from the text; going beyond the author.

Another way to view reading comprehension is to look at the specific reading skills that make up comprehension (Harris & Sipay, 1975). Each of the following is a specific comprehension skill and can be taught separately:

1. *Reading to note and recall details.* There are many occasions when one must read to remember the details in a selection. In fact, American education has been criticized for overemphasizing this component of reading. Children should be helped to learn to relate the details to each other and to the main idea.

2. *Reading for main ideas.* One of the most valuable of comprehension skills is the ability to find the main idea or central thought in a selection. This is more difficult to learn than reading for details.

3. *Following a sequence of events or steps.* This skill is one of organizing—being able to see the steps of a process or the events in a story. Seeing such order is important to thinking, understanding, language, and reading.

4. *Drawing inferences and reaching conclusions.* This skill requires thoughtful reading and interpretation. The reader must go beyond the facts that are given in order to reach a conclusion. If the reader can answer the question, "What does the author mean?" then the reader is thinking along with the author.

5. *Organizing ideas.* This skill refers to the ability to see interrelationships among the ideas of a reading selection. It involves seeing cause and effect, comparing and contrasting relationships, and seeing the author's general plan for structuring the material. Studying the table of contents, looking at topic headings, and outlining are all techniques to help the student see how the ideas are organized.

6. *Applying what is read to solve problems and verify statements.* If reading is to be a functional skill, reading material must be adapted to new situations and integrated with previous experiences. Many children, particularly slow and disabled learners, have difficulty acquiring the ability to integrate the knowledge and skills gained in reading.

7. *Evaluating materials for bias, relevancy, and consistency.* This skill is similar to what was earlier called *critical reading*. This includes the ability to make judgments about the author's bias, to compare several sources of information, to detect propaganda techniques, to determine the logic of an argument or approach. Even children who are able readers need much help in acquiring this skill. It may be beyond the ability of some slow and disabled learners.

Another important aspect of comprehension skills for the older student is the group of skills known as *study skills* (Harris & Sipay, 1975).

1. Learning to locate information. Use of index, libraries, table of contents.
2. Comprehension of informational materials. Understanding technical vocabulary, reading maps, charts, tables.
3. Outlining and summarizing. Taking notes, outlining material, and summarizing what has been read.
4. Reading in the content areas. Specific reading skills are needed for reading in the various content areas: literature, mathematics, social science, science. Reading in each of these areas requires a different set of skills. Instruction in reading in content textbooks may be helpful for slow and disabled learners. It is often possible to obtain content materials suited to the student's reading level. For example, if the social studies textbook for the grade level is too difficult, the teacher could search for a

126
Adaptation of
Methods and
Materials:
Advanced
Stages

book with the same content but on an easier reading level. Some use of a lower grade level book solves the problem. Some publishers put out content-area books for disabled readers. Several content-area books written at an easier reading level are listed in Appendix B.

Exercises and activities that aid comprehension and evaluation are given below.

Free Reading or Individualized Instruction

After the children have mastered the basic elements of reading, books and pamphlets with a variety of topics and varying degrees of difficulty should be provided in the classroom. Interesting stories with limited vocabularies of first- to fourth-grade levels can be purchased for this purpose. This procedure is followed in classrooms where the library technique is utilized.

The children should be allowed to select any book they wish to read in school or to take home. They should not be forced to answer a variety of questions related to a book. Such a procedure may halt their interest. However, some children may wish to talk about an interesting story they have read. They should be encouraged to discuss it with the teacher or with the other children. In this way the teacher will have a clear notion of their comprehension.

Mentally retarded and slow-learning children, as well as most disabled learners, will not develop all the necessary skills through the free reading of stories. *Direct instruction is needed to provide these skills.* However, free reading does create interest in books and stories, develops concentration, and provides pleasurable experiences. Free reading stimulates comprehension, since the child is reading to see what will happen next. Free reading activities probably promote little evaluation and critical thinking.

Reading Directions or Answering Questions

Many projects and activities are needed to encourage comprehension and evaluation of reading materials.

After discussing a project and the manner in which it is to be executed, the teacher may mimeograph or write directions for the children. The children may then read the directions to find their individual roles in the activity. The directions may require modification or extension, depending upon the ability of the children. This introduces them to the process of evaluation and stimulates thinking about the reading material.

Another method is to write the story of a project and give correlated seatwork in the form of questions and answers in order to determine what reading progress the children have made.

To increase comprehension, atypical learners should continually be provided with reading materials and activities that will enlarge their reading vocabulary. These activities include learning new words and enriching the meaning of known words. The activities given in Chapter 2 for language development should be continued. These provide for oral expression, enriching experiences, study of pictures, and story reading or story telling by the teacher or children. An excellent method of increasing the children's vocabulary and enriching their experiences is through projects and excursions. Stories about these experiences may be written and then read by the children. One teacher working with a group of intermediate mentally retarded children brought her camera to school and took a picture of each child. The children wrote about their pictures and described the developing process. In that way the children enlarged their vocabulary in connection with a new and interesting project. Older and more advanced children can of course use the dictionary to look up words.

Directed Reading-Thinking Activity

The Directed Reading-Thinking Activity (DR-TA) is an approach to teaching reading comprehension based on the thinking process that occurs during the reading activity (Stauffer, 1969). The key to teaching with this approach is to guide students to set up their own questions and purposes for reading. Students read to solve problems that they have set up for themselves. For example, the child guesses what will happen in the story and reads to determine the accuracy of those speculations. Thereby, the relationship between reading and thinking is stressed. Both reading and thinking require a context to be read or thought about, both embody the dynamics of discovery, and both entail a systematic examination of ideas.

Reading, like thinking, involves continuous change. At every turning of a page, or even a phrase, the reader has to take into account the context—its parts, its problems, its perplexities. From these, he or she must be able to follow the threads of a plot that point the way toward the plot's end. Or the student must follow the course of ideas in nonfiction that lead to an outcome or solution. The student must assess what he or she finds, weigh it, accept or reject it, or alter his or her objectives.

Both reading and thinking start with a state of doubt or desire to learn. Thus the process of reconstruction is a process of inquiry or discovery until the doubt is resolved, the knowledge acquired, or the pleasure attained (Stauffer, 1969, p. 38).

In Directed Reading-Thinking Activity, then, teaching reading becomes a way of teaching thinking. Important questions the teacher asks in directing the process are: "What do you

128
Adaptation of
Methods and
Materials:
Advanced
Stages

think? Why do you think so?" "Can you prove it?" The goals are to teach children to examine, hypothesize, find proof, suspend judgment, and make decisions.

This method is essentially a discovery method and can readily be recommended for superior and average children. The goals and methodology for the slow and disabled learner are more often focused on specific skills than on the thinking process. However, it would be interesting to try the DR-TA method with atypical children as it provides a means of improving cognitive as well as reading skills.

The Effect of Competition

Psychologists and educators agree that too much competition in the classroom may do more harm than good, although it does furnish an incentive for some children. It may be true that learning-disabled children will function better if they are successful in competition. Not everyone can be at the head of the class, however, and those who are at the foot suffer from it.

If competition must be used as an incentive for further achievement among atypical children, it is best that each child competes with himself or herself. Children may read one book one week, mark it in their record books, then improve their records by reading two books the next week, three the third week, and so on. Many children like to break their own records, and there is no harm in this. In many cases it may furnish an incentive for accuracy in reading.

Having a child graph progress from day to day is a common method of providing incentive. An elaborate system of recording daily progress is known as the Precision Teaching System developed by Ogden Lindsley (1974).

Goals for Teaching Advanced Reading for the Various Classifications of Slow Learners and the Learning Disabled

Advanced reading for mildly retarded children is similar to that offered in the third, fourth, and fifth grades of the regular school. Few mildly retarded children advance beyond the sixth-grade reading level. For the most part, they remain between the third and fifth grades in academic skills; hence this level may be considered advanced reading for the mildly retarded. The borderline child may achieve up to the secondary school level. Many disabled learners may achieve beyond the secondary school level, some approaching levels consistent with their chronological age.

By the time slow-learning children have reached third-grade reading level, they have attained a fair degree of reading ability. They have read a number of books with simple vocabulary, have become interested in reading, have developed methods of word recognition, are reading a great deal silently and without obvious lip reading, and have increased their speaking and reading vocabularies.

129
Methods of
Teaching
Advanced
Reading to
Slow and
Disabled
Learners

Disabled learners may continue schooling through post-high school or college levels. The upper limit of reading may be substantially higher for the disabled learner than for the slow learner. The teacher must be careful not to limit the reading achievement of the disabled learner by setting goals that are too low.

For advanced reading instruction, the teacher should endeavor to accomplish the following:

1. Broaden the child's experiences through wide reading.
2. Stimulate the child to read for information and pleasure.
3. Increase the child's ability to recognize new words in oral and silent reading.
4. Increase the child's speed and comprehension in reading.
5. Increase the ability to understand increasingly difficult words, phrases, and entire selections.
6. Stimulate the reading of newspapers and magazines, and encourage other adult reading activities.

Methods of Teaching Advanced Reading to Slow and Disabled Learners

Most of the approaches to reading utilized with normal children in the third, fourth, and fifth grades are applicable to the slow and disabled learner and the mildly retarded child at the corresponding level of achievement. The main difference is that adult activities will be given more extensively to normal children because they are likely to reach a higher level of attainment. For example, it would be futile to prepare mildly retarded children to appreciate better literature and technical scientific materials since these children will not attain the level of literary appreciation or scientific thinking reached by mentally normal adults.

The following procedures should be emphasized in teaching advanced reading to slow and disabled learners:

1. Continue efforts to enlarge their reading vocabulary. Many readers and work type materials provide for such instruction. The methods for increasing vocabulary and comprehension given in the earlier part of this chapter are applicable here.

130
Adaptation of
Methods and
Materials:
Advanced
Stages

2. Provide for recreational reading by stimulating interest in stories. Book clubs can be formed and each week in class children can relate interesting stories they have read.

3. Provide for instruction in the use of the dictionary, the use of the table of contents, the index, and the methods of selecting and withdrawing books from the library.

4. Provide for continuation of methods of word recognition by context clues, visual and phonic analysis, and the use of suffixes and prefixes.

5. Provide for increase in speed of silent reading and for accuracy in study-reading. Special exercises may improve fluency, accuracy, and independence in word recognition.

6. Integrate reading with the social studies, arithmetic, and other activities of the classroom that are not always a part of the reading lesson.

7. Provide for instruction in reading newspapers and popular magazines that are within the children's level of comprehension. During early reading, the comic strips attract their attention. Later, other features of the daily newspaper can be utilized. Many older mentally retarded children read the newspaper daily and appear to keep abreast of the news. Newspapers are seldom used with normal children in the third, fourth, and fifth grades. Nevertheless, mentally retarded children who are from 13 to 16 years of age and have achieved the corresponding reading level should be given instruction in reading newspapers and magazines. A work-textbook entitled *Newspaper Reading* by Gary D. Lawson (1960) can be used effectively with learning-disabled and retarded teenagers. The daily newspaper is used as a basic text, with exercises and comprehension questions to be completed in the workbook. A similar workbook by Ardelle Manning (1964) entitled *Magazines* is designed to teach retarded and slow-learning teenagers how to read and profit from magazine articles. *Know Your World* (Xerox Education Publications) is a high-interest, low-reading level newspaper for poor readers.

Mentally retarded children are older than normal children by the time they reach a functional level of reading. They have less time for reading instruction since they are nearing the end of their formal schooling. The normal child has more time to learn and will later reach a higher level of reading achievement. The final achievement level of the disabled learner is more uncertain.

8. Provide for instruction in the use of timetables, graphs, road maps, telephone books, city directories, and other reference materials used by the average adult. Many of these reading activities can be accomplished through projects and activities. Many normal children learn these incidentally, but atypical learners may require specific classroom instruction. This is reading in preparation for life.

More and more printed materials are being published that are geared particularly to the adult-life needs and interests of the retarded and slow and disabled learners. Topics such as budgeting, taxes, applying for and holding a job, civic responsibility, establishing a home, and so on are treated in workbooks published by a number of publishers. A list of these materials is given in Appendix B.

9. Take into consideration individual differences and individual difficulties. The teacher should try to determine whether the pupil is developing in all phases of reading. If he or she is deficient in one phase, exercises should be introduced to correct that particular weakness.

Reading Fundamentals for Teenagers, a workbook for basic skill building by Rose G. Neufeld (1963), contains a series of corrective reading exercises for the young adolescent who reads on a third- or lower fourth-grade level. While the text and exercises are on this level, the content of the reading material is geared to the interests of the young teenager. The book includes skill-building exercises for vocabulary development, word attack skills, and comprehension.

Functional Literacy

The concept of functional literacy was formulated in part by the Right to Read program, a federally sponsored effort to enable every child to cultivate the reading skills necessary for full participation in our society (*Right to Read,* 1970). These essential reading skills have been referred to as *survival skills* (Ahmann, 1975; Northcutt, 1975). The important questions raised by the concept of functional literacy are: (a) *what* reading skills are necessary? and (b) *how* can they be measured?

What reading level and what kinds of reading achievement are needed to survive in our society today? What are the reading tasks that an ordinary American adult must perform in order to function adequately in American society today? Traditional reading measurements that give information on grade level (such as 3.5 or 4.6) are not sufficient to answer these questions. They do not specify survival skills for functional literacy. An individual with a 5.3 reading score may not have these skills, while a person with a 3.5 score may have them.

Definition and measurement of functional literacy has become a thorny problem among reading researchers, career educators, and vocational specialists. Certainly, reading is a fundamental vocational skill in our society. A person must be able to read to learn about available jobs, to get a job, to keep a job, to get ahead on a job, and to change to another job. In the Adult Performance Level Study, an attempt was made to describe and assess functional literacy (Northcutt, 1975). The following kinds of reading tasks were required:

132
Adaptation of
Methods and
Materials:
Advanced
Stages

1. Reading newspaper Help-Wanted advertisements to obtain specific information.
2. Determining deductions from wages from the information on gross salary and deduction.
3. Reading a W-4 form to enter correct number of exemptions in the appropriate block.
4. Completing an incomplete business letter with the return address section.
5. Addressing an envelope.
6. Reading and understanding an equal opportunity notice.
7. Distinguishing between net and gross pay.
8. Reading a tabular payment schedule to determine monthly payment for a given amount of indebtedness.
9. Calculating gasoline consumption rate of an automobile when given odometer readings and fuel consumption.
10. Reading catalogue advertising to calculate the difference in price between new and used appliances.
11. Writing up a mail order form correctly when given an advertisement with price information.
12. Ordering from a restaurant menu a meal for two persons not to exceed a certain amount.
13. Writing a check on an account without an error so serious that it could not be processed by the bank or would be processed incorrectly.
14. Determining the cereal box with the lowest unit cost from three boxes of cereal displayed with name, weight, and price.
15. Determining the correct amount of change on a purchase when given a cash register receipt and the denomination of a bill used to pay for the purchase.

A national survey of 5,073 persons to determine what reading tasks people actually perform in day-to-day living was reported in 1975 by Murphy. The amount of time spent reading ranged from a few minutes per day to seven or eight hours, with an average of about one and one-half hours. The most important reading tasks performed by adults were the following (in order of importance) (Murphy, 1975):

1. Price, weight, and size information
2. Street and traffic signs
3. Main news in the newspapers
4. Writing on packages and labels
5. Manuals and written instructions
6. Forms, invoices, and accounting statements
7. Tests, examinations, and written assignments
8. Letters, memos, and notes
9. Order forms
10. Local news in the newspapers
11. School papers and notes
12. Bills and statements (p. 52).

A study of the reading levels needed for various careers showed that the general literacy requirement for many seemingly low-skill jobs was surprisingly high (Sticht & McFann,

133
Mainstreaming
Slow and
Disabled
Learners in
the Regular
Classroom:
Advanced
Reading
Instruction

1975). For example, reading requirements for a ground vehicle repairman (mechanic) varied from seventh-grade to eleventh-grade level, depending upon the measurement technique used.

Becker (1970, 1972) recommends the use of the language-experience approach with reading disabled young adults. He successfully used the language-experience method with illiterate adolescent Job Corps trainees.

Advanced reading instruction for slow and disabled learners should focus on functional literacy and survival skills. Specifically, what reading skills will these students need to get along in the world on a day-to-day basis? Teaching should concentrate on these skills. Advanced reading instruction should be both practical and useful.

Mainstreaming Slow and Disabled Learners in the Regular Classroom: Advanced Reading Instruction

Most slow and disabled learners are not in special classes but are in the regular grades of the elementary school. As noted previously, recent federal legislation (Public Law 94–142, 1975) has specified that handicapped children are to be placed with nonhandicapped pupils whenever possible. The law refers to this effort as "the least restrictive alternative."

Most slow-learning and learning-disabled children are far below average in reading ability. They are often considered laggards or lazy children because they are unable to keep up with the requirements of the grade.

An elementary school teacher can do much to increase the mildly retarded child's efficiency in reading, although the class curriculum does not provide for elementary instruction in reading. Most children in a fourth-grade class have learned a method of word recognition. They are reading rapidly, silently, and with comprehension. Some children may not have developed an efficient method of word recognition. They sometimes use their lips in silent reading in an attempt to recognize words and to understand the assignment. They are slow readers and invariably fail to complete the reading lesson. As a result they do not obtain as much information from books as the other pupils.

Twelve-year-old Joe has been promoted each year since he repeated the fourth grade at the age of 9. His IQ on the *Stanford-Binet* was 107. In arithmetic computation he tested at the fifth-grade level. His reading level was barely second grade. He participated in discussion in class but was unable to read the assignments. He was a child with a severe reading disability. What he knew about the world around him had been learned through observation, television, and what he heard in class. What this child needed was an adequate diagnosis of his reading problem and an assignment one hour

134
Adaptation of
Methods and
Materials:
Advanced
Stages

a day to a resource room for intensive remediation of his reading problem.

Suggestions for increasing the slow and disabled learner's efficiency in reading in the elementary grades are given below:

1.   Many of the suggestions for beginning reading instruction given in Chapter 4 are applicable in the upper elementary grades as well. The teacher may find another child in class who could give the atypical child some individual help in reading. The teacher should give disabled learners every opportunity to do tasks in which they can excel.

2.   The child can be helped to develop an independent and efficient method of word recognition. This may be accomplished by teaching the child phonics, syllabication, structural analysis, and context clues.

3.   The child may be given books with a reduced vocabulary containing information similar to that in the advanced books used by the rest of the class. In this way the slow and disabled learner can read about Lincoln or Washington from a simple book while the other children read about the same person from a more advanced social studies book.

4.   Any project or activity in which the atypical child participates should be used to increase vocabulary, to broaden comprehension in reading, and to increase reading efficiency. If the class is instructed to write a composition about some experience, the disabled learner can do likewise. Of course, he or she will require more guidance from the teacher or from some other pupil.

5.   Recreational or free reading should be encouraged. The teacher should provide the atypical learner with interesting books with a reduced vocabulary.

Summary

To increase efficiency in reading with slow and disabled learners, a method of word recognition should be taught. Phonics, context clues, structural analysis, and syllabication aid word recognition. Mildly retarded and borderline children in particular are deficient in generalizing ability and have difficulty developing a method of word recognition.

Silent reading should not be required too soon. Oral reading should be prolonged since it aids learning and gives the teacher a guide to the methods of reading the child is using. Good teacher judgment should prevail on the balance between oral and silent reading for atypical learners.

Interesting reading materials for mentally retarded and slow-learning children are difficult to obtain, since most elementary books are written for younger normal children. The atypical child should be given reading materials with elements of surprise, liveliness, and animalness. These materials must be simple enough to ensure mastery on the part of the child.

Comprehension of reading materials should always be stressed. The reading program should include free reading, reading directions and answering questions, correlating project work, and increasing the reading vocabulary of the disabled learner.

Retarded and slow-learning children who read at the third-, fourth-, and fifth-grade levels can be given reading programs similar to those given to normal children in the corresponding grades. Interest in recreational reading and in the use of newspapers, timetables, directories, maps, and the like should be developed before the child leaves school.

Direct remedial phonics instruction is advocated for certain reading disability cases. When remedial procedures are followed carefully, they can be very useful with mildly retarded, borderline, and learning-disabled children.

6 Specialized Remedial Reading Techniques

This chapter presents special methods, called *remedial methods,* for teaching reading. These approaches are to be differentiated from the developmental methods discussed in Chapters 3, 4, and 5.

The methods presented in this chapter are select, highly specialized ways of teaching reading. These methods are not ordinarily used by the regular classroom teacher, nor are they included in the developmental approach. These methods are reported to be effective with some severely disabled readers.

The remedial methods discussed in this chapter include the VAKT approach, the Fernald method, the Gillingham method, the Hegge-Kirk-Kirk approach, the Neurological Impress procedure, the Edmark method, the Distar method, the Cloze technique, the Rebus approach, and the Glass Analysis method.

VAKT Approach

The *VAKT approach* to reading makes a concerted effort to have the child use several sensory modalities in the learning process. V-A-K-T represents four sensory modalities: *visual, auditory, kinesthetic,* and *tactile.* The *multisensory approach,* a term also used in reference to the VAKT method, is based on the assumption that if the child uses all of the sensory avenues in the learning process, learning will be reinforced and enhanced. For example, the child is asked to *say* the word (auditory), *see* the word (visual), and *trace* the word (kinesthetic) on a surface that has a high degree of tactile sensory input such as sandpaper (tactile). Tracing offers the learner a tactile and kinesthetic sensation for learning that is not available in the usual developmental methods. The theory underlying the VAKT or multisensory approach is that the more avenues of sensory input that are activated and combined in a single learning experience, the greater the probability of success.

The multisensory approach has been used successfully to teach reading to students who had been considered nonreaders, even after they had been in school for a number of years.

Some research data support this specialized approach to reading instruction for atypical learners (Cawley, 1972; Kirk, 1933; Linn & Ryan, 1968; McCarthy & Oliver, 1965).

Caution against indiscriminate use of multisensory techniques has been advised by other writers. They argue that some atypical learners cannot process the stimulation of several modalities simultaneously; as a result, such teaching may confuse the child and actually prevent learning (Berry, 1969; Johnson & Myklebust, 1967; Wepman, 1964).

Two specialized methods often associated with multisensory approaches are the Fernald method and the Gillingham method. While both approaches utilize a tracing procedure, they differ in other essential respects. The Fernald method (Fernald, 1943) uses a multisensory approach to teach the entire word as a unit. The Gillingham method (Gillingham & Stillman, 1968; Orton, 1966) uses a multisensory approach to beginning reading by teaching discrete units of sounds or letters of the alphabet.

The Fernald Method

The *Fernald method,* which was reported to be successful with severely disabled readers at the clinic school at the University of California at Los Angeles in the 1920s, was developed by Grace Fernald and Helen B. Keller (Fernald, 1943). The method incorporates both language-experience and tracing techniques in a multisensory procedure. Because it is a laborious method and student progress is usually very slow, it is recommended only when other methods have proved to be ineffective.

Pupils must be highly motivated. From the beginning, pupils dictate their own stories, which provide the material for teaching. Thus, the vocabulary learned is selected by the students. The students must use several modalities in learning. The student *says* the word, *sees* it written by the teacher, *traces* the word with a finger, *writes* the word from memory, *sees* the word again, and *reads* the word aloud for the teacher.

The word is taught as a whole unit; that is, it is not broken into small components that emphasize the phoneme. The approach can be classified more as a sight method than as a decoding method. The Fernald method consists of four stages:

Stage 1. The teacher writes the word on paper with a crayon in manuscript or cursive letters. It must be large enough for the child to trace. The child then traces the word with finger contact and says each part of the word as it is traced. This process is repeated until the child can write the word without looking at the copy. The child writes the word once on scrap paper and then in the story, which is constructed from the child's experience. The length of the tracing period varies with the individual child. The story is then typed so that the child can read it in print.

Stage 2. This stage is reached when the child no longer needs tracing in order to learn new words. Students are now able to learn by saying the words to themselves, provided they are written by the teacher as in stage 1. They continue to write freely and to read the typed copy of what is written.

Stage 3. Pupils learn from the printed word by saying it to themselves before they write it. The child learns directly from the printed word without requiring the teacher to write it. Many children eventually acquire the ability to glance over words of four and five syllables, say them once or twice, and then write them without a copy. This occurs at a stage when the child still reads poorly and sometimes fails to recognize even simple words after being told many times what they are. At this point the child begins to want to read from books, and a basal reader can be introduced. When the reading of a selection is completed, the new words are reviewed and written from memory and later checked to ensure their retention by the child.

Stage 4. Now the child is able to recognize new words from their similarity to words already learned. After pupils have learned from the printed word, they begin to generalize and to recognize new words from their resemblance to previously learned words. These resemblances may have to be pointed out to slow and disabled learners until they are able to make the generalizations themselves. The students can now expand into more reading materials.

By this time, the remedial teacher should have (a) supplied enough reading to develop concepts that will help the child recognize new words from their similarity to ones that have been experienced in other combinations, (b) developed the child's reading vocabulary sufficiently for the comprehension of the materials to be read, and (c) taught the child to apperceive the meaning of word groups when reading any new content.

The student must be given the wealth of experience necessary for intelligent and rapid reading. Remedial instruction should not be discontinued until the child has achieved a satisfactory reading ability.

If the four stages are followed in sequence and mastery assured at each stage before moving on, the slow learner and the learning-disabled pupil should learn to read and become eager to use reading materials.

The Fernald method was developed primarily for teaching reading to children and adults with normal intelligence who had extreme difficulty learning to read. However, Fernald also advocated the method for use with retarded children.

At present, the method is used with both slow and disabled learners. For some children, the stages are short-circuited and the child learns words or phrases by writing these symbols from memory.

The Gillingham Method

Whereas the Fernald method uses a multisensory approach to teach the entire word as a unit, the Gillingham method (Gillingham & Stillman, 1968) uses a multisensory approach to reading, writing, and spelling by teaching units of sounds or letters of the alphabet. This method was developed by Anna Gillingham and Bessie Stillman in the 1930s as an instructional treatment for the kinds of children diagnosed by Samuel Orton as language-disordered. The theory formulated by Orton (1937) stated that reading problems occurred in these children because of an incomplete cerebral hemispheric dominance. The lack of dominance (especially left-hemispheric dominance) produces confusion, orientation errors, and a general delay in learning to read (J. Orton, 1966). The Gillingham method is based upon Orton's research on the relationship between cerebral dominance and reading and language disorders.

Gillingham and Stillman refer to their method as an *alphabetic method*. The sounds represented by the letters of the alphabet are learned one at a time using a multisensory approach. The learner *sees* the letter, *hears* the sound it represents, *traces* it according to certain specified hand movements, and *writes* it. In this way, the visual, auditory, and kinesthetic modalities are used simultaneously. The authors refer to multisensory phonic relationships set up within the brain in this process as *associations*.

Once ten letters are learned, they are blended in a specified fashion to form words. The blended words are consonant-vowel-consonant (CVC) words such as *Sam, hit, ran*. The words are then put into sentences and stories as specified in the manual. A sample sentence is: *Fat Sam has a bat.*

The materials are to be used and the directions are to be followed as specified in the manual (Gillingham & Stillman, 1968). According to the authors, the omission of any one of the sequential steps jeopardizes the success of the procedure. The materials include: phonic drill cards, phonic words ("Jewel Case"), syllable concept cards, and little stories. These materials are designed to accompany the lessons outlined in the manual.

The "phonic associations" (V = visual, A = auditory, K = kinesthetic) designated by Gillingham and Stillman (1968) are the following:

Association I. This association consists of two parts—association of the visual symbol with the name of the letter, and association of the visual symbol with the sound of the letter: also the association of the feel of the child's speech organs in producing the name or sound of the letter) as he hears himself say it. Association I is V-A and A-K. Part b is the basis of oral reading.

Part a. The card is exposed and the name of the letter spoken by the teacher and repeated by the pupil.

Part b. As soon as the name has been really mastered, the sound is made by the teacher and repeated by the pupil. It is here that most emphasis must be placed if the case is primarily one of speech defect. The card is exposed, the implied question being, "What does the letter (or phonogram) say?," and the pupil gives its sound.

Association II. The teacher makes the sound represented by the letter (or phonogram), the face of the card not being seen by the pupil, and says, "Tell me the name of the letter that has this sound." Sound to name is A-A, and is essentially oral spelling.

Association III. The letter is carefully made by the teacher and then its form, orientation, etc., explained. It is traced by the pupil over the teacher's lines, then copied, written from memory, and finally written again with eyes averted while the teacher must keep the principles laid down in the "Penmanship" chapter in mind. Now, the teacher makes the sound saying, "Write the letter that has this sound." This association is A-K and is the basis of written spelling (p. 41).

The Gillingham method emphasizes drill and repetition. The method requires exclusiveness; that is, other kinds of reading, writing, or spelling instruction and materials are not to be used while the Gillingham method is in use. Other lessons, such as social studies, literature, or science, therefore, must be read to children in this program. The authors also require that the remedial sessions be held daily for a minimum of two years to be effective.

The Gillingham method was designed for children identified as dyslexic, described as having normal or superior intelligence but unable to acquire reading skills by ordinary school methods. Such children could also be classified as disabled learners. Gillingham and Stillman have stated that some retarded children may also profit from use of the Gillingham method.

In 1974, Slingerland produced an adaptation of the Gillingham method called a *Multi-Sensory Approach to Language Arts for Specific Language Disability Children* (1974). The Slingerland materials include a teacher's guide and a set of auxiliary teaching materials. The manual for these materials details the Gillingham approach for classroom use for primary grade teachers.

Another variation of the Gillingham material is presented in *Recipe for Reading* (Traub & Bloom, 1970). There are twenty-one supplementary readers for use with *Recipe for Reading*.

The Gillingham approach has been criticized on several grounds (Dechant, 1970; Frostig, 1966; Gates, 1947; Wepman, 1960). According to these authors, the method does not make accommodation for children with auditory discrimination and auditory perception problems; the procedures are overly rigid; the reading material in the program is not interesting; the reading of other materials is delayed; and children instructed in this approach have a tendency to develop a labored reading style with much lip movement.

Nevertheless, there is much value in the Gillingham method. Teachers need not follow the program rigidly but may use it as an element in any ongoing program. Otto, McMenemy, and Smith (1973) comment that the approach has been reported to be successful when used with modifications. They urge that teachers use only those aspects that can be implemented practically and that do not violate good principles of instruction. The good teacher becomes the master rather than the servant of this approach or any other.

The Hegge-Kirk-Kirk Remedial Reading Drills

The *Hegge-Kirk-Kirk Remedial Reading Drills* were developed at the Wayne County Training School for mentally retarded children (Kirk, 1936). The reading drills are systematically developed, using principles now known as programmed instruction. In the initial stages it is primarily a phonics method that differs from the conventional phonics systems in its completeness and in its emphasis on certain principles of learning and retention. It uses the principles of minimal change, one response to one symbol, repetition, social reinforcement, and so on. Kirk contends that many experiments and discussions on phonics are not usually applicable to the individual treatment of reading defects among slow and disabled learners but rather for the classroom teaching of the normal child. This method has proved successful with children who had failed to profit from various conventional school methods (Hegge, 1934).

Gross Organization of Drills

The Remedial Reading Drills are divided into four parts.

Part I consists of the most frequent sounds, namely, the sounds of the consonants, the short vowels, and the sounds of *ee, sh, oo, ch, tch, ar, ay, ai, or, old, ea, oa, ck, ow, ou, ing, all, ight, th, wh, qu, er, ir, ur,* and final *e.*

Part II consists of certain combinations of sounds previously learned in isolation: *an, in, un, en, on, ink, ank, unk, ang, ong, ung, and, ound, est, ill, ell,* and consonant combinations.

Part III consists of more advanced and less frequently used sounds presented in word wholes: *jaw, Paul, new, took, find, boy, boil,* mud*dy,* bad*ly,* litt*le,* seem*ed,* ask*ed, age, ice,*

ci*ty,* fan*cy, taught, ought, p*rotest, *other, r*eturn, *be*fore, *de*fend,
*prevent, pen*sion,* addi*tion,* plan*tation,* solu*tion.*

Part IV includes supplementary exercises that teach exceptions to sounds presented in Parts I to III, configurations
not previously taught, word-building exercises, and exercises
on sounds whose letters are frequently confused, such as *b, d,
p, m, n.*

Organization Within the Drills

Figure 6.1 presents a sample of the organization of the drills.
The following should be noted:

Figure 6.1   *Remedial Reading Drills*

PART I. Introductory Sounds

Drill 1

a

sat	mat	rat	bat	cat	fat
cap	sap	map	tap	lap	rap
am	ram	Sam	ham	dam	jam
rag	bag	tag	wag	hag	lag
can	man	ran	tan	fan	pan
sad	mad	had	lad	pad	dad

sat	sap	Sam	sad
map	man	mad	mat
tan	tap	tag	tax
cab	cat	cap	can
bag	bad	ban	bat
hat	ham	hag	had
rap	rat	ran	rag
lad	lap	fan	fat

sat	man	fat	tan	pat	ban
map	can	mad	cat	man	cab
rag	cat	lap	ham	bat	tap
jam	fan	dam	had	tag	rap

sat	cap	rag	can	sad	mat	sap
ram	bag	man	mad	rat	map	Sam
tag	ran	had	bat	tap	ham	wag
tan	lad	cat	lap	dam	hag	fan
pad	fat	rap	jam	lag	pan	dad

Source: T. G. Hegge, Samuel A. Kirk, and Winifred Kirk. *Remedial
Reading Drills.* George Wahr Publishing Co., Ann Arbor, Michigan, 1935.
Used by permission.

1. Drill I uses the short vowel *a* and the consonants.

2. In the first section, only the initial consonant changes (minimal change); in the second section, only the final consonant changes; in the third section, the initial and final consonants change.

3. In the first three sections, the letters are spaced so that the child must sound each letter individually.

4. In the fourth section, the letters are brought together since the child tends to read the whole word after successive presentations are given earlier.

5. The words are to be read from left to right for the purpose of developing dextrad eye movements. The child reads the words across the page rather than down a column.

Whenever possible, every drill in part I follows this general method. Drill 2 is similar to drill 1, except that the sound of short *o* (as in *hot*) is presented instead of short *a* (as in *cat*). Drill 3 is a review of both ă and ŏ to help the child discriminate the vowels. Drill 4 introduces the sound of short *i* (as in *sit*), and drill 5 reviews ă, ŏ, and ĭ. Drill 6 introduces the short sound of ŭ.

By the time drill 7 is reached, the child has had much repetition of the consonants and of the short vowels *a, o, i,* and *u.*

Drill 8 introduces the sound of *ee* as in *k-ee-p.* The grapheme *ee* is presented as a sound in itself just as short *a* was presented as a sound in drill 1. The sound of *ee* is presented as a configuration, separate from the consonants, so that the child will learn to respond to *ee* as a whole and not by any rules. The words are presented thus: *d-ee-d, f-ee-d,* and so on. As in drill 1, only the initial consonant is changed at first, then only the final consonant, and ultimately both consonants. Other common configurations such as *ay, oo,* and so on are presented in successive drills.

Applications of the Hegge-Kirk-Kirk Method

The method of remedial training described is not a general method of teaching reading to all children or to children in the higher grade levels. It is applicable to clinical reading cases, children who have failed to learn to read after a number of years in school. In *Why Johnny Can't Read* (1955), Rudolf Flesch criticized many reading methods but advocated the *Remedial Reading Drills.* To counter the use of the Hegge-Kirk-Kirk drills as a general method of teaching reading, Kirk and Kirk (1956) refuted Flesch's claims for the drills and reiterated that the drills should be used only with those children who need this approach. The following general principles should be kept in mind when this method of treatment is used:

1. The method is applicable to children whose reading status is only first-, second-, or third-grade level. It is not a remedial method for retarded readers in the higher grades.

2. The child must have a reading problem; that is, there must be a discrepancy of approximately two or more years between reading grade and the grade consistent with the child's mental age.

3. Any extreme visual or auditory deficiencies must have been corrected.

4. A child must be trainable in sound blending. A deficiency in this ability may not be very frequent, but in about 2 percent of the cases that have come to the authors' attention, the child has been unable to learn to blend sounds after prolonged training.

5. The child must be willing to learn and must develop cooperation. It should be remembered that at the outset, many children appear uncooperative and uninterested. In many cases, after they achieve some success they cooperate splendidly. Some children, however, due to an extreme emotional reaction toward any type of teaching, continue to show poor cooperation. The present method is probably not applicable to psychopathic or neurotic children who are unable to pay attention and who do not appreciate progress. Usually a child who has been in school and who has failed to learn is very conscious of his or her disability and any method that brings hope of success is likely to be accepted wholeheartedly.

6. The child must lack the perceptual-motor abilities developed by the drills and must need to develop skills in recognizing details (Stage II of the reading process). For example, a disabled reader who is very accurate but extremely slow should be given exercises to develop reading speed rather than phonic drill materials. In the upper grades, this type of reading problem is frequent, but in the primary grades the retardation is rarely the result of accurate phonics reading, and therefore the drills are used for the development of accurate perception and response.

7. It is necessary that the teachers of slow and disabled learners transfer the ability to sound words to a natural reading situation.

Neurological Impress Method

The *Neurological Impress Method* is a relatively new approach to reading instruction designed for students with severe reading disabilities (Heckelman, 1969; Langford, Slade, & Barnett, 1974). It is a system of unison reading in which the

student and the instructor read together, the voice of the instructor being directed into the ear of the student at a fairly
close range. The student or teacher uses a finger as a locater
as each word is read. The finger should be at the location of
the spoken word. At times, the instructor may be louder and
faster than the student and at other times the teacher may
read more softly and slightly slower than the student. No
preliminary preparations are made with the material before
the student sees it. The object is simply to cover as many
pages of reading material as possible within the time available
without causing fatigue to the student. The theory underlying the method is that the auditory feedback from the
reader's own voice and from someone else's voice reading the
same material establishes a new learning process.

Few research studies investigating this approach have been
reported. The studies that were reported were conducted with
pupils in the average IQ range who had severe reading difficulties, and these offer contradictory findings. Nevertheless,
individual cases of children who improved markedly in reading using this method are of interest and warrant further
investigation (Langford, Slade, & Barnett, 1974; Otto, Mc-
Menemy, & Smith, 1973).

Edmark Reading Program

The *Edmark Reading Program* (Edmark Associates, 1972) is
designed for pupils with extremely limited skills. It is based
upon principles of behavior modification and programmed
instruction (Bijou, 1965). Each lesson contains a stimulus,
student response, and reinforcement.

The program teaches a total of 150 words in 227 separate
lessons. The lessons are of four kinds: word recognition,
direction books, picture-phrase matching, and storybooks.
The approach used in this program is a whole-word sight
vocabulary rather than a code structure system. The reasoning
of the developers (Bijou and associates) is that students who
are failing need the fastest start possible to regain their interest in learning. They feel the whole word approach is
faster and therefore more functional than a decoding process
for a starting point in reading.

The developers report that students with IQs lower than 35
have learned to read the entire 150-word vocabulary and have
been able to use those words functionally. The only student
prerequisites are the ability to repeat a word that the teacher
says and the ability to point to indicate a response. Language
meaning is learned during the program. To use the Edmark
program, it is necessary to obtain the teacher and student
materials designed for it (Edmark Associates, 1972). The program, which has been used primarily with the retarded, is
reported to be successful by its developers, Bijou and associates
(Lent, 1968).

Distar

The *Distar Reading Program* (Engelmann & Bruner, 1969) was designed to teach academic skills to children with below-average communication abilities. It was developed through work with preschool culturally different children. According to its developers, the program should enable virtually all children who have mental ages of 4–0 or above to learn to read (Engelmann, 1967). This means that the materials are intended for both slow and disabled learners. The suggested beginning mental age of 4–0, it is interesting to note, conflicts with the advice of both the reading and early childhood professionals. The period before the child reaches a mental age of 6–0 to 6–6 years has traditionally been considered the period for developing prerequisite or readiness skills for reading. Rather than waiting for the child to mature, the Distar program begins teaching the academic and reading skills that the Distar developers believe the child must learn in order to read.

The children are placed in small groups, initially no more than five in a group. One full thirty-minute lesson is presented each day. Everything that the teacher is to say and do is specified in the manuals, including tone of voice and hand movements. The children sit on chairs in a quarter-circle, each within reach of the teacher. Correct responses are reinforced in a specified manner, wrong answers are corrected.

The materials and methods make use of a behavioral approach to teaching and specify the teacher's wording and actions. The Distar program includes the following:

1. Symbol-action games. Used to teach skills, such as left-to-right orientation and linear sequence.

Figure 6.2   Sample of *Distar* Reading Program

a littlₑ fish sat on a fat fish.

thē littlₑ fish said, "wow."

thē littlₑ fish did not hātₑ thē

fat fish. thē littlₑ fish said,

"that fat fish is mom."

Source: From *Distar® Reading I* by Siegfried Engelmann and Elaine C. Bruner. © 1974, 1969, Science Research Associates, Inc. Reprinted by permission of the publisher.

2. Blending tasks. Used to teach children to spell words by sounds (say it slow) and to blend quickly (say it fast).
3. Rhyming tasks. Used to teach children to recognize the relationship between sounds and words.

The Distar system is a highly structured, step-by-step program with emphasis on code-breaking skills. Directions for the teacher are specified to meet the educational objectives set for the program.

Because of the emphasis on auditory skills required for the decoding lessons in Distar, some teachers have reported that the system is not effective with children who have difficulty with auditory processing. In addition, some teachers reject the instructional rigidity of the program. Other teachers, however, find the system to be well organized, well written, and highly effective in teaching children to read (Boyd, 1975). At present, there is relatively little published research evidence relative to the effectiveness of the Distar reading program (Boyd, 1975; Gillespie & Johnson, 1974). Research is in progress, however. Becker and Englemann (1976) have reported an extensive follow-up study in twenty school districts of disadvantaged children who were taught with Distar and compared with children of the same socioeconomic status who used other reading approaches. They stated, "The evidence shows that the model has been effective in building basic skills and intelligence for a wide variety of disadvantaged children. On our measures our low income students are at the national norms by the end of the third grade." They also state that the procedure was very effective with low IQ children.

An advanced remedial reading program following Distar concepts is the *SRA Corrective Reading Program,* intended for grades four through twelve. The teachers' materials accompanying this program include a management and skills manual, presentation books, and placement tests. The student materials include stories, student contracts, and progress charts.

The Cloze Procedure

The *Cloze procedure* is a relatively recent development that has been used (a) to determine the readability (or difficulty level) of a selection, (b) to test reading comprehension, and (c) to provide instruction in reading (Bloomer, 1962; Bormuth, 1968; Jongsma, 1971). It is discussed here as a remedial technique to improve reading comprehension.

The following technique is used to prepare material for Cloze instruction:

1. Passages are selected that are to be used as instructional material.

2.   The passage is retyped with every *n*th word (for example, every fifth word or every eighth word or every tenth word) deleted. The deleted word is replaced by an underlined blank of a standard length.

3.   Students are instructed to read the passage and to fill in the word that they think is deleted. The missing word is usually written by the child but it could be given orally.

Unlike most of the procedures discussed in this chapter, which are designed to improve decoding skills, word analysis skills, or word recognition abilities, the Cloze procedure is used to help pupils use the structure and grammatical patterns of oral language to comprehend written language. It is viewed as a psycholinguistic approach because it forces the reader to deal with the syntactic and semantic cue systems of written language.

The Cloze procedure is based on the gestalt idea of closure —the impulse to complete a structure and to make it whole by supplying a missing element. The reader is asked to make closure by supplying the missing word from a printed passage. If words are deleted at random, both lexical words and structural words are omitted. *Lexical words* carry primary meaning and are usually verbs, nouns, adjectives, and adverbs. *Structural words* indicate relationships and are usually articles, prepositions, conjunctions, and auxiliary verbs. The advantage of the Cloze technique is that the reader must bridge gaps in both language and thought. What is developed with this method is the psycholinguistic process underlying reading.

Several variations of the Cloze procedure have been suggested (Gove, 1975; Lopardo, 1975; Jongsma, 1971). While the Cloze procedure for testing and judging readability level is generally accomplished by deleting every fifth word, a number of authors have suggested deleting every tenth word for instructional purposes. In another variation, only lexical words (such as nouns and verbs) are deleted. Still another suggested technique is to delete only structural words (such as prepositions).

Lopardo (1975) suggests combining the Cloze procedure with a language-experience approach. In this procedure, a language sample is either dictated or written by the student. The sample is typed as dictated and is read by the child. The material is rewritten as a Cloze paragraph, with words deleted. The student fills in the Cloze passage and compares it to the original sample.

A sample passage using the Cloze procedure with every tenth word deleted is shown below:

In the late afternoon sunlight, Henry Carver gazed with
_____ at the pail of blueberries in front of him.
_____ were six quarts in that pail and another six
_____ a pail in the canoe.

"Won't the fellows over _____ camp be surprised
when they see me come back _____ a dozen quarts of
the finest blueberries in the _____!" he said to himself.

He was about to pick _____ the pail when a stick
snapped behind him. Facing _____ about, he saw
something that made him feel as _____ someone had
poured icy water down his spine. There _____ the
trail, between him and where he had left _____ canoe,
stood a bear—big and black and ugly! (McKee, Harrison, Cowen,
& Lehr, 1962, p. 228)

(Answers: pleasure, there, in, at, with, state, up, quickly, if, on, the)

When the Cloze procedure is used to determine readability,
the exact word that has been deleted is typically the only
selection that is accepted as correct. This policy simplifies
the scoring procedure. However, when using the Cloze procedure for instructional purposes, synonyms for the deleted
word are usually counted as correct.

The Rebus Approach

A *rebus* is a picture or a symbol of a printed word, and it is
used in reading material instead of certain printed words. For
example, a picture of an eye substitutes for the printed word *I*.
The *Peabody Rebus Reading Program* (Woodcock & Clark,
1969) attempts to simplify the initial stages of reading with
the use of rebus symbols. A sample from the Peabody Rebus
Reading Program is presented in Figure 6.3.

The Glass Analysis Method

The *Glass Analysis method* for teaching the decoding skills of
reading is described by Glass (1973) as a method of developing
perceptual conditioning for the decoding of letter clusters
within words. Essentially, the student is guided to recognize
common letter clusters easily and quickly while looking at the
whole word. The method concentrates on the decoding of
words through intensive auditory and visual training focused
on the word being studied (Glass, 1973; Glass & Burton, 1973).

This method relies on several assumptions about the function of decoding in reading: First, the processes of decoding
and reading are clearly separated. *Decoding* is defined as the
act of correctly determining the accepted sound connected
with a printed word. *Reading* deals with word meaning.

Second, decoding precedes reading. Reading is viewed as
the act of deriving meaning from the printed word. However,
reading cannot occur until the person has developed the ability to decode. If one does not learn to decode efficiently and
effectively, one will never be able to read.

Third, decoding should be taught separately from reading. The teaching of decoding is easier and less complex than the teaching of reading; therefore the teaching of decoding should be separated from instruction in reading.

The Glass Analysis method proposes eight points about the teaching of decoding:

1. Decoding is not reading and should be taught separately from reading.

2. Children should learn to decode words whose meanings they already know.

3. Emphasis should be on decoding skills. Lessons should not permit the intrusion of pictures or include the context of phrases or sentences.

Figure 6.3   Sample of Rebus Reader

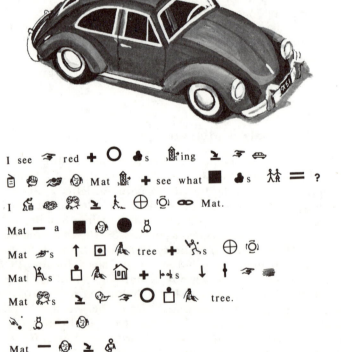

Source: From Woodcock and Clark, *Peabody Rebus Reading Program,* Reader One. American Guidance Service, Inc., Circle Pines, Minn. Used by permission.

4. Syllabication is not useful in teaching decoding and should not be part of the decoding program.

5. Successful decoders do not apply prescribed rules or a conscious reasoning process in decoding. Therefore, the teaching of decoding should not include the teaching of rules and principles. Successful decoders use perceptual conditioning abilities.

6. Words are first seen as wholes and then as parts or letter clusters that combine to form the correct sound. The learner should not respond to each letter as a separate part of the word.

7. The student needs correct visual and auditory clustering perception to learn the decoding process.

8. Correct decoding requires that the child learn the correct mental set to see and respond to the appropriate letter-sound structures within a word.

The materials needed to teach recognition of letter clusters through the Glass Analysis method can be teacher-made. Essentially, they consist of flash cards about three inches by six inches in size. Commercially published materials are available from Easier-to-Learn Materials and Walker Educational Book Corp. (Appendix D). On each card is printed a carefully selected word containing letter clusters. The words selected for study are within the child's meaning vocabulary. *Letter clusters* are defined as two or more letters that, in a whole word, represent a relatively consistent sound.

For example, in the word *catch,* the clusters are *at* and *ch*; in *play,* the clusters are *pl* and *ay*; in *standard,* the clusters may be *st, an* or *and, ar* or *ard* (Glass, 1973).

Four steps are required to teach each word:

1. Identify the whole word and the letters and sound of that target cluster.

2. Pronounce the sound or sounds and ask the child for the letter or letters.

3. Give the letter or letters and ask for the sound or sounds.

4. Take away letters and ask for the remaining sound.

The teacher is advised to not separate letters from a blend, digraph, or vowel cluster; to avoid covering up any part of the whole word; and to make sure that the student never sees less than the entire word.

The following specific instructions are recommended to teach the word *song* (Glass, 1973, p. 27):

The child is shown the word *song* on the card.

The teacher asks, "In the word *song* what sound does the letter *s* make? What sound does the *ong* make? If I took off the *s,* what sound would be left? What is the whole word?"

According to Glass (1973), this method shapes perception by examining whole words in a way that will help the child when he or she sees other words containing the same letter clusters. The child responds visually as well as auditorily to letter clusters. Glass suggests that this is what all successful decoders do—recollect how letters cluster into whole words. The method literally forces the issue of clustering.

Summary

This chapter reviewed the major specialized techniques that are used for teaching reading to atypical learners. Some of these techniques are procedures that have been developed or popularized by a particular program. Some are dependent on the use of particular materials. There is little research available on any of these specialized techniques, which are sometimes referred to as *remedial methods*. Each seems to have certain value, but each also has certain shortcomings. Knowledge of these remedial methods certainly should be among the competencies of the teacher who is helping atypical learners in reading. It is important that the teacher be able to choose and select the valuable and workable elements of a remedial program for a particular child. In this way the teacher becomes the master of the reading material or method, rather than a servant to the material.

The following specialized methods were discussed in this chapter:

1. The VAKT approach to reading is a multisensory approach, in which the child uses the auditory, visual, tactile, and kinesthetic modalities to learn to read.
2. In the Fernald method, the learner goes through several stages, the first being the tracing and remembering of a whole word as a first step in learning to read. Emphasis is placed on the visual memory of the whole word or phrase.
3. The Gillingham method is an alphabetic approach. The child uses a multisensory approach to learn individual letters, including the names of the letters, the sounds of the letters, and the visual symbols of the letters. The child also learns to blend the letters into words.
4. The Hegge-Kirk-Kirk method is a systematic phonics approach, based on accepted principles of learning and retention.
5. The Neurological Impress method is a system of unison oral reading in which both the teacher and the student participate.
6. The Edmark reading program teaches a 150-word vocabulary with materials and lessons based on principles of behavior modification and programmed instruction.

7. Distar is a code-emphasis reading program that uses highly specified and structured materials and directions for the teacher. It was developed in work with disadvantaged children.

8. The Cloze technique has been used to test comprehension and has also been used to teach comprehension. The reader must replace words that are deleted.

9. The Rebus method uses pictures or symbols instead of some printed words to simplify beginning reading.

10. The Glass Analysis method helps children learn to decode by guiding them to recognize common letter clusters quickly and easily while looking at the whole word.

Informal Assessment Procedures

This chapter and Chapter 8 deal with the topic of evaluation and diagnosis. Evaluation of reading means determining the reader's skills and needs and judging progress that has been made. Evaluation procedures can be classified into two types: informal assessment procedures, which are discussed in this chapter, and formal assessment procedures, which are discussed in Chapter 8.

The Purpose of Evaluation and Diagnosis

All teachers use informal assessment methods routinely during teaching, whether or not they label the procedure *assessment*. In dealing with any child a teacher determines at what grade level the child can read; how well or how poorly the child reads at that grade level; and what problems the pupil has in reading (for example, does the child read with apparent comprehension, at what rate does the child read, and how does the child decode words?). These observations help the teacher to adjust the reading program to the child's level of functioning and to devise procedures to decrease inefficiency in reading.

Ordinarily, teachers in the elementary grades are able to design instruction in reading for the children in their classes and to provide some variation for children of varying abilities. But in each class there will be children who deviate markedly from the group in reading ability. A teacher of fourth-grade children may find that 60 to 70 percent of the children can read the fourth-grade reader and its supplementary equivalents satisfactorily. Some of the children will be able to read in a fifth- or sixth-grade reader, while one or two may be reading beyond the sixth-grade level. However, there may also be one or two children in the class who read at the first- or second-grade level, and there may be one child in the class who does not read at all.

It is the children who are reading significantly below their chronological age reading grade expectancy who require more intensive evaluation of reading problems and who need a systematic diagnosis.

Evaluation serves several purposes: it provides information about current reading level, about errors in reading, about learning styles and needs, and it helps the teacher plan instruction. In addition, evaluation serves to test teaching effectiveness by assessing progress that has been made.

Many diagnosticians use a mathematical formula as part of the evaluation to determine the extent of the child's discrepancy in reading in relation to his or her ability to learn. The various formulas used for this purpose are discussed in Chapter 8.

Evaluation should go hand-in-hand with instruction. That is, information gathered in the diagnostic evaluation shapes the teaching; the teaching in turn gives information that leads to further diagnosis and evaluation. Figure 7.1 illustrates the relationship between evaluation, diagnosis, and teaching.

The evaluation-teaching process can be viewed as a cycle whose phases are: (a) diagnosis; (b) planning; (c) implementation; and (d) evaluation, leading to (e) modification of the diagnosis, new plans, and implementation of new teaching strategies. Evaluation and diagnosis occur in phases a, d, and e of Figure 7.1.

Diagram of the Diagnosis-Teaching Cycle   Figure 7.1

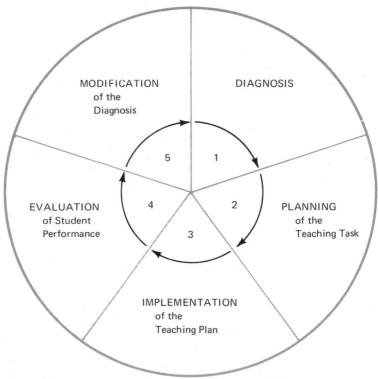

Source: Janet W. Lerner. *Children with Learning Disabilities: Theories, Diagnosis, and Teaching Strategies,* 2nd edition. Copyright © 1976 by Houghton Mifflin Company. Used by permission of the publisher.

Informal Evaluation

Informal measures differ from formal methods in many ways. Informal procedures have not been tested on large populations, nor are data available to permit comparison of a student's performance with that of a normed sample (discussed in Chapter 8). Moreover, the nature of informal assessment permits leeway in administration and interpretation. Because informal procedures have not been standardized, the teacher is free to make adjustments such as giving the student additional time for taking the test or encouraging the student during the testing process. Such adjustments put students at ease and help assure that they put forth their best effort. Informal assessment procedures include the use of teacher-made tests, observation of the student's reading behavior, diagnostic teaching, and other special procedures. Each of these techniques is discussed in this chapter.

Farr (1969) notes that there have been relatively few studies investigating the validity and usefulness of informal assessment measures. However, those research studies that have been undertaken indicate that informal procedures are often reliable and valid measures of the child's reading. Farr reasons that informal measures are often reliable because (a) more samples of reading behavior may be taken with informal measures than with formal measures, (b) they are taken over a period of time rather than in a single session, and (c) a wide variety of assessment techniques is used. Other advantages of the informal test are that they require less time, can be accomplished in a group, can be used during regular instruction periods and with classroom materials, are less expensive, and can be used to determine the effectiveness of specific classroom materials for particular children.

Informal reading measures, then, can serve to help the teacher (a) plan instruction, (b) evaluate the student's ability in various learning tasks, (c) analyze the student's reading errors, (d) learn about a student's attitudes toward reading, and (e) determine the student's reading interests.

Inter- and Intraindividual Assessment

A major reason for evaluating a pupil, whether it be accomplished informally or formally, is to help organize a teaching program. In general, a child is assessed on the basis of: (a) interindividual evaluation and (b) intraindividual evaluation (Kirk & Kirk, 1971). The more common type, *interindividual testing,* determines the level of functioning of an individual in comparison to others of the same age. The IQ score is an example of interindividual testing, for it compares one child with another. The formal reading test yields a grade level score, such as 1.8 or 3.2, which also compares one child with another. While such methods compare one child with another and are used primarily for classification and placement purposes, they do not aid in organizing a remedial program for a particular child.

Intraindividual testing procedures, in contrast, require an analysis of what the child can do and cannot do in a specific situation or in a variety of reading situations. This analysis is made without comparing the child with other children. In this approach, the emphasis is on the child's behavior on various tasks. The purpose of intraindividual testing is to provide a teaching program for a particular child. Both formal and informal measures can be used for both interindividual and intraindividual testing.

Kinds of Informal Tests

There are many informal assessment procedures. The most practical approach is for the teacher to use ordinary materials and procedures found in every school. As noted earlier, the purpose of both informal and formal testing is to gather two kinds of information: (1) the child's level of reading and (2) the child's reading errors and learning style. Both kinds of information are necessary if the teacher is to develop a reading program that will ameliorate or compensate for a deficiency or difficulty that has inhibited the child's ability to learn to read.

To determine the child's level of reading and to observe reading errors, the teacher must have the child read in different contexts. The most common dimensions of reading to observe are: (a) oral reading of passages in a book; (b) reading graded words in isolation; (c) discriminating between words; (d) silent reading, including reading comprehension; and (e) listening comprehension. All of these dimensions of reading can be examined with the typical basal graded reading books found in the school.

An example of informal testing is illustrated with the case of Johnny, who was admitted to a third-grade class at the age of 8. Within a few days of the opening of the class his teacher, Ms. Martin, noted that Johnny was not following in the reading lesson and was not participating in the assignments. At an opportune moment, Ms. Martin called Johnny to her desk and asked him to read in the basal reader used in the class. Johnny was unable to read the first page in the third-grade book except for a few words. The teacher then gave him a second-grade reader and found that Johnny could not decode all of the words. In a first-grade book he read the materials with some difficulty and needed help from the teacher. From these observations Ms. Martin estimated that Johnny's reading level was in the middle first grade in oral reading of paragraphs. In addition, she noted that Johnny guessed at the words, seemed unable to decode words he did not know, and made numerous repetitions, substitutions, and other errors.

To determine Johnny's listening comprehension level, Ms. Martin read the next story in the first-grade reader and asked Johnny questions. He knew the answers. She then read a story in the second-grade reader and also in the third-grade reader and found that Johnny understood these stories very well. She classified his listening comprehension at the third-grade level.

In the back of the first-grade reader Ms. Martin found a list of the vocabulary of that reader. She asked Johnny to read these words in isolation and found that Johnny knew only a few of the words. She estimated that his level of word reading was even lower than middle first-grade. In addition, she noted that Johnny had no method of word analysis. He either knew the word or he did not try to decode it by sounding the first consonant and guessing at the word, or trying some other method of word attack.

To test Johnny's word discrimination ability, Ms. Martin covered the words in the back of the first reader except for the first five words and said to him, "Look at these words and find the word *on*." "Now find the word *the;* now *boy*," and so on. She found that Johnny could recognize and point to three of the words, whereas he could recall only one of these words in word reading. Ms. Martin estimated Johnny's word discrimination ability to be at a high first-grade level.

From this informal examination, using only graded readers in the classroom, Ms. Martin assessed Johnny's reading level as first-grade, with word reading lowest and word discrimination highest, but with listening comprehension at the third-grade level or above. She also noted that Johnny had not yet developed a method of word attack, that he had learned a few sight words but did not use phonics or other analytic means of word recognition. She then proceeded to find out whether he had any phonic knowledge and to determine his style of learning. She did not examine his silent reading ability by having him read a page by himself silently and answer questions, since he was reading very little.

Below is a more detailed discussion of reading levels, word recognition skills, and guides to the informal analysis of reading ability.

Estimating Reading Level

Reading level refers to the difficulty level at which the child can read, and it is stated in terms of grade level. That is, in determining reading level, the teacher is trying to discover whether the child is reading at the primer level, first-grade level, second-grade level, third-grade level, and so on. While the formal standardized test is often used to determine reading level, informal methods can be useful.

The Oral Reading Level

The *Informal Reading Inventory* (IRI) is a method of determining the child's reading level by judging oral reading of graded reading passages. The following suggestions are given for determining the oral reading level:

1. Select several graded readers that you think the child can read.

2. Ask the child to read orally a passage in each of the books selected. If the child reads a first-grade reader fluently and without hesitation, ask him or her to read a second-grade reader, then a third-grade reader, and so on, until the child reads the passage with great difficulty.

3. Since the child reads at several levels, the teacher can estimate his or her reading informally at three reading grade levels: (a) the independent reading level, (b) the instructional reading level, and (c) the frustration reading level.

  (*a*) A child is rated at the *independent reading level* when he or she can read the passage in a graded reader accurately and without help from the teacher. This is the reading level at which independent work can be assigned without undue concern as to success.

  (*b*) The child is rated at the *instructional level* when he or she needs some help reading. This is the level at which the child can profit from instruction and the materials are considered not to be too easy or too hard.

  (*c*) The child is rated at the *frustration level* when he or she can read the materials, but with considerable difficulty.

Table 7.1 shows the criteria that are commonly used to determine the three reading levels with the Informal Reading Inventory.

Table 7.1 Criteria for Scoring IRI

Reading Level	Word Recognition	Comprehension
Independent	98%–100%	90%–100%
Instructional	95%	75%
Frustration	90% or below	50% or below

The criteria shown in Table 7.1 for determining reading levels were first suggested by Betts (1946) and later by Johnson and Kress (1965).

There has been some controversy among reading experts as to how to score and interpret the Informal Reading Inventory (Powell, 1967, 1971). However, the criteria indicated in Table 7.1 are the scoring standards currently used by many reading specialists. Since the IRI is an informal test, leeway can be given in administration, scoring, and interpretation.

If a resource or itinerant teacher or a regular class teacher frequently estimates the reading grade levels of many children, it is advisable that the teacher prepare a list of readings to be used with different children. This is best accomplished by typing several stories of about one-quarter page length from two or three primers, first-grade readers, and so on through the sixth grade. These materials, taken from several basic readers, can be used over and over again with different children for the purpose of estimating their reading levels. The compilation of these materials will save the teacher from spending time looking for different graded readers. They will also serve as a norm, permitting the teacher to compare different children's responses to the same materials. Through this procedure teachers can create their own reading inventory.

The Silent Reading Level

To determine whether the child can read silently and understand the materials, the teacher can have the child read a passage silently at his or her estimated instructional reading level and then ask the child questions about the passage. By having the child read silently a passage at the oral reading frustration level, the teacher can similarly estimate the silent reading level. A rough guide to estimating the silent reading level is:

Independent Level	100 percent comprehension
Instructional Level	75 percent comprehension
Frustration Level	50 percent or less comprehension

The Listening Grade Level

By reading a paragraph to the child a teacher can determine through questioning whether the child is above or below his or her instructional level in listening and understanding. Some mentally retarded children who have learned to read mechanically and who have word recognition skills sometimes do not understand materials read to them. They may be at the third-grade level in word reading and at the first- or second-grade level in listening and understanding. On the other hand, many disabled learners may be reading orally and silently at the first- or second-grade level but have listening skills at the fourth- or fifth-grade level.

By reading graded passages to the child, the teacher can get an estimate of the child's listening comprehension level—the difficulty level at which the child understands materials being read to him or her. To obtain the listening grade estimate, the teacher reads graded level passages to the child and asks comprehension questions about the material. The student should be able to relate the experiences that are heard and to use the vocabulary and language structure of the selection being read. The listening comprehension level refers to the child's ability to understand approximately 75 percent of the material and is determined by asking the child four questions on the material after it is read. If the child answers three of the four questions, he or she has a 75 percent comprehension score on that level.

The comprehension level is sometimes referred to as an *expectancy level*. It indicates the level at which children could comprehend satisfactorily if they were able to read the material for themselves.

The Word Recognition Grade Level

A teacher can assemble a word test from the glossaries of the basal readers used in assessing oral reading. If taken from the graded reader, the list of words is of course graded and can constitute a word recognition test from the primer level to the sixth-grade level. This test is designed to determine at what grade level a child can recognize words. As with oral reading, if the child reads all or most of the words in the first-grade list, his or her independent level would be first grade; if the pupil reads a second-grade list with 25 percent errors or less, he or she would be rated at the second-grade instructional level; when the child reads a list with 50 percent errors, he would have reached his frustration level in word reading.

An example of a graded word list is shown in Figure 7.2. This informal list presents ten words at each level from pre-primer to grade six. This list was constructed by selecting words at random from graded basal reader glossaries ranging from the preprimer to third-grade level; the Durrell-Sullivan reading vocabularies were used to construct the lists of grades four, five, and six (Durrell, 1956).

This informal graded word list can be used as follows:

1.   Type the list of words selected for each grade on separate cards (one list on each card).

2.   Duplicate the entire list on a single sheet of paper.

3.   Have the child read the words from the cards while the teacher marks the errors on a duplicate sheet, noting and recording the child's method of analyzing and pronouncing difficult words.

4. Have the child read from increasingly difficult lists until he or she misses three or more words on a card.

5. Start with a list that is very easy for the child and continue until three or more words are missed. By doing this the teacher can determine three reading levels (Lerner, 1976):

(*a*) The level at which the child misses one word suggests the independent reading level. The child can read accurately and without instructional help at this level.

(*b*) The level at which the child misses two words suggests the instructional level. The child has only slight difficulty and can read at this level with help from the teacher.

(*c*) The level at which the child misses three or more words suggests the frustration level. The child is having a great deal of trouble and the material at this level is probably too difficult for the student.

6. While the child reads this list (or any other prepared list of words), the teacher should observe how the child reads the words. When recording the child's errors, the teacher should note how the reader mispronounces a word and should transcribe the mispronunciation as accurately as possible. These observations will help the teacher determine what word

Figure 7.2   Informal Graded Word Reading List

Pre-Primer	*Primer*	*Grade 1*	*Grade 2*
see	day	about	hungry
run	from	sang	loud
me	all	guess	stones
dog	under	catch	trick
at	little	across	chair
come	house	live	hopped
down	ready	boats	himself
you	came	hold	color
said	your	hard	straight
boy	blue	longer	leading

Grade 3	*Grade 4*	*Grade 5*	*Grade 6*
arrow	brilliant	career	buoyant
wrist	credit	cultivate	determination
bottom	examine	essential	gauntlet
castle	grammar	grieve	incubator
learned	jingle	jostle	ludicrous
washed	ruby	obscure	offensive
safety	terrify	procession	prophesy
yesterday	wrench	sociable	sanctuary
delight	mayor	triangular	tapestry
happiness	agent	volcano	vague

recognition skills need to be taught. This phase of the assessment will be discussed further under "The Analysis of Reading Errors."

Another list of words that can be used as an informal word recognition list is contained in Table 4.1, The 220 Basic Word Sight Vocabulary. This list is divided into preprimer, primer, first, second, and third grade words. If these words are printed on cards, they can be used as a quick means of checking sight vocabulary.

The Word Discrimination Grade Level

The word discrimination test is used to determine if the child can recognize a word even though he or she cannot recall the word by naming it. To determine word discrimination grade level, the teacher can select words from the word recognition list and ask the child to read the words. If the child cannot read the words, the teacher can say, "Point to the word *chair*," or "Point to *horse*," and so on. If the child points to the right word, the child can discriminate or recognize words at a particular level, even though he or she cannot read or recall them.

The words selected for the word discrimination test may be taken from the back of a graded level book or from the Informal Graded Word Reading List shown in Figure 7.2. To test word discrimination at the preprimer level, for example, list the words, *see, run, me, dog,* and *at* on a piece of paper. Show the child the entire list and say, "One of these words is *dog*. Look at all the words in this list and point to *dog*."

Recognizing or discriminating words is, of course, an easier task than reading or naming the word. Sometimes children can read only three words out of ten presented to them but are able to point to six of the words when the teacher says the word. Hence the reading grade level for word discrimination should be higher than for word recognition. Again, the word discrimination test helps the teacher determine whether the child can recognize the word even though the child cannot recall it.

Comparison of Reading Grade Levels

When teachers have completed testing the children on their own test or inventory, they can compare the estimated reading grade levels on the five dimensions of reading. Sandra, for example, may rate as follows:

Oral reading of paragraphs	Grade 2.5
Word recognition	Grade 1.5
Silent reading	Grade 3.0
Listening and comprehension	Grade 4.0
Word discrimination	Grade 2.0

The teacher concludes from this information that Sandra's understanding of story material that she hears is quite high; that her word recognition skills are low; and that if it is possible to determine the specific problems in word recognition that Sandra is encountering, these problems might be remediated.

The Analysis of Reading Errors

Estimating the reading grade level of a child in terms of independent, instructional, and frustration levels by means of teacher-made tests, is referred to as an *Informal Reading Inventory*. This inventory, consisting of passages and words from basal readers, is used to determine the child's reading levels in the five dimensions of reading. The most important function of assessment, however, is to analyze reading errors, problems, and their correlates. Such analysis is needed if the teacher is going to organize effective and relevant remedial programs.

The following sections describe procedures of analyzing oral reading and of analyzing word reading. The two procedures are described separately, but they should be performed at the same time. While the child is reading a paragraph or a word list, the teacher should record the child's errors.

Analysis of Oral Reading

As the child reads a passage from the Informal Reading Inventory, the teacher should use a recording sheet containing the same materials to report the child's errors and answers to comprehension questions and the teacher's comments. The child's copy should be suitable in type, size, and spacing for the reading of that level. As the child reads orally, the teacher records any errors: omissions, insertion of words and word parts, substitution of words, repetition of words, unknown words, and so on. Indicate errors on the teacher's record sheet in the following manner:

Omissions. Encircle the words or parts of words omitted.
Example: Mike saw ⓐ boy.

Insertions. Use a caret (∧) and write the word inserted.
Example: He ran after ∧the dogs and cats.

Substitutions. Cross out the word and write the child's response.
Example: Dandy ~~was~~ is a good dog. The ~~store~~ star is ~~far away~~ from here.

Repetitions. Use a wavy line under the word or words repeated.

Example: Look at the red automobile.

Hesitations. If the child hesitates for a period of time and then reads the word correctly, mark it with two checks.

Example: He saw the lightning.

Unknown Words. If the child hesitates (5 seconds) but does not respond or ask for the word, tell him the word. Underline the word and mark it DK (doesn't know).

DK
Example: This is a <u>practical</u> plan.

Reversals. If the child reverses a word or letters in the word, write the reversal word over the word.

was
Example: The cat ~~saw~~ a bird.

Omission or Addition of Sounds. Circle a sound omission. Insert any sounds added by the student.

is   on
Example: The cattle ~~are with~~ the farmer.

A protocol of a paragraph read could be:

clear
Reading errors are ~~clues~~ to inefficient reading. They reveal the differences   was   DK
~~difficulties~~ the child ~~is~~ having in reading. These errors require attention by the teacher.

These reading errors will give the teacher clues to the major needs of the child in oral reading.

Analysis of Word Reading

To determine the level of word reading from the list of words in Figure 7.2, the teacher should have the same list of words on a record form. On this form the teacher records misread words in the same manner as in the oral reading analysis. This record will give the teacher information on the types of error the child makes consistently. The teacher also notes the learning style of the pupil as follows:

1. If the pupil reads some words he or she knows by sight but does not try to analyze or respond to words he or she does not know, the teacher might infer that the child has not learned a method of word attack. The child does not know how to sound letters or break words into syllables in order to decode them. This may mean that he or she needs to be taught a method of word attack. For this type of child it is customary to test sound blending to determine whether the youngster can learn phonics.

2. The child may not know words as wholes but may try to decipher the word by spelling out some of the letters. Such a child guesses at a number of words, probably from the sound of the letters. If the child spells out words in order to know them, it may mean that he or she has not learned a systematic method of word attack but has learned letters and is trying to use this knowledge to decode words. The child could probably profit from a phonic attack method.

3. The child may sound the first consonant and guess at the rest of the word. This means that the child has only a partial knowledge of phonics—not enough to do much good.

4. The child may know some sight words and may attempt to decode words by spelling or sounding some of the letters. This means that the child has probably been taught some phonics but not enough to help.

5. The child may know a number of words but may mispronounce them. This means that the child needs his or her phonic skills analyzed, since he or she may be making vowel or consonant errors, or both.

6. The child may read sight words but make a number of errors, particularly reversal errors. This means that the child may be having trouble perceiving the words correctly.

7. Sometimes one can obtain insight into the learning strategies of children by asking them to describe how they learned something.

In addition to teacher-made Informal Reading Inventories, teachers may use other assessment materials to gather information on oral reading skills. Publishers of basal reading series often provide IRI based on their materials. For example, Houghton Mifflin has the *Houghton Mifflin Informal Reading Inventory*. There are several commercially published reading inventories such as the *Classroom Reading Inventory* (Sivaroli, 1973) and the *Standard Reading Inventory* (McCracken, 1966). These are described in more detail in Chapter 8.

Other Approaches to Assessment

In addition to, or sometimes in place of, the Informal Reading Inventory assembled by the teacher, other procedures can be used to determine reading levels, errors in reading, and learning style. These include observation, diagnostic teaching, miscue analysis, and Cloze procedures.

Careful observation is very important in informal diagnosis of a child's reading. Strang (1969) recognized the crucial importance of observation when she encouraged teachers to be child watchers. She emphasized that teachers should learn to observe students to obtain valuable diagnostic information that can be put to immediate use. Strang advised that:

1. Teachers should have a background knowledge of the behavior and conditions frequently associated with the child's reading achievement and difficulties.
2. Teachers should know how to make accurate, insightful observations.
3. Teachers should be able to understand or interpret the behavior they have observed.

Strang believed that day-by-day observation by trained teachers who respond immediately to the strengths and difficulties they observe in a child's reading may be as effective as and far more practical than elaborate test batteries.

For example, while the child is reading orally from any material, including the teacher-made inventory, the teacher should observe the child with the following questions in mind:

1. Does the child recognize words from context clues?
2. Does the child repeat a great deal?
3. What kinds of error does the child make in oral reading?
4. Is the child a word-by-word reader?
5. Does the child jump over words that are not known in an attempt to read faster?
6. Does the child seem to pay much attention to the meaning of the material being read?

The child can be observed on many occasions during the day: during the testing sessions, during teacher lessons, during the child's free time, on the playground, and during group activities. Although observations are not always recorded, some systematic recording of the most significant student behavior can be useful to the teacher, the student, the parent, and the following year's teacher (Strang, 1969). Records may be kept as dated observations or anecdotal observations that are recorded and filed as a checklist.

A checklist is a list of reading skills and behaviors. The teacher simply checks appropriate items. Such lists can be made by the teacher, adapted from another list, or purchased commercially. A detailed reading checklist is provided by Guszak (1972). The *Pupil Record Booklet* of the *Gates-McKillop Reading Diagnostic Tests* also includes a good checklist of reading difficulties. An illustration of a checklist of reading behaviors is shown in Figure 7.3.

Diagnostic Teaching

The term *diagnostic teaching* means an extension and continuation of the search for diagnostic information about the child during the process of teaching. Such an approach is also referred to as *trial lessons* or *task analysis* (Gillespie & Johnson, 1974; Lerner, 1976; Myers & Hammill, 1976; Roswell & Natchez, 1971). After giving the pupil both informal and formal tests, there is still much for the teacher to learn about

Figure 7.3   Sample Diagnostic Reading Checklist

	Acceptable	Needs Improvement
Word Recognition Skills		
Sight vocabulary		
Knows initial consonant sounds		
Knows ending consonant sounds		
Knows consonant blends		
Knows consonant digraphs		
Knows short vowels		
Knows long vowels		
Blending skills		
Recognizes little words		
Uses context clues		
Word-meaning Skills		
Uses structural analysis		
Understands prefixes, suffixes, and roots		
Observes punctuation		
Uses dictionary		
Uses glossary		
Knows meaning of technical words		
Comprehension Skills		
Recognizes main idea		
Recognizes relevant details		
Knows relationships among main ideas		
Organizes ideas in sequence		
Follows directions		
Reads maps, tables, and graphs		
Can draw inferences		
Reading Behavior		
Holds book at proper distance		
Reads with fluency (not word-calling)		
Does not fingerpoint or lose place		
Volume of voice is appropriate		
Shows confidence in reading		
Reads on his own without assignments		

the child. This can be accomplished by developing lessons
that teach and test simultaneously. Two examples of diagnostic teaching are given below.

169
Other
Approaches to
Assessment

Visualization (Visual Memory)

The teacher may obtain diagnostic information about the
child's learning styles or modalities through short teaching lessons. Children with reading difficulties are commonly found
to have poor visualization ability; that is, poor ability to remember what is seen. To test this ability informally, the
teacher can write words on the board, erase them, and have
the child write them from memory. It is better to try words
that are nonphonic first, since children who know phonics
can write parts of them from their phonics knowledge. However, a word like *horse* is not known by most nonreaders, and
when it is written on the board and the child is asked to write
it from memory, the child will have to remember what was
seen. The usual procedure is to write *horse* and ask the child
what the word is. If the word is unfamiliar, the child is told
that it is *horse*. Then the word is erased, and the child is
asked to write it from memory. After the child writes it from
memory, the teacher writes *horse* on the board again and asks
the child whether he or she wrote it correctly. If incorrect,
both words are erased; the word *horse* is written again and
the child asked to write it from memory a second time, a
third time, and a fourth time. Children who have fairly good
visualization ability can write words that they have not learned
before in one or two repetitions. Those who have difficulty
will take three or four trials before they learn.

This is an informal test of the child's ability to learn words
visually. If the child is deficient in the ability to learn words
as wholes or reproduce them after seeing them, he or she has
a visualization problem and may require a remedial procedure similar to the Fernald kinesthetic method. This method
requires the child to look at unknown words, say them after
prompting, write them from memory, and say them again.
This procedure develops visualization in relation to words
and phrases. The Fernald method is described in detail in
Chapter 6.

Auditory Blending

If children do not have a method of word recognition, that
is, if they do not try to decode words through phonics or
equivalent methods, they might have a disability in sound
blending. The teacher should test informally the child's
sound-blending ability by presenting two-sound words, then
three-sound words, then four-sound words as follows: *sh-oe,
m-e, g-o, t-a-p, r-a-t, t-r-a-p, s-t-o-p, c-l-a-m*, and so on. These
sounds are presented orally; no visual representation is used.

If the child can blend these sounds when they are presented one per second, he or she has good sound-blending

ability. If the child is unable to blend three-sound words presented one per second, then the child can be considered to have a sound blending disability. If the remedial method decided upon is phonics, the remedial program should start with auditory training in sound blending.

Since most remedial methods for so-called nonreaders bear some resemblance to the Fernald kinesthetic method or the phonics method, or a combination of the two, diagnostic teaching can begin by testing visualization and sound blending.

If the kinesthetic method is being used, it is necessary to teach words and phrases that will lead to book reading, that is, to teach the vocabulary of the book to be used later.

If a phonics method is going to be used, then a system such as the Hegge-Kirk-Kirk Remedial Reading Drills, the Gillingham system, or some other phonics system should be selected. Whatever is selected should be pursued consistently.

Reading Miscue Analysis

Reading miscue analysis is a method of recording and analyzing oral reading errors (called miscues) in a systematic fashion (K. Goodman, 1965, 1969; Y. Goodman, 1972). The concepts and techniques for recording miscue analysis were developed by Kenneth and Yetta Goodman and their associates at Wayne State University.

The premise underlying miscue analysis is that oral reading errors provide valuable diagnostic information about the child's reading. The errors provide clues about the child's language, reasoning skills, and reading process. This type of analysis is viewed by Goodman as a psycholinguistic approach to reading that gives insight into the reader's underlying language patterns. When the student does not produce exactly what is on the printed page in oral reading, the discrepancies are traditionally counted as errors. In Goodman's view, these discrepancies should be seen as miscues and analyzed for their diagnostic and remedial implications. The precise method for doing this is described in Burke and Goodman's *Reading Miscue Inventory* (1972).

From the reading miscue viewpoint, reading the word *can* for the word *car* would be a lower-order error than substituting *automobile* for *car*. In the second case the child is using context and meaning of the material; in the first, there is a phonological error. In this system, errors can be analyzed as phonic errors, grammatical errors, semantic errors, dialect errors, and so on. Errors in reading may reflect the child's own language pattern rather than poor reading skills. For example, the child may read, "My mother, she be going," instead of "My mother is going."

Miscue analysis of oral reading errors in retarded children conducted by Levitt (1972) and Ramanauskas (1970) found little difference in the errors made by normal children and those made by retarded children. While miscue analysis is a relatively new concept in assessment, the theory behind it is provocative. More research on the use of this technique with slow and disabled learners is very much needed.

The Cloze Procedure

The Cloze procedure is another informal method for obtaining diagnostic information about the child's reading. The Cloze method for teaching reading comprehension is described in Chapter 6. In addition, the Cloze method can be used for testing.

Karlin (1973) suggests that the Cloze procedure can be used as an informal method to estimate the difficulty children will have with reading materials. Research relating Cloze scores to instructional level has been done with Cloze tests in which every fifth word was deleted (Rankin & Culhane, 1969). However, Karlin believes that deleting every tenth word is less formidable for the child and is more appropriate for informal diagnostic assessment.

Specific procedures for designing Cloze materials are presented in Chapter 6. For informal testing purposes, however, the following modifications can be made. Two or three excerpts from the material the child is to read are typed with every tenth word removed; the word is replaced by a blank of standard length. The child reads the typed material and tries to supply the missing word. If the reader can supply somewhat less than half the missing words, the material is judged to be appropriate for the student for instructional purposes (Karlin, 1973).

Summary

A child's reading can be evaluated by informal assessment procedures. Interindividual testing gives information for comparing a child with other children. Intraindividual testing gives information on an individual child's various abilities and disabilities.

Informal measures differ from formal methods in that they have not been tested on large populations to gather standardization data. More leeway can be given in administering and scoring informal tests. There are two kinds of informal assessment procedures: (a) methods that determine the child's reading grade level; and (b) methods that diagnose the child's reading errors and learning style. Reading grade level is determined by checking different dimensions of reading, including: (a) oral reading of paragraphs, (b) word recognition, (c) word discrimination, (d) silent reading, and (e) listening comprehension.

Procedures that diagnose reading errors and learning style give information about the kinds of mistakes or miscues the child makes and the way the child approaches the reading-learning situation. This information is helpful in developing the remedial plan.

Informal assessment is a very important means of gathering data about the child's reading. The purpose of informal assessment is to provide clues to effective instruction and remediation.

Formal tests are commercially prepared instruments that have been used with and standardized on large groups of children. Such formal tests are useful as part of the diagnostic procedures for analyzing the reading problems of slow and disabled learners. Unlike informal methods of reading evaluation, formal assessment procedures make use of standardized instruments that yield numerical scores. When formal reading tests are used, strict procedures in administration, scoring, and interpretation are required.

Both formal tests and informal measures can offer important information. When trying to diagnose or evaluate a student's reading abilities, teachers should use both kinds of measurement in order to learn as much as possible about the student. The information from one type of measure can corroborate that from the other. It is dangerous to depend on any single measure as an indicator of student performance. Farr (1969) recommends that if the teacher wants an accurate assessment of the child's reading abilities, he or she should use a wide variety of assessment procedures, including informal inventories, observations, and standardized tests.

There are three types of formal tests: (a) standardized or norm-referenced tests, (b) diagnostic tests, and (c) criterion-referenced tests. In some cases, a particular test may be placed within several of these categories. For example, a criterion-referenced test can be used as a diagnostic test; the diagnostic test can be either a norm-referenced test or a criterion-referenced test or both. Despite these crossover tendencies, these three categories are a useful way of classifying formal tests.

Standardized or Norm-Referenced Tests

Norm-referenced or standardized tests are interindividual tests, generally standardized on thousands of children in the different grades. Ordinarily, reading survey tests are administered to a whole class at a time (group tests), although there are some individual norm-referenced tests. They are called *norm-referenced* because they have scores derived from their administration to a large group of children. Most of the tests have the following characteristics:

1.   The test is usually available in more than one form so that children can be examined more than once without obtaining a higher score due to practice.

2.   The test is accompanied by a manual giving directions for administration, scoring, and interpretation.

3.   The manual contains grade norms, age norms, and possibly percentile ranks or some form of scaled scores.

4.   Figures on reliability (the degree to which the test gives results that are consistent) and validity (the degree to which the tests measure what they are supposed to measure) are included in the manuals. The manual might show a reliability score of .90, indicating that if the test were given to the child again, it is 90 percent likely that the same score would be obtained.

As for validity, if the test purports to test "speed of reading," it should measure speed and not word knowledge or comprehension.

The tables in the manual present different methods of reporting scores. A raw score is usually the number of correct items. The meaningful scores are: (a) grade scores, (b) age scores, (c) percentile ranks, and (d) stanines or scaled scores.

Intelligence Tests

One kind of standardized test is the intelligence test. Intelligence tests are important in the assessment of reading problems, for they help determine the child's potential for learning, usually in terms of an IQ score (see Chapter 2, "Measuring Mental Maturity," for methods of interpreting IQ scores). Reading tests, in contrast, help determine the child's present reading achievement level. The numerical difference between the child's scores on these two kinds of tests (intelligence and reading tests) is the discrepancy between potential and achievement. The size of this discrepancy helps the teacher determine if the child does have a significant reading problem. Techniques to determine this discrepancy are discussed later in this chapter.

Intelligence tests can be divided into two types: (1) individually administered intelligence tests, and (2) group administered intelligence tests.

Individual Intelligence Tests

Individual intelligence tests are administered by a trained examiner to a single child. Administration can take from ten minutes to several hours, depending on the test. The individual intelligence test is considered useful for estimating the general mental capacity of a child. While testing, the examiner has an opportunity to observe the child and to make sure that the subject puts forth his or her best effort. Furthermore, the examiner usually obtains clinical information about the child's attitudes, attentiveness, and approach to tasks.

The most widely used individual intelligence tests are described below:

The *Stanford-Binet Intelligence Scale,* revised in 1960, is applicable to children as young as age 2 and also to adults. It yields a single IQ score (deviation IQ) and requires about an hour to administer. Both administration and scoring are fairly complicated and a highly trained examiner is required. Ordinarily this kind of test is administered, scored, and interpreted by a school psychologist.

The *Wechsler Tests* consist of three different tests for three age ranges. The *Wechsler Preschool and Primary Scale of Intelligence (WPPSI)* is used with children between the ages of 4–0 and 6–0; the *Wechsler Intelligence Scale for Children–Revised (WISC–R)* is used with children ranging in age from 6–0 to 16–11, and the *Wechsler Adult Intelligence Scale (WAIS)* is used for those over age 16–11. These tests require about an hour for administration and are administered by school psychologists. The Wechsler tests yield several IQ scores (deviation IQ): a verbal IQ, a performance IQ, and a full-scale IQ. In addition, the verbal section and the performance section each have several subtests that yield scaled scores. In the *WISC-R,* for example, the verbal tests include these subtests: information, similarities, arithmetic, vocabulary, comprehension, and digit span. The performance tests consist of: picture completion, picture arrangement, block design, object assembly, coding, and mazes.

Less widely used individual intelligence tests include:

The *Peabody Picture Vocabulary Test (PPVT)*, an individually administered intelligence test for children aged 2–5 to 18–0. The *PPVT* takes about ten minutes to administer. The child is shown a card with four different pictures; the examiner asks, "Show me globe," and the child points to one of the four pictures. In a sense, this is also a test of receptive language ability for single words. The Peabody can be administered by a minimally trained examiner.

The *Slosson Intelligence Test for Children and Adults,* revised in 1963, is an individually administered test that can be given by a minimally trained examiner. It is a verbal test, requiring about twenty minutes to administer.

The *Goodenough Draw-a-Man Test,* revised by Harris in 1963, is also used to measure intelligence. In this test, the child is instructed to draw a picture of a man, a woman, and himself or herself. The drawing is scored according to the child's accuracy of observation and on the development of conceptual thinking. This is a nonverbal test. It can be given by a minimally trained examiner and requires about ten minutes to administer.

Group Intelligence Tests

There are a number of group intelligence tests that measure functions similar to those measured by individual intelligence tests. These tests are comparatively simple to administer to groups of children. Directions are given orally and the children indicate their answers by marking in the booklets. Widely used group intelligence tests include: *Otis-Lennon Mental Ability Test, SRA Primary Mental Abilities Test, California Test of Mental Maturity,* and *Kuhlmann-Anderson Intelligence Test.*

Standardized Reading Tests

It is useful to differentiate two kinds of standardized reading tests: the survey reading test and diagnostic reading test. The first provides general information about the child's reading level; the latter gives an in-depth view of the child's (a) reading subskill abilities, (b) reading errors, and (c) learning style in reading. The survey reading test is discussed in this section; the diagnostic reading test in a later section.

The Survey Reading Test

The purpose of the survey test is to give general information about the child's reading level. The survey test usually has at least two parts: one measuring the pupil's reading vocabulary and the other measuring paragraph comprehension. Some survey tests also have sections that measure sentence comprehension and rate of reading. Survey tests are usually designed as group tests; students read silently and then answer multiple-choice questions. The tests usually have fairly long time limits so that the pupil is stopped by the increasing difficulty of the reading material rather than by the time element. Usually a survey test is one of the first tests given to assess reading ability.

Survey tests can be viewed as interindividual tests, since the score compares the child's reading with that of other children of the same age or grade. The teacher can use such scores to determine how a particular pupil reads in comparison with other children of similar age.

Overreliance on reading grade scores obtained from survey tests can be dangerous. The score shows the level at which comprehension can be achieved with difficulty rather than the level at which fluency and reasonable accuracy can be expected (Strang, 1968). For many children, particularly those who are good test-takers and do well at guessing, the score obtained does not indicate the grade level at which the child can read with ease. Research suggests that a book at the grade level indicated by standardized reading tests would actually be at the child's frustration reading level and would be much too difficult for instructional purposes (McCracken, 1962; Sipay, 1964).

There is also a question about how accurately standardized tests measure the reading ability of pupils who are actually reading way above or way below the grade levels for which the test is intended. For example, Bonnie is reading at about second-grade level but she is in the sixth grade. A test designed for sixth graders will not assess Bonnie's reading performance accurately. Harris and Sipay (1975) suggest that the solution for so-called out-of-level testing is to have the child tested at a level commensurate with the estimated level of reading ability. With such an approach, Bonnie would take the test designed for second graders rather than for sixth graders.

In addition to the objective data given by the test scores, the teacher can gather much additional subjective information about the child and the child's reading through careful observation during the testing session and by examining the child's performance on individual test items.

Scores on Reading Tests

The raw score on a reading test is simply the total number of correct items. For interpretation, this must be converted to a more meaningful score, such as the grade score, the age score, the percentile rank, or stanine or scaled score.

Reading Grade Score

To obtain a reading grade score, the raw score is converted to a grade level score, such as 3.5 (fifth month of the third grade), which indicates that the child's reading level is the same as the median score of children in the middle of the third grade. For example, if Sandra scores 5.1 on the XYZ reading test, she receives the same raw score as the median of the children in the first month of the fifth grade who took this test. That is, one-half of these children in grade 5.1 scored 5.1 or higher and the other half scored 5.1 or lower. Reading grade scores are typically reported in years and tenths of a year because there are ten months in a school year.

It is important to emphasize that the reading grade score indicates the score obtained by the median of pupils in a given grade. Thus a score of 4.5 means that half of the pupils in the fourth grade scored 4.5 or higher and half scored 4.5

or lower. The grade score indicates a kind of average—not a base—for students at grade 4.5. One should not expect all students to score above 4.5; statistically only one-half will do so. If 50 percent of a school's students score at or below grade level on a reading test, this result implies that they are statistically average. It does not mean that half of the pupils in the school must be brought up to some nonexistent baseline.

Reading Age Score

A *reading age score* is similar to a reading grade score except that norms are based on the age of the pupils rather than grade placement. A reading age score of 7–11 means that the child scored the same as the median of the norm population aged 7 years and 11 months. Reading age scores are reported in terms of years and twelfths, as chronological age is based on a twelve-month year. The difference between a person's reading age and reading grade is roughly five years. To convert a reading grade to a reading age, simply add five years. For example, Betty's reading grade is 3.2; her reading age, therefore, is 8–2. (If one wishes to be more precise, the difference between the age score and grade score is 5.2. This is because the average child beginning first grade (grade 1.0) is 6 years and 2 months of age. There is a 5.2 difference between 1.0 and 6.2.)

Reading grade and reading age scores are useful when trying to determine the reading growth of an individual child over a period of remediation time. For example, Sam scored at the 2.1 level in September and at the 3.4 level in March following six months of remediation. This means that in six months Sam gained 1.3 grades in reading. Grade level scores are easy for parents or boards of education to understand. These scores are also useful in making decisions about placement in a reading group or grade.

Percentiles

Percentiles are a way of stating how a child compares with other children in terms of his or her own grade or age. Percentiles can be regarded as ranks in groups of 100; percentiles are expressed in numbers from 1 to 99. If Bill gets a percentile of 85, this means that Bill's score is better than those of 85 percent of the students with whom he is being compared, and it is poorer than those obtained by 15 percent. The fiftieth percentile is the median score—50 percent of those tested received higher scores and 50 percent received lower scores. Percentiles are useful for comparing a student with others of the same age or grade or to rank students of a given grade. It is difficult to measure reading growth with percentile scores.

Stanines and Standard Scores

179
Standardized
or Norm-
Referenced
Tests

Stanines are another type of derived scores used in some reading tests. The stanine score ranks pupils of a given age or grade from 1 to 9. The lowest stanine score is 1, the median stanine is 5, and the highest is 9. The name *stanine* is a contraction of "standard nine" and is based on the fact that the scores run from 1 to 9. Stanines are normalized standard scores with a mean of 5 and a standard deviation of 2. This means that 68 percent of children tested would have a stanine of 3 to 7.

Standard scores are normalized scores. That is, scores are put into a convenient form by transforming them mathematically to a normal distribution, with the mean and standard deviation being preassigned. For example, on the *Wechsler Intelligence Scales,* the mean is 100 and the standard deviation is 15; on the *Illinois Test of Psycholinguistic Abilities,* the mean is 36 and the standard deviation is 6; on the *College Entrance Examination Board (CEEB),* the mean is 500 and the standard deviation is 100. This means that 68 percent of the population score between 400 and 600.

Each of the derived scores described above has certain advantages, and each has certain shortcomings and is subject to statistical criticism (Anastasi, 1975). Teachers should select the scores that will serve the purpose at hand. When working with an individual child on a clinical basis, a grade level score is often one of the most useful types of derived scores. It is also readily understood by most parents. It indicates the grade level at which a child is reading in the test administered. It is an interindividual score, however, and does not give clues about remediation.

Examples of Survey Reading Tests

There are many standardized or norm-referenced survey tests on the market. The survey tests used at the primary, elementary, and intermediate levels include the following:

California Reading Test (California Test Bureau)

Comprehensive Reading Scales (Van Wagen Psycho-Educational Laboratories)

Gates-MacGinitie Reading Tests (Teachers College Press)

Iowa Every-Pupil Tests of Basic Skills (Houghton Mifflin)

Iowa Silent Reading Tests (Harcourt Brace Jovanovich)

Metropolitan Achievement Tests: Reading (Harcourt Brace Jovanovich)

New Developmental Reading Tests (Lyons and Carnahan)

SRA Achievement Series: Reading (Science Research Associates)

Stanford Achievement Tests: Reading (Harcourt Brace Jovanovich)

Wide Range Achievement Test (WRAT) (Guidance Testing Associates)

Survey tests at the secondary or high school level include:

California Reading Test (California Test Bureau)

Comprehensive Test of Basic Skills (California Test Bureau)

Diagnostic Reading Tests (Committee on Diagnostic Reading Tests)

Iowa Silent Reading Test (Harcourt Brace Jovanovich)

Iowa Tests of Educational Development (ITED) (Science Research Associates)

Iowa Tests of Basic Skills (Houghton Mifflin)

Gates-MacGinitie Reading Tests (Teachers College Press)

Nelson-Denny Reading Test (Houghton Mifflin)

Cooperative English Tests: Reading Comprehension (Educational Testing Service)

Sequential Tests of Educational Progress (STEP) (Educational Testing Service)

Traxler Silent Reading Test (Bobbs Merrill)

Davis Reading Test (Psychological Corporation)

In addition there are several reading tests designed for adult basic education students:

Tests of Adult Basic Education (TABE) (California Test Bureau)

Adult Basic Learning Examination (ABLE) (Harcourt Brace Jovanovich)

Basic Reading Inventory (BRI) (Scholastic Testing)

Several of the most widely used standardized survey tests are described below.

California Reading Tests. Level 1 (grades one to two); *Level 2* (grades two to four); *Level 3* (grades four to six); *Level 4* (grades six to nine); *Level 5* (grades nine to twelve). Each level has subtests on vocabulary and comprehension. Levels 1 and 2 have word attack subtests. There are two or more forms available at each level. Administration time: ranges from thirty-five minutes at *Level 1* to eighty minutes at *Level 5*. (California Test Bureau)

Gates-MacGinitie Reading Test. *Primary A* (grade one); *Primary B* (grade two); *Primary C* (grade three). Each Primary contains two subtests—vocabulary and comprehension. *Primary CS* (grades two to three) tests speed and accuracy. *Survey D* (grades four to six); *Survey E* (grades seven to nine); *Survey F* (grades ten to twelve). Each Survey test includes subtests of vocabulary, comprehension, and speed and accuracy. All of the tests consist of two or more forms. Administration time: ranges from forty-five to fifty-five minutes. (Teachers College Press)

Iowa Tests of Basic Skills. *Primary Battery* (grades 1.7 to 3.5); *Levels Edition* (grades three to eight). Reading comprehension, vocabulary, word analysis, work-study skills. Two forms at each level. Administration time: sixty minutes and eighty-five minutes. (Houghton Mifflin)

Metropolitan Achievement Tests: Reading. *Primer* (grades K.7 to 1.4). Listening for sounds, word knowledge, comprehension. Two forms. Administration time: approximately one hour. *Primary I* (grades 1.5 to 2.4); *Primary II* (grades 2.5 to 3.4). Word knowledge, word analysis, comprehension. Three forms. Administration time: approximately one hour. *Elementary* (grades 3.5 to 4.9); *Intermediate* (grades 5 to 6.9); *Advanced* (grades 7 to 9.5). Word knowledge, comprehension. Three forms. Administration time: forty-three to forty-six minutes. (Harcourt Brace Jovanovich)

SRA Achievement Series: Reading. *Primary I* (grades 1 to 2.5); *Primary II* (grades 2.5 to 3); *Multilevel Blue* (grades 4 to 5); *Multilevel Green* (grades 6 to 7); *Multilevel Red* (grades 8 to 9.5). Vocabulary and comprehension subtests. Two forms. Administration time: approximately one hour. (Science Research Associates)

Stanford Achievement Tests: Reading. *Primary I* (grades 1.5 to 2.4); *Primary II* (grades 2.5 to 3.4); *Primary III* (grades 3.5 to 4.4); *Intermediate I* (grades 4.5 to 5.4); *Intermediate II* (grades 5.5 to 6.9). Vocabulary, reading comprehension, and word study skills. There is also a listening comprehension subtest. *Advanced* (grades 7 to 9.5). Vocabulary and reading comprehension. Two forms at each level. Administration time: thirty-five to ninety-five minutes. (Harcourt Brace Jovanovich)

Samples of a standardized or norm-referenced survey reading test are shown in Figure 8.1.

Diagnostic Reading Tests

In contrast to the survey test, which gives general information about the pupil's reading ability, the *diagnostic reading test* is designed to give a more detailed analysis of specific reading skills and difficulties. The diagnostic reading test consists of a battery of subtests of several reading achievement skills, which provide detailed information about the individual's reading. Often, these subtest skills tap pivotal or diagnostically sensitive reading behaviors. Such diagnostic batteries enable the teacher to construct a child's test profile from the subtest scores (Hill, 1974).

Diagnostic reading tests are intraindividual tests in that they test the individual child's reading abilities and disabilities. They also tell what errors the child is making in reading and the kind of errors that are made. In short, diagnostic reading tests give information on how the individual is reading, what kinds of errors are made, and the reading strengths and weaknesses.

Many diagnostic reading tests are standardized or norm-referenced; some, however, are not. Reading researchers who

Figure 8.1   Samples of Survey Reading Test

Words: Part A

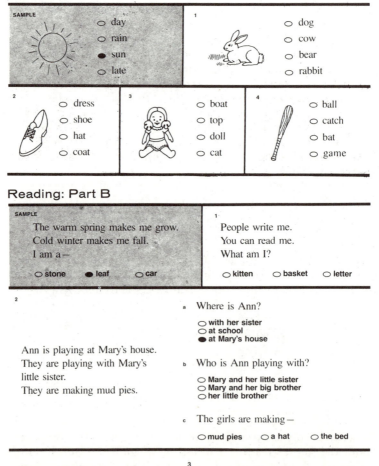

Reading: Part B

Source: Reproduced from the Metropolitan Achievement Tests, copyright © 1970 by Harcourt Brace Jovanovich, Inc. Reproduced by special permission from the publisher.

have studied the specific reading subskills in norm-referenced diagnostic tests question the diagnostic validity of the subtests of reading (Farr, 1969). Because a single subtest is often very short, it may not be a discrete and valid measure of the sub-skill being measured. For this reason, if the diagnostic test shows a weakness in a specific subskill, it is wise to support such a finding with other information from other diagnostic tests, informal measures, and observations.

There are some commercial diagnostic reading tests that are not norm-referenced tests, that is, they include no norm-referenced data. Such tests, then, are more similar to informal tests. When interpreting the results of a diagnostic test, the teacher should know whether the test is norm-referenced.

Diagnostic tests are often designed for individual rather than group administration. As noted above, they are likely to have many subtests that measure various skills, such as oral reading, silent reading, special phonics skills, sight vocabulary, spelling, auditory and visual reading abilities, and blending skills. Administration and scoring are usually more complex than for the survey test, and therefore administration of diagnostic reading tests requires a certain amount of training. There are two types of diagnostic reading tests: (a) diagnostic reading test batteries that test many reading subskills and (b) specific skills tests that measure abilities in a single area.

Examples of Diagnostic Test Batteries

Widely used diagnostic test batteries include: *Durrell Analysis of Reading Difficulty, Gates-McKillop Reading Diagnostic Tests, Spache Diagnostic Reading Scales, Stanford Diagnostic Achievement Test, Peabody Individual Achievement Test (PIAT)*, and the *Woodcock Reading Mastery Tests*.

Durrell Analysis of Reading Difficulty

The Durrell battery has been used for many years as a diagnostic test. There are many parts to the test, and the examiner usually uses selected subtests for a particular child. There are oral reading paragraphs along with comprehension questions after each paragraph. There are also paragraphs for silent reading and listening comprehension. There is a word recognition subtest given with a tachistoscope that comes with the test, and separate grade norms are given for flashed and untimed presentations.

In addition to the oral reading, silent reading, listening, and word recognition subtests, there are numerous supplementary tests on naming, identifying, matching, and writing letters; visual memory of words; hearing sounds and letters in words; learning to hear sounds in words, giving sounds of letters and letter groups; visual memory of words; spelling; and handwriting. (Harcourt Brace Jovanovich)

Gates-McKillop Reading Diagnostic Tests

This diagnostic battery contains many subtests. There are two forms of the test, I and II. The oral reading test scores the child on reading accuracy and classifies the errors that the child makes. There are no comprehension questions. A word list of forty words is given to obtain a measure of sight vocabulary. Each word is exposed for a short time. Words are also exposed untimed to measure the child's word analysis abilities. There is a timed phrase recognition section.

Word analysis subtests test knowledge of word parts, recognition of visual forms representing sounds, auditory blending, spelling, oral vocabulary, syllabication, and auditory discrimination. (Teachers College Press)

Spache Diagnostic Reading Scales

In this test the child reads from one of three word lists and the teacher notes the child's sight vocabulary, analyzes the method of decoding, and estimates reading level. The child then reads orally from passages ranging in difficulty from primer to eighth-grade reading level. The child is given comprehension questions following each passage. These are evaluated like an Informal Reading Inventory, determining independent, instructional, and frustration levels. There are also supplementary phonics tests and a listening test. (California Test Bureau)

Stanford Diagnostic Reading Test

This is a group test with separate measures of comprehension, vocabulary, syllabication, auditory skills, phonic analysis, and rate. There are two levels of this test: *Level I* (grades 2.5 to 4.5) and *Level II* (grades 4.5 to 8.5). There are two forms. Administration time: approximately two and one-half to three hours. (Harcourt Brace Jovanovich)

Peabody Individual Achievement Test (PIAT)

This is an individually administered test for kindergarten through high school. It tests students for general information and reading recognition. It also tests letter names, letter sounds, visual discrimination of letters and words, mathematics, spelling, reading comprehension, comprehension of sentences. Thirty to forty minutes are required to administer the entire battery. (American Guidance Service)

Woodcock Reading Mastery Tests

This is an individually administered reading diagnostic test battery. It contains subtests on letter identification, word identification, word attack, comprehension, and passage comprehension, and a total reading score. Scores are both norm-referenced and criterion-referenced. (American Guidance Service)

Examples of Diagnostic Tests of Specific Skills

The tests described above are batteries with many diagnostic subtests. Some reading diagnostic tests are designed to measure a specific subskill. Four categories of tests of specific skills are: oral reading tests, phonics tests, standardized reading inventories, and tests of reading aptitude.

Oral Reading Tests

Gray Oral Reading Test. This is an individually administered test with thirteen graded reading passages. Reading accuracy and rate of reading are measured in a combined score. Comprehension questions are included but not used in the scoring system. Grades one to twelve. There are four forms. (Bobbs-Merrill)

Gilmore Oral Reading Test. This is an individually administered test with ten reading paragraphs. Scores measure reading accuracy, comprehension, and rate. Grades one to eight. Two forms. (Harcourt Brace Jovanovich)

Slosson Oral Reading Test. This is a brief individually administered test of word recognition for words presented in isolation. Grades one to twelve. (Slosson's Educational Publications)

Wide Range Achievement Test (WRAT) (Reading). This is an individual brief test of word recognition that also tests spelling and arithmetic computation. *Level I* (grades one to six); *Level II* (grades seven to twelve). (Guidance Testing Associates)

Phonics Tests

Botel Reading Inventory. This is a group-administered test on phonics, word recognition, word opposites (in reading and listening). It also determines instructional level. Grades one to twelve. (Follett Educational Corp.)

Sipay Word Analysis Tests (SWAT). This is a set of sixteen diagnostic subtests: specific visual analysis, phonic analysis, blending skills, word analysis survey test. (Educator's Publication Service)

Roswell-Chall Diagnostic Reading Test and *Roswell-Chall Auditory Blending Test.* These are two quick check tests.

The first checks the child's knowledge of letter and phono-gram sounds, one-syllable words, short and long vowels, and syllabication. The second is a brief standardized test of auditory blending. (Essay Press)

Doren Diagnostic Reading Test of Word Recognition. This is a diagnostic reading test with twelve subtests measuring letter recognition, beginning sounds, whole-word recognition, words within words, speech consonants, ending sounds, blending, rhyming, vowels, discriminate guessing, spelling, and sight words. (American Guidance Service)

McCullough Word Analysis Tests. This is a set of seven subtests on phonic and visual analysis skills. Grades four to six. (Personnel Press)

Standardized Reading Inventories

The following reading inventories are similar to the informal reading inventories described in Chapter 8; however, these reading inventories have been standardized on large populations and have accompanying norming data. Some have additional kinds of information.

Classroom Reading Inventory (Sivaroli, 1973). This is an oral reading test accompanied by comprehension questions, which gives results in terms of instructional levels. (William C. Brown)

Standard Reading Inventory (McCracken, 1966). Oral reading passages, comprehension questions, and word lists. Scoring gives independent, instruction, and frustration levels. (Klamath)

Reading Placement Inventory (Sucher & Allred, 1973). Word lists and reading passages. Each selection has comprehension questions. (Economy Co.)

220 Basic Word Sight Vocabulary. This list (see Chapter 3) can be used as a quick word recognition inventory. Dechant (1971) suggests that the following criteria be used to correlate number of words recognized with grade level.

Number of Words	Grade Level
75	Preprimer
120	Primer
170	First reader
210	Second reader
220	Third reader

The following tests measure reading aptitude:

(Slingerland) *Screening Test for Identifying Children with Specific Language Disability.* This screening test is intended

Sample of Diagnostic Reading Test: *Durrell Analysis of Reading Difficulty*

Figure 8.2

Durrell Analysis of Reading Difficulty

NEW EDITION

INDIVIDUAL RECORD BOOKLET

BY Donald D. Durrell *Professor of Education and Director of Educational Clinic, Boston University*

NAME _____   DATE _____

SCHOOL _____   EXAMINER _____

AGE _____ GRADE_____   REPORT TO _____

DATE OF BIRTH _____   ADDRESS _____

Profile Chart

GRADE	READING ANALYSIS TESTS							ADDITIONAL TESTS								AGE
	Reading		Listen-ing	Flash Words	Word Analysis	Spell-ing	Hand-writing	Durrell-Sullivan				Revised Stanford-Binet				
								Capacity		Achievement						
	Oral	Silent						Word	Para.	Word	Para.	Vocab.	M.A.			
H																12-0
6.5 M																11-8
L																11-4
6.0																11-2
H																11-0
5.5 M																10-8
L																10-4
5.0																10-2
H																9-11
4.5 M																9-8
L																9-5
4.0																9-2
H																9-0
3.5 M																8-8
L																8-5
3.0																8-2
H																8-0
2.5 M																7-9
L																7-5
2.0																7-3
H																7-0
1.5 M																6-9
L																6-6
Record scores here →																

for use in locating children who have or are likely to de-velop disabilities in several language areas: reading, spell-ing, and handwriting. There are tests designed for group and individual administration, including visual copying, visual memory and discrimination, three auditory group tests, and one individual auditory test. There are tests for grades one,

Figure 8.3   Sample of Diagnostic Reading Test: *Gates-McKillop Reading Diagnostic Tests*

PUPIL RECORD BOOKLET FORM **1**

G A T E S - M c K I L L O P
READING DIAGNOSTIC TESTS

ARTHUR I. GATES
Professor Emeritus of Education
Teachers College, Columbia University

ANNE S. McKILLOP
Professor of Education
Teachers College, Columbia University

Pupil's Name _____ School _____ Date _____

Pupil's Age _____ Birthday _____ Grade _____ Examiner _____ Teacher _____

AGE, GRADE, INTELLIGENCE	1 Raw Score	2 Grade or Other Score	3 Rating	READING AND OTHER TESTS Date Given	1 Raw Score	2 Grade or Other Score	3 Rating ( ) , ( )
1 Chronological Age			( ) ¦ ( )	1 _____			
2 Grade Status (A.G.)				2 _____			
3 Binet___I.Q. _____ MA			(Date Given)	3 _____			
4 _____ I.Q. _____MA				Average Silent Reading Gr. (ASRG)			

READING DIAGNOSTIC TESTS

I. Oral Reading (OR)			( ) ¦ ( )	**V. Knowledge of Word Parts**			(OR)
Total Score				1. Recognizing and Blending Common Word Parts			
Analysis of Total Errors				2. Giving Letter Sounds			
a. Omissions, Words		%		3. Naming Capital Letters			
b. Additions, Words		%		4. Naming Lower-Case Letters			
c. Repetitions		%		**VI. Recognizing the Visual Form of Sounds**			
d. Mispronunciations (g through k)		%					
Analysis of Mispronunciations				1. Nonsense Words			
e. Full Reversals				2. Initial Letters			
f. Reversal of Parts				3. Final Letters			
g. Total Wrong Order (e+f)				4. Vowels			
h. Wrong Beginnings							
i. Wrong Middles				**VII. Auditory Blending**			
j. Wrong Endings							
k. Wrong Several Parts							
II. Words: Flash Presentation			( ) ¦ ( )	**VIII. Supplementary Tests**			( )
III. Words: Untimed Presentation				1. Spelling			
				2. Oral Vocabulary			
				3. Syllabication			
IV. Phrases: Flash Presentation				4. Auditory Discrimination			
				5. _____			

two, three, and five to six. The teachers' manual gives directions for administration and scoring but does not give standardization data. Evaluation is subjective in nature. (Educator's Publishing Service)

Monroe Reading Aptitude Test. For beginning reading at grade one to nonreaders age 9. Tests of visual perception, auditory perception and memory, motor control, speed, articulation in speech, and language development. (Houghton Mifflin)

Monroe-Shermand Group Diagnostic Reading Aptitude and Achievement Test. Grade three and up. Reading achievement test of paragraph meaning, rate, word discrimination, arithmetic, spelling. There are also tests of visual memory, auditory memory and discrimination, motor speed, and oral vocabulary. (Nevins Printing)

Samples of score sheets from two diagnostic tests are shown in Figures 8.2 and 8.3.

Criterion-Referenced Tests

Teacher-made criterion-referenced measures have been used for many years. Commercially published *criterion-referenced tests* (CRT) are relatively recent developments in measurement and have been introduced for several reasons: (a) there are serious shortcomings with standardized reading tests; (b) there is an increasing demand for more accountability; and (c) behavioral psychology, which advocates using criterion-referenced tests because such tests are closely related to treatment, has influenced measurement in education. The basic purpose of criterion-referenced measurement is to determine if the pupil has met specific instructional objectives. For example, does the pupil recognize *ing* endings? Can the student use the initial digraph *sh*? Does the pupil know the meaning of the prefix *dis-*? Criterion-referenced tests are a way of measuring mastery levels rather than grade levels; they describe performance rather than compare performance (Wormer, 1974). They can also be viewed as intraindividual tests.

Norm-referenced tests are standardized on large populations; criterion-referenced tests are developed in a very different manner. The aim is not to compare an individual's reading performance with that of the norming sample. Instead, each individual's achievement in reading is determined by assessing his or her performance on a hierarchy of specific reading skills. The basic goal of criterion-referenced testing is to describe behavior as accurately as possible in relation to standards of performance deemed important to the test developer. That is, the test developer selects items that reflect mastery in reading. These items are placed in an ordered sequence or hierarchy. Students are tested for mastery of the items to see whether they have attained specific reading competencies. The child's performance is compared to his or her previous performance to determine growth; the individual is not compared to the standardization population. For example, when Billy has mastered skills twenty-eight through fifty in the test developer's hierarchy of skills, Billy's reading growth can be readily documented. (In nonreading terms, a test to determine if Mary can float on her back is a criterion-referenced measure. A test that shows that Mary can swim as well as the average six-year-old is a norm-referenced measure.) When a reading subskill is learned sufficiently to meet the established criterion (such as 90 percent accuracy), the pupil progresses on to the next subskill in the sequence. For example, when Tony learns skill number 9 (the *ch* consonant digraph) at an acceptable level of proficiency (95 percent), he can then move on to skill number 10. The number of specific reading skills identified in criterion-referenced tests range up to 450 (Rude, 1974; Thompson & Dziuban, 1973).

A number of criterion-referenced measurement and teaching programs for reading have appeared on the market in the past few years, including the following:

Croft In-Service Reading Program (Croft Educational Service)

Fountain Valley Teacher Support System (Richard L. Zweig)

Individual Pupil Monitoring System—Reading (Houghton Mifflin)

Prescriptive Reading Laboratory (CTB/McGraw-Hill)

Read On (Random House)

Skills Monitoring System—Reading (Harcourt Brace Jovanovich)

Wisconsin Design for Reading Skills Development (National Computer Systems)

Woodcock Reading Mastery Tests (American Guidance Service)

Samples from one criterion-referenced test, the *Individual Pupil Monitoring System—Reading* (*IPMS—Reading*) are shown in Figures 8.4 and 8.5. The *IPMS—Reading* includes five levels, each of which measures performance on behavior objectives. Each level is divided into three reading skill areas: word attack, vocabulary and comprehension, and discrimination/study skills. The minitest for behavior objective 231 of the vocabulary and comprehension test appears in Figure 8.4. There are two record-keeping systems in the *IPMS—Reading*. The first is a *Pupil Progress Record*. The top portion contains a bar graph. Figure 8.5 shows that the

Sample of Criterion-Referenced Test

Figure 8.4

VOCABULARY

231.   **Place Relationships:** Choose the printed phrase that describes the placement of objects or people (*in*, *on*, etc.) in a picture.

1. The boy is walking _____ .

A) to the house
B) from the house
C) into the house

4. The dog is _____ .

A) under the box
B) in the box
C) by the box

2. Jane is going _____ .

A) to the store
B) from the store
C) around the store

5. The dog is _____ .

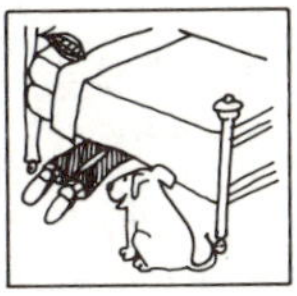

A) on the bed
B) under the bed
C) by the bed

3. He put his arms _____ .

A) around the dog
B) under the dog
C) over the dog

Source: *IPMS Reading Test, Level 2, Form B: Vocabulary and Comprehension,* Houghton Mifflin Company, Boston, 1974, p. 1. Used by permission of the publisher.

Sample of Criterion-Referenced Test

Figure 8.5

TO THE PUPIL

On the front cover, circle A or B for the form you are using.

How to Fill in Your Progress Chart

1. Find the right skill number.
2. Write in the <u>number correct</u>.
3. Fill in the same amount of boxes as the <u>number correct</u>.

Sample Chart: This is how one student filled in the chart.

Skill Number	Skill Name	Number Correct	1	2	3	4	5
231.	Place Relationships	*3*					
232.	Likes & Opposites	*5*					

Skill Number	Skill Name	Number Correct	1	2	3	4	5
231.	**Place Relationships:** Choose the phrase for a picture (*in the box,* etc.).						
232.	**Likes & Opposites:** Identify 2 words as being the same or different.						
233.	**Synonyms:** Identify the synonym for a word in a sentence.						

Source: *Pupil Progress Record: Vocabulary and Comprehension, IPMS Reading, Level 2,* Houghton Mifflin Company, Boston, 1974. Used by permission of the publisher.

Figure 8.6   Sample of Criterion-Referenced Test

VOCABULARY & COMPREHENSION Level 2 Skills	Names of Students	Paula C.	Susan C.	Robert K.	Karen H.	Bill S.	Class Average
231. **Place Relationships:** Choose phrase (*in*, *on*, etc.) for picture		2	5	4	4	5	4
232. **Likes & Opposites:** Identify words as same or different		2	5	4	3	2	3.2
233. **Synonyms:** Choose from context		1	4	2	3	3	2.6
234. **Antonyms:** Choose from context		2	4	4	3	4	3.4

Source: Teacher's Management Record, IPMS Reading, Level 2, Houghton Mifflin Company, Boston, 1974, p. 2.

Figure 8.7   Sample of Criterion-Referenced Test

Test 10—Contractions

Example	____a warm day.	Ⓐ I've Ⓑ Is Ⓒ Its Ⓓ It's

1. Mother said, "____ eat lunch now."

Ⓐ Let's
Ⓑ Lets
Ⓒ It's
Ⓓ We

2. Jane said, " ____ water the plants now."

Ⓐ III
Ⓑ I've
Ⓒ We
Ⓓ I'll

3. ____you go to school?

Ⓐ Let's
Ⓑ Didn't
Ⓒ Did
Ⓓ Didnt

Source: From *Wisconsin Design for Reading Skill Development: Word Attack, Level B, Form P.* © 1972 by The Board of Regents of the University of Wisconsin. Reproduced by permission of the publisher, National Computer Systems, Inc.

student had three correct items on skill number 231. The second record-keeping system is the *Teacher's Management Record*. Figure 8.6 shows the scores of a group of children on skills 231, 232, 233, and 234. A sample subtest, *Rhyming Elements,* from the *Wisconsin Design for Reading Skill Development* is shown in Figure 8.7.

193
Limitations
of Norm-
Referenced
and Criterion-
Referenced
Tests

Limitations of Norm-Referenced and Criterion-Referenced Tests

Criticism of criterion-referenced and norm-referenced tests should be known by teachers, since they will be selecting tests to diagnose children. Whether norm-referenced tests or criterion-referenced tests better measure children's abilities and disabilities is currently under intensive debate among educators and reading specialists. In studying these two approaches to formal testing for use with slow and disabled learners, we must consider the values and inadequacies of each approach.

Limitations of Norm-Referenced Tests

Problems with standardized reading tests have been described by several authorities of reading measurement (Anastasi, 1975; Farr, 1969; Otto, 1973; Thorndike, 1973).

1. Standardized norm-referenced tests give little information about the pupil's specific abilities and disabilities in reading. Information about such strengths and weaknesses is particularly important for use with slow and disabled learners.
2. Short norm-referenced tests are convenient and more marketable than longer criterion-referenced tests. However, the brevity may impose unrealistic time limits and actually restrict the sample of reading behavior obtained. This is undesirable, as an adequate sample is needed to establish an instructional program for slow and disabled learners.
3. Group administration is often used with norm-referenced tests. This may be disadvantageous for the individual who does not understand the directions and cannot perform well in a group testing setting.
4. The format of some normed tests, particularly the machine-scored format, makes test-taking difficult for some slow and disabled learners.
5. The child may be given a norm-referenced test that is either too difficult or too easy for him or her.
6. The grade score on a norm-referenced test may overestimate the child's actual reading ability.

7. Statistical criticisms of standardized tests are well documented. A serious drawback in using standardized tests to diagnose reading achievement is the lack of discriminate validity for the various subtests of reading (Farr, 1969). The confidence level of many norm-referenced diagnostic reading tests has been called "distressingly" low (Thorndike, 1973).

Limitations of Criterion-Referenced Measures

Criterion-referenced measures have been noted to have a number of shortcomings and limitations (Davis, 1974; Otto, 1973; Thompson & Dziuban, 1973).

1. A disproportionate amount of time must be spent monitoring students, keeping records, and doing paperwork.
2. Hard-to-measure qualities, such as appreciation or attitude toward reading, may be overlooked.
3. Students who test at an acceptable criterion level for a specific skill may be unable to transfer that skill to a reading situation.
4. Students may test at an acceptable criterion level on a specific skill one day but be unable to perform that skill a few days later.
5. The hierarchy, or ordered sequence of skills, selected by the testmaker may be inappropriate for a particular child. That is, Peter may do better by learning skill number 89 before skill number 25. Moreover, testmakers do not agree about sequence.
6. Determining the appropriate criterion for proficiency may be difficult. That is, 60 percent proficiency may be sufficient for some skills, while in other skills a 95 percent proficiency may be required.
7. The sequence of skills to be learned does not take into account the unique strengths and weaknesses of a specific child. That is especially important for slow and disabled learners.
8. Criterion-referenced tests need better test construction to determine valid and reliable content-referenced interpretations (Davis, 1974).

Need for Both Norm-Referenced and Criterion-Referenced Tests

Values and shortcomings have been noted in both norm-referenced and criterion-referenced tests. Test developers are beginning to design reading tests that combine elements of all three types of tests: norm-referenced, diagnostic, and criterion-referenced. One such test is the *Woodcock Reading Mastery Scales,* published in 1973. According to Proger (1975), who

195
Limitations
of Norm-
Referenced
and Criterion-
Referenced
Tests

reviewed this test, it includes several soundly constructed options for both criterion-referenced and norm-referenced interpretations. In addition, it is also a diagnostic test, containing subtests on letter identification, word identification, word attack, word comprehension, and passage comprehension. The interpretation page of the *Woodcock Reading Mastery Scales* is shown in Figure 8.8.

Many authorities believe that both norm-referenced and criterion-referenced measures are needed, and that they can complement each other when each type is used for the proper purpose (Davis, 1974; Otto, 1973; Wormer, 1974). Norm-referenced survey tests are valuable for test-retest procedures to determine progress, while diagnostic and criterion-referenced tests are used best initially in organizing a remedial program.

Impartial judgments of reading tests made by reading authorities are presented in the source book *Reading Tests and Reviews* (Buros, 1968, 1975), which can be found in most reference libraries.

Woodcock Reading Mastery Scales   Figure 8.8

See the manual for additional interpretive procedures including age scores, standard scores, separate percentile rank norms for boys and girls, SES-adjusted norms, and use of the Reference Scales in criterion-referenced interpretations.

Source: Richard W. Woodcock. *Woodcock Reading Mastery Test, Interpretation of Test Results.* American Guidance Service, Circle Pines, Minnesota, 1973. Reproduced by permission of the publisher.

Evaluating Discrepancies in Reading

Determining the discrepancy between a child's reading achievement and intellectual ability is a means of judging the severity of the reading problem. The teacher should determine this discrepancy in order to: (a) use it as an aid in selecting children who are eligible for special services, (b) judge the progress made by children, (c) evaluate programs, (d) fulfill reporting and accountability requirements, and (e) meet legal requirements. Several techniques have been suggested for determining discrepancies between reading achievement and intellectual ability:

The Mental Grade Method (Harris, 1961)

This is the simplest method. To estimate reading expectancy, five is subtracted from the mental age.

RE (reading expectancy) = MA (mental age) − 5

Jimmy is 10–0 and has a mental age of 12–0. His reading expectancy is therefore grade 7.

7 (RE) = 12 (MA) − 5

If Jimmy reads at the 3.0 grade level, he has a four-year discrepancy in reading.

Years-in-School Method (Bond & Tinker, 1967, pp. 198–203)

This method takes into account the school exposure the child has had.

$$RE \text{ (reading expectancy)} = \frac{\text{years in school} \times IQ}{100} + 1.0$$

Ten-year-old Jimmy is in the middle of fifth grade, that is, he has been in school for 4.5 years. His IQ score is 120. Using this formula, we find that his reading expectancy grade is 6.4.

$$RE = \frac{4.5 \times 120}{100} + 1.0 = 6.4$$

Since Jimmy reads at the 3.0 grade level, the discrepancy between expectancy and achievement levels is 3.4 years.

Learning Quotient Method (Myklebust, 1968)

This method determines discrepancy in terms of a quotient, that is, what percentage of his or her ability to learn has the child fulfilled? There are two steps in this method:

(1) EA (expectancy age) $= \dfrac{\text{MA} + \text{CA} + \text{GA (grade age)}}{3}$

(2) LQ (learning quotient) $= \dfrac{\text{AA (achievement age)}}{\text{EA (expectancy age)}}$

Note that in this method, all scores are converted from grade scores to age scores (grade score $+ 5 =$ age score). What is Jimmy's learning quotient with this method?

(1) EA $= \dfrac{12.0 + 10.0 + 10.5}{3} = 10.8$

(2) LQ $= \dfrac{8.0}{10.8} = .74$

If the cutoff point is 85 percent, then Jimmy would be considered learning disabled. It is possible to compute the learning quotient using the verbal IQ or the performance IQ, as well as the full-scale IQ.

Of course, the use of methods such as those described above has many shortcomings. These methods do not take into consideration the results of informal tests or clinical factors and judgments; they produce negative values for early childhood and preschool children; and the use of IQ scores is highly criticized. Nonetheless, discrepancy measures may provide useful information in many situations.

Summary

This chapter discussed formal assessment procedures in reading as they affect slow and disabled learners.

Three kinds of formal reading tests are: (1) standardized or norm-referenced tests, (2) diagnostic tests, and (3) criterion-referenced tests. Standardized, norm-referenced tests are standardized on large populations and give standardization data. The meaningful scores include reading grade scores, reading age scores, percentile scores, and stanine scores. Two kinds of norm-referenced standardized tests are the survey reading test and the diagnostic reading test. The survey test gives general information about the person's reading level; the diagnostic test gives analytic information. Criterion-referenced tests yield a description of reading behavior in terms of a predetermined sequence of reading skills.

In general, norm-referenced survey tests determine the reading grade level of a child. They are also used to measure progress over time. Criterion-referenced tests are used to determine the mastery of specific instructional objectives.

Reading Research:
Slow and Disabled Learners

The body of research concerned with the teaching of reading is both extensive and exhaustive. The literature is replete with investigations of the reading process itself, levels and methods of instruction, books and appropriate materials for teaching, the use of programmed texts, teaching machines, and so forth. No attempt is made here to review the extensive literature on reading and reading disabilities, since that effort would encompass volumes. This chapter will discuss research related to the reading of slow and disabled learners.

Some of the studies that are reviewed in this chapter investigated the reading of children diagnosed as slow-learning or mentally retarded. Other studies analyzed the reading of youngsters categorized as disabled learners, brain injured, or having minimal brain dysfunction. The two groups of research findings are intermingled in this chapter because the characteristics, learning patterns, and diagnostic and teaching procedures used with these two groups of children (slow and disabled learners) overlap to a great extent. The research findings for one group have obvious implications for the other.

The Relationship of Mental Age to
Reading Achievement

Investigators have tried to determine the potential for reading achievement of slow and disabled learners. One question studied was the reading level of these children. Do they read above, at, or below their expectancy level as determined by mental age? The criterion ordinarily used to answer this question is based on the assumption that reading achievement develops according to mental age, and that children develop one year in reading as they grow one year in mental age. For example, children with a mental age of 6–0 would have a reading achievement grade of 1.0; children with a mental age of 6–5 would have a reading grade of 1.5; children with a mental age of 7–0 would have a reading grade of 2.0, and so forth. This correlation between mental age and reading expectancy is represented in the following table:

Mental Age	Reading Grade Expectancy
6–0	1.0
6–5	1.5
7–0	2.0
7–5	2.5
8–0	3.0
8–5	3.5
9–0	4.0
9–5	4.5

It has been suggested that reading grade expectancy can be determined by subtracting 5–0 from the mental age or chronological age. For example, a child with a mental age or a chronological age of 7 would have a reading grade expectancy of $7–0 - 5–0 = $ grade 2.0.

The earliest studies on the relation of reading achievement to mental age were made by Merrill. The first study, conducted in Minnesota, involved a group of public school special-class children and a group of mentally retarded children in a Minnesota residential school (Merrill, 1918). The mental age of the children in both groups ranged from 5 to 11. In oral reading, the groups reached only 75 percent of expectancy based on mental age. Merrill also found that as chronological age increased, the percentage of children able to do oral reading up to their reading expectancy level decreased.

In a second study, conducted in Oakland, California, Merrill (1921) found that the majority of the 210 special-class children examined were achieving below expectancy based on the mental age criterion. They were most retarded in reading, less so in arithmetic, still less in writing, and least in spelling.

Following Merrill's work, there was a series of studies to investigate the relationship of mental age to reading. For example, Renshaw (1919) reported that only 13.5 percent of three hundred retarded adolescents in prevocational special classes in Detroit were reading at a level commensurate with their mental age. Burt (1921), Hoyt (1924) and Witty and McCafferty (1930) found similar results. Their investigations resulted in the conclusion that the large majority of mentally retarded children read below their mental age.

Studies have also been conducted to determine how far below mental age retarded children are in their reading achievement. In a survey of 1,500 retarded children in Newark, New Jersey special classes, Kelly (1934) found the children to have an overall reading retardation of one year below their mental age. Furthermore, over 30 percent of the children with a mental age between 8 and 9 were nonreaders. Hill (1939), studying a group of retarded children enrolled in the Schenectady, New York special classes, reported that they were one-half year below their mental age expectancy. Scarborough (1951) and

Mullen and Ilken (1952) reported findings of reading retardation of 1 year and 1.4 years, respectively, in special classes in Chicago. In the Mullen and Ilken study, only 27 percent of the subjects read at or above expectancy.

Not all studies demonstrated that retarded children are significantly below their mental age–reading grade expectancy. Some studies showed that some groups of retarded children are up to or above their mental age expectancy in reading. Bennett (1929) investigated the reading achievement level of seventy-nine retarded students in six primary special classes in Yonkers, New York. In this study, close to 75 percent of the subjects achieved up to or slightly above their mental ages in reading. Similar findings were reported by Chapman (1939), who conducted a study of 368 mentally retarded children in special classes in Portland, Oregon. Mean reading age was compared with mean mental age at each mental age level from 6 through 13. In Chapman's study, reading age exceeded mental age by two-thirds of a year, on the average.

In an investigation comparing the academic achievement and mental age of ninety-eight children in eight special classes in Malden, Massachusetts, Ring (1951) found that the reading level was up to expectancy, arithmetic level was slightly above expectancy, and spelling level was slightly below expectancy.

Daley and Lee (1960) compared the actual reading ability and the expected reading level of a group of seventy-seven institutionalized retardates. The chronological age range was 10–2 to 18–6; the mental age range 6–1 to 12–7; IQ ranged from 45 to 86 with a mean of 61. Mental age equivalents were used to determine expected or potential reading level. Actual reading grade level was determined by the *Durrell Analysis of Reading Difficulty*. The reading ability of 62 percent of the subjects was found to be compatible with or exceeding their mental age reading grade level.

The following conclusions can be drawn from the studies on the relationship of mental age to reading achievement:

1. The majority of mentally retarded children in special classes or in institutions are below their mental age in reading achievement. This can be accounted for by the fact that many special teachers do not stress academic achievement but emphasize social adjustment. Furthermore, children assigned to special classes are generally those who are academically as well as mentally retarded.

2. Some mentally retarded children read up to or exceed their mental age. This can be explained by the fact that the correlation of mental age and reading is around .50 and .60, far from a perfect correlation. Also, the progress of a retarded child in reading, although dependent upon mental age or maturity, is also contingent upon the efforts made by the teacher in teaching reading. Retarded children in regular classrooms tend to achieve more, due to the emphasis on academic achievement.

3.   Group results on reading achievement are generally of
little value when estimating the achievement of a particular
child. Each child is unique, and progress cannot be predicted
from an IQ or a mental age alone. Other factors such as
motivation, lack of a specific disability, systematic instruction, ability of a teacher, reinforcements, and numerous other
unknown factors determine the progress and reading achievement of all children, including those with low intelligence.
That is why we occasionally find a child with a mental age
of 6 reading at the third-grade level.

Mental Age and Beginning Reading

One of the major problems in teaching atypical children to
read is determining the mental age level at which to introduce
such instruction. Studies conducted in the 1930s involving
children of normal intelligence strongly advocated delaying
reading instruction until a mental age of 6 had been attained.
Thomas (1946) stated, "Children who do not have a mental
age of 6–0 are bound to have difficulty in learning to read,
while children who have a mental age of 6–6 are likely to
achieve success in first grade reading without too much difficulty" (p. 30). While advocates of earlier reading instruction
continue to have a strong impact, the 6-year minimum age is
still supported by a large number of reading authorities.

   Results of investigations of the minimum mental age required for beginning reading instruction for the retarded or
learning-disabled child are neither clear-cut nor decisive.

   Davidson (1931) conducted an experimental study of bright,
average, and dull children whose mental age was 4. Each subject participated in ten-minute lessons on word recognition
each day for six weeks. All the groups were able to recognize
the words, but the bright children were found to be greatly
superior to the other subjects. The dull group's performance
was poorest.

   Moore (1964) taught educable mentally retarded children
with mental ages of 3 and 4 to read and write by means of the
talking typewriter technique. While authorities may believe
that these children are not ready to learn to read, Moore has
shown that with somewhat unconventional methods they can
learn to do so.

   Despite the growing evidence that children can be taught to
read before reaching the mental age of 6, a number of investigators advocate delaying formal reading instruction until that
level of mental maturity has been reached.

   Harris (1961) stated his position as follows:

It has been demonstrated that normal five-year-olds can make satisfactory progress in reading under some forms of instruction, and
that with patient, individual instruction the ability to recognize a

few words can be acquired even by dull children with mental ages between four and five. In view of these results, there seems to be some warrant for introducing dull children to the beginnings of reading before they reach a mental age of six or six and a half. Children with mental ages between five and six may be expected to make some progress in word recognition, even if truly meaningful reading is beyond them. They can at least learn to recognize their names and a few common signs and labels. Systematic reading instruction, however, should be delayed until the necessary level of mental maturity has been reached. Until then, emphasis should be placed on the development of readiness for reading (p. 481).

Hegge (1934) reported on an intensive reading program that increased the reading grade of a group of older retarded subjects from 1.6 to 4.2 in a little less than two years. He concluded that high-grade mental defectives should be able to absorb all that is needed of academic learning in a much shorter period if beginning instruction is delayed until they reach a more advanced level of mental maturity.

In a prolonged preacademic program conducted at the Wayne County Training School, Melcher (1940) found that the retarded subjects for whom reading instruction had been delayed until they had attained a mental age of 8 made more rapid progress during their first year than would have been predicted for normal children of the same mental age. Weiner's (1954) follow-up study of some of the same subjects indicated that at age 11 this group was inferior to a control group from the same training school whose preacademic instruction had not been delayed. At the time of the final testing, however, when both groups were approximately 15 years, 6 months of age, no differences were found between the groups. Both groups were reading at the fourth-grade level.

Jordan (1965) studied the effects of prolonged prereading verbal activities on the subsequent reading achievement of eighty-three educable retarded children. Experimental subjects received readiness training that stressed auditory and visual skills, concept development, verbal reasoning, vocabulary, comprehension, and sequencing. Control subjects followed the usual curriculum for educable retarded children. Progress was assessed at the end of the first four grades. Initially, the control subjects were superior to the experimental subjects, but by the end of the fourth year the experimental group was performing better than the control subjects.

These latter investigators contend that postponement of instruction in reading leads to more rapid learning and to superior achievement in the long run. Yet many slow and disabled learners are faced with reading tasks as they enter school, even though their mental age may be only 4–0 or 5–0. If reading instruction were delayed until they reached a mental age of 6–0 or 6–6, they would be nine or ten years old and would have been in school from two to four years (Kirk, 1964). Stevens and Orem (1968) present a case for early

203
Reading
Achievement of
Retarded,
Average, and
Superior
Children

reading. According to these authors, the child's language aptitude decreases with age, and the older a person becomes, the more difficulty he or she will have mastering language. Therefore, it is inferred that the longer reading experience is delayed, the more difficult its mastery will be.

The more recent trend seems to be in the direction of earlier reading instruction for retarded and slow learners. In the light of somewhat conflicting evidence, however, it seems irrelevant to pursue the issue further. A matter of far greater concern is the adequacy of the instructional program—at whatever age it is provided.

Reading Achievement of Retarded, Average, and Superior Children

Researchers have been interested in comparing the reading achievement of retarded, average, and superior children. It is obvious that superior children generally read at a higher level than average or retarded children of the same chronological age. Generally, a superior child of eight years reads better than an average child of eight years, and both of these read better than a retarded child of eight. The question, however, is whether there is a difference among these three groups when mental age is controlled. Specifically, will a thirteen-year-old retarded child with a mental age of 9 read the same or different than a nine-year-old child with a mental age of 9, or a seven-year-old child with a mental age of 9? The purpose of this kind of question is to determine the variables that influence learning, namely, life experience or general mental ability.

Studies on this problem have been done since 1920, when Jones (1919–1920) compared bright subjects with dull subjects and concluded that the young bright subjects scored higher on silent and oral reading tests than did older dull subjects. Merrill (1924), Monroe (1932), Bliesmer (1954), Dunn (1956), and Shotick (1960) also compared retarded subjects and average or superior subjects on various reading tests and concluded that, on the whole, older retarded children are slightly inferior to younger bright children in reading ability.

In a more recent extensive study, Blake, Aaron, and Westbrook (1969) studied achievement in fifty basic reading skills among retarded, normal, and superior pupils taught at primary and intermediate reading instructional levels. The subjects were 308 pupils enrolled in forty-four public school elementary classes (grades two through five) and in intermediate and secondary special classes for the mentally retarded from three Georgia school systems. The mean reading achievement grade at the beginning of the study for primary level retarded and normal subjects (matched on mental age and sex) was 2.39 and 2.46, respectively. At the intermediate level, mean reading achievement for the retarded group was 4.31, and 4.43 for the matched normal group.

In level of acquisition, the primary level mentally retarded group compared favorably with the normal subjects on thirty-nine of forty-eight comparisons. Six of the nine skills in which the primary level retarded subjects' performance was inferior centered on comprehension. This was not true for the intermediate students. The comprehension category most clearly differentiated among the groups. At the intermediate level the retarded subjects compared favorably on five of the comprehension skills measured but were inferior to the normal subjects on twice as many tasks. The same areas of language deficit noted at the primary level were evident at the intermediate level, with the exception of interpreting metaphors, where performance of the two groups was similar.

While no definitive conclusions can be drawn from this review of studies comparing relative achievement of retarded, normal, and superior children of the same mental age, results strongly indicate that mentally retarded children tend to be poorer achievers in reading than others of the same mental age. It is believed that age and experience are not the major factors that produce reading ability, but that mental age is the primary factor.

Regular Classes Versus Special Classes

The efficacy of special classes for handicapped children has been questioned repeatedly. Following is a review of research comparing the relative reading achievement of retarded children placed in special classes with that of retarded children retained in the regular grades.

Three studies (Bennett, 1932; Pertsch, 1936; Wassmann, 1933) conducted over forty years ago indicate that the reading achievement of retardates in regular classes is superior to that of retardates in special classes.

The first study, by Bennett (1932), compared fifty retarded children in regular grades with fifty retarded children (ages 12 and 13) enrolled in special classes. She found that the children in the special classes achieved less than children enrolled in the regular grades. Pertsch (1936) conducted a similar study with 278 children in the New York schools. He concluded that the children in the regular grades were superior in academic achievement to those enrolled in the special classes. Cowan (1938) reevaluated the Pertsch study, questioning the selection factor, and reversed Pertsch's conclusions. Cassidy and Stanton (1959), Blatt (1958), Elenbogen (1957), Thurstone (1959), and Ainsworth (1959) all compared the reading achievement of mentally retarded children in special classes with the reading achievement of those retained in the regular grades.

They concluded that either there was no difference in educational achievement between the two groups or that those enrolled in the regular grades were superior. The only exception was children in the lower IQ range (50 to 60). These children tended to do better in the special classes. Many of these studies, however, did not control for the selection factor.

A more definitive study was conducted by Goldstein, Moss, and Jordan (1965). This comprehensive investigation attempted to control for the uncontrolled variables criticized in previous studies. Subjects were randomly assigned to an experimental (special class) group or to a control (regular class) group. The fifty-seven experimental subjects had a mean IQ of 76.7 and a mean chronological age of 77.3 months, as compared with sixty-nine control subjects with a mean IQ of 78.5 and a mean chronological age of 79.0 months. While this study involved all areas of the curriculum, only the results of reading achievement are reported here.

The Goldstein, Moss, and Jordan study showed that children with an IQ of 80 or below and those with an IQ of 81 or above responded differently to regular classroom placement. The children with an IQ of 81 and above who attended regular grades tended to score slightly (but not significantly) higher than similar children placed in special classes. The reverse seemed to prevail for children with an IQ of 80 or less —children placed in special classes tended to score slightly higher than similar children placed in the regular grades.

The earlier efficacy studies comparing special class placement with regular class placement for mentally retarded children presented somewhat conflicting findings. To explain the differences in findings, two very plausible reasons were advanced, namely, selective placement of pupils in special classes prior to the investigation, and uncontrolled differences in curriculum content and teacher preparation. Yet even when these factors were controlled, as in the Goldstein, Moss, and Jordan (1965) study, differences noted between the groups were negligible. Perhaps one is still faced with the question, "For *which* retarded child is special class placement or regular class placement preferred?"

Logically, one would expect greater achievement among children in small special classes with expertly trained teachers. However, the results of research studies do not bear out this expectation. There may be a number of explanations for these results, including the following:

1. Special class teachers tend to emphasize social adjustment and not academic achievement. This explanation seems plausible, since most studies show that the personal adjustment of mentally retarded children in special classes is superior to that of their counterparts in the regular grades.

2. The expectations of regular teachers for the academic achievement of their pupils could be greater than the expectations of special class teachers.

3. The retarded child is exposed to better models of oral reading, study habits, and language when he or she is placed in the regular classroom.

These may or may not be adequate explanations. A more crucial issue is to discover the most appropriate reading instructional program for slow or disabled learners, regardless of the educational setting in which they are placed.

The Reading Process of Deviant Learners

Reading is an exceedingly complex process. Despite decades of research on reading, its nature is not yet fully understood. Adequate reception or decoding, discrimination among sounds and symbols, visual and auditory sequential memory, relating facts and concepts to earlier learned material, and effective expression or encoding of ideas are some of the major elements involved in reading (Smith, 1974).

Only a few studies have been designed specifically to investigate the reading processes that may be characteristic of mentally retarded and learning-disabled individuals. These few have dealt with reversal errors, specific processes, and the effects of brain injury on the reading process. Investigations utilizing the *Illinois Test of Psycholinguistic Abilities* (Kirk & McCarthy, 1961) have yielded some information concerning the psycholinguistic functions as they relate to the reading process.

Reversal Errors

Mintz (1946), Kirk (1934), and Kirk and Kirk (1935) investigated reversal errors among retarded readers. Mintz (1946) found no clear-cut relationship between reversals and lateral preference. Kirk (1934), using mirror writing, studied the relationship between ocular and manual preference and reading in a group of older institutionalized retardates. The left-eyed, right-handed subjects were not superior in mirror reading to the right-eyed, right-handed group, as previously reported by Monroe (1932).

Kirk and Kirk (1935) later reported on a study that dealt with the effects of the teacher's handedness and reversal tendencies in writing. Young superior children with mental ages of 6 made more reversal errors in writing than did older institutionalized retarded subjects of the same mental age regardless of the hand the teacher used when writing the symbols. No differences were found in reversal errors in writing within the retarded group, regardless of which hand the teacher used.

It would appear from these studies that retardates do not make an excessive number of reversal errors. This conclusion does not necessarily apply to disabled learners.

Specific Processes

Dunn's 1956 study was the first to investigate qualitative differences in the reading process between mentally retarded and normal boys of the same mental age. The retardates were found to be inferior readers. An analysis of the reading errors made by both groups disclosed the following: (a) the retarded subjects made more vowel errors, omitted more sounds, made fewer repetitions, and had significantly more aided and refused word errors than did the normal group; (b) there were no differences between the groups on consonant or reversal errors; (c) the normal children added more words in oral reading than did the retarded subjects; and (d) the retarded subjects tended to be word-by-word readers with less concern for meaning.

The special-class boys were found to be markedly inferior to normal boys in their ability to use context clues. They were also inferior on flashed presentations of words and phrases as well as on untimed presentations of the same materials.

No significant differences were found between the two groups in their ability to blend sounds, in reading rate, in comprehension, or in the number of fixations and regressions per one hundred words. The groups were similar in reading capacity, but the retarded group was generally inferior to the normal group in reading achievement.

In a study similar to Dunn's, Sheperd (1967) investigated the reading process of two groups of retarded boys whose mental age ranged from 7–5 to 9–10. One group was composed of twenty adequate readers (reading age above projected mental age); the other group consisted of twenty inadequate readers (reading age below projected mental age). Reading age scores were based on the *Gates Advanced Primary Reading Test*. An extensive battery of tests was administered individually to each subject in order to measure selected factors in the reading process.

A significant difference was found in favor of the good readers on all measures of silent and oral reading ability as well as on the test of ability to use context clues. The poorer reading group had significantly more faulty vowels, faulty consonants, reversals, omission of sounds, word substitutions, and words aided and refused. More repetitions were made by the adequate readers. There were no significant differences between the two groups on addition of sounds or on addition or omission of words. The poor reading group was markedly inferior in sound-blending ability, suggesting a possible lack of phonic word attack skills.

Sheperd's good reading group performed significantly better on the text of basic information, particularly on the section requiring word recognition ability. However, the two groups had comparable funds of basic information where no reading ability was required. On tests of auditory discrimination, memory for designs, and visual closure, no differences were found between the groups. Neither group made an excessive number of reversal errors. There were no differences between adequate and inadequate readers in handedness, eyedness, or lateral dominance. These results accord with those already reported by Mintz (1946), Kirk (1934), Kirk and Kirk (1935), and Cawley and associates (1968).

It would seem from the research on the reading process in the mentally retarded, that there is a lack of word attack skills among retarded readers, particularly in the area of phonics, as well as an inability to use context clues. A teaching method designed to overcome these deficiencies would seem appropriate.

Brain Injury

A very limited number of studies investigated the effects of brain injury on the reading process of the mentally retarded.

In a comparison of brain-damaged and non-brain-damaged institutionalized children, Vance (1956) matched subjects on chronological age, mental age, and IQ. The chronological age range was from 7 to 13; the IQ range, from 40 to 70. All subjects (brain-damaged and non-brain-damaged) participated in an eight-month specialized instructional program. No significant differences were found between the groups at the completion of the study or after a three-year period.

Capobianco and Miller (1958) replicated Dunn's (1956) study with a group of exogenous (brain-damaged) and endogenous (non-brain-damaged) institutionalized subjects. The groups were matched on chronological age and IQ, using the Riggs and Rain classification system and the *Syracuse Visual Figure Background Test*. The exogenous group scored higher (but not significantly so) on measures of silent and oral reading, on word discrimination, and word recognition. No significant differences were found between the groups on faulty vowels, faulty consonants, reversals, repetitions, omission and addition of sounds or words, and words aided or refused. The groups were also comparable in performance on tests of auditory acuity and visual perception.

In these studies (Capobianco & Miller, 1958; Vance, 1956), the fact that no significant differences were found between groups is in itself highly significant. It had been assumed that distortions of perception and conception, confusion of figure and background stimuli, and so on, characteristic of brain-damaged children, would interfere with school progress and especially with reading. Research data do not substantiate this assumption. Reading achievement can be attained by brain-damaged children just as it can be attained by the non-brain-injured. What makes the difference is the quality of the instructional procedures employed!

Frey (1961) compared the reading behavior of a group of brain-injured children who attended a specialized program for such children (of average and retarded mental development) with that of a matched group of non-brain-injured children. The two groups were compared on standardized achievement tests, diagnostic reading tests, and types of reading errors made. The mean test age equivalent was 8–2 for the brain-injured children and 8–1 for the non-brain-injured group.

On the *Gates Primary Reading Test,* the *Monroe Word Discrimination Test, Gray Oral Reading Test,* the *Iowa Word Recognition Test,* and the *Monroe Sound Blending Test,* the brain-injured group was significantly superior to the non-brain-injured group. There were no significant differences between the two groups on the *Monroe Word Discrimination Test,* the *Monroe Visual Memory Test,* or the *Gates Reversible Words Test.*

The *Monroe Diagnostic Battery* was used to compare the groups on the qualitative aspects of the reading process. Compared to the brain-injured group, the non-brain-injured subjects showed a significant excess of faulty vowels, faulty consonants, omissions of sounds, and word substitutions. There were no differences between the groups on reversals, addition of words, repetitions, addition of sounds, omission of words, and words aided and refused.

Frey's findings substantiate those of Vance (1956) and Capobianco and Miller (1958) and indicate further that not only can brain-injured children learn to read, but in some areas of reading they can, with specialized training, perform better than non-brain-injured children.

It seems reasonable to conclude that the adequacy of the training given is a far more crucial variable than organic signs in predicting the reading success of brain-injured or non-brain-injured children. This conclusion applies to both slow and disabled learners.

ITPA Research

The *Illinois Test of Psycholinguistic Abilities* (Kirk & McCarthy, 1961, 1968) has been used with retarded children, although it was not specifically designed for or standardized on a retarded population. The *ITPA* is an individually administered diagnostic test providing a diagnosis of children's abilities and disabilities that guides the remediation of language problems. Nine subtests in the experimental edition (1961) and ten basic subtests plus two supplementary subtests in the revised edition (1968) measure various facets of psycholinguistic development so that remediation can follow, should a disability exist. Results of *ITPA* research have pinpointed the areas of greatest deficit in the psycholinguistic processes of retarded children.

Ragland (1964) studied the variables differentiating retarded and nonretarded readers among thirty institutionalized educable mentally handicapped students. Their chronological age ranged from 12 to 16; mental age, from 6–5 to 10–0. Readers were considered retarded if they were reading one year or more below reading expectancy level based on mental age. The retarded readers averaged a grade level of 1.43 in reading achievement, while the nonretarded group achieved a mean grade level of 3.47.

The retarded readers were significantly inferior in performance on the total *ITPA,* on the total automatic-sequential level, and particularly on the auditory-vocal automatic subtest (test of grammatical usage). The retarded group was generally inferior on all subtests except visual decoding and vocal encoding. No significant performance differences were observed between groups at the representational level.

Sheperd's (1967) research included a comparison of the automatic psycholinguistic functions of adequate and inadequate readers among educable mentally retarded boys. Results were similar to Ragland's (1964) in that both groups scored below their mean mental age level on all three subtests. The adequate group was significantly superior to the inadequate group on auditory sequential memory (digit repetition). Unlike Ragland, however, Sheperd found no significant difference between groups on the grammatic closure subtest. The two studies found the total performance of both groups (adequate and inadequate readers) to be below the theoretical mean for their mental age.

Bateman and Wetherell (1965) summarized that the typical *ITPA* profile of retarded children reflected a deficit in the entire automatic-sequential level as compared with a relative strength at the representational level. They reported further that many culturally disadvantaged children of low IQ show relatively stronger performance on the visual-motor channel than on the auditory-vocal channel. This auditory-vocal deficit is noted particularly on the auditory-vocal automatic subtest, which assesses the subject's ability to use the redundancies of grammar.

Like retarded children, normal children with severe reading disabilities or disabled learners show relatively inferior performance at the automatic (nonmeaningful) level of the *ITPA* (Celebre, 1971; Kass, 1966; Macione, 1969; Ruhly, 1970).

The consistency of research findings relative to the psycholinguistic processes of the mentally retarded has important implications for curriculum planning, especially in the area of reading instruction.

1. Beginning reading instruction should include automatic-type tasks that stress mechanical, rote kinds of learning. The need for repetition, memorization, overlearning, and drill is apparent.

2.   *All* learning situations need not be made meaningful for slow or disabled learners. If they are helped to develop the automatic "tools" of language they will be better able to process information and derive meaning on their own.

3.   Weakness in the auditory-vocal area suggests a need for a more direct teaching approach geared toward this channel, emphasizing phonic instruction, sound blending, auditory closure, and so on.

Teaching Methods

There are a number of studies relating to the method of instruction used in teaching slow and disabled learners to read. Studies conducted prior to 1950 have been reviewed by Dunn (1956), Kirk (1964), and Cegelka and Cegelka (1970). It appears from these reviews that no *one* method has been found successful with all slow and disabled learners. The need for teaching word attack skills is generally acknowledged, but little agreement is noted regarding the best method by which this can be accomplished. The phonics approach has been strongly advocated by some researchers, while others report success from a more eclectic approach combining phonic, sight, and kinesthetic methods. The studies on methodology seem to indicate the need to match the method to the learner in an individualized program of reading instruction.

General Methods

In a study of eleven-year-old English children, Burt and Lewis (1946) compared four groups of slow-learning subjects (IQ range: 79 to 83) who were retarded in reading based on their mental age–reading grade expectancy. A different approach to reading instruction was used with each group—visual (sight or whole word), kinesthetic (tracing and writing the words), alphabet (spelling), and phonic (sounding). Improvement was found in all groups. The visual group improved the most, but only 10 percent more than the least improved group. The kinesthetic approach was more effective than the alphabet and phonic approaches. The teachers who participated in the study felt that, for slow and retarded pupils, the best procedure is "active learning" based predominantly on a visual approach. They also felt that a phonics approach is too hard for such children.

Jordan (1967) states that current introductory reading methods could be divided into three categories, namely: (a) those emphasizing sight vocabulary; (b) phonics methods; and (c) the experience-chart (language-experience) approach. While the purpose of all three methods is to teach children to read, their emphases differ. Sight vocabulary methods stress visual skills, whereas phonics methods demand good auditory discrimination and memory. The primary emphasis in the experience-chart method is on comprehension, with only secondary emphasis on learning words. According to Jordan, these differences can be important to the retarded child with a generally lowered learning ability who also happens to possess a specific disability in the particular skill emphasized by the method chosen.

The language-experience approach rejects the idea of a controlled vocabulary for beginning readers, and the development of a basic sight vocabulary is dependent on the child's oral expression. Allen (1964) states that using the child's own language as a basis of reading instruction results in a high degree of independence in writing and reading.

While the language-experience approach has been advocated for retarded children (Jordan, 1965; Kirk, 1940; McCarthy & Oliver, 1965; Remington, 1956), it appears that preference for this method is based more on testimonial than empirical evidence. Only one research study known to the reviewers (Woodcock & Dunn, 1967) has systematically compared the reading performance of retarded children taught by this method with that of retardates taught by any other method. A definitive statement as to its rank among successful teaching methods for the retarded awaits further research.

Promising new approaches to developmental reading instruction for deviant learners have been suggested in recent years, including the Progressive Choice method, the initial teaching alphabet (i/t/a), modality blocking, operant conditioning, and various attempts at programmed instruction.

Progressive Choice

Davy (1962) reported favorable results with a two-year reading program utilizing Woolman's Progressive Choice method with retarded children at the Emmorton Special School, Harford County, Maryland. This method simplifies the presentation of stimuli and eliminates response alternatives. In the initial phase of the program, each letter has only one related sound and only one shape since upper-case letters alone are used. The pupil must combine a new shape (letter) with previously learned letters to produce a meaningful word before the next new shape is introduced.

The thirteen subjects in Davy's study (whose mental age ranged from 3–1 to 6–4) constituted two groups, an advanced and a beginners' reading group. Each group had a twenty-minute instructional session daily. Initial learning of words as well as retention by both groups after the three-month summer vacation was sufficiently great as to lead the author to suggest that Progressive Choice may be a more efficient and effective method than approaches commonly used with retarded children.

The use of the initial teaching alphabet (i/t/a) with retarded children has been the topic of considerable research. Varying degrees of purported success, however, continue to cloud the issue of its effectiveness with retarded readers.

Orman (1966) and Smith (1974), in independent small group studies using i/t/a with educable retardates, reported similar satisfactory results. Orman found that his subjects (mental age range: 4 to 9) gained confidence and satisfaction in reading. They found i/t/a symbols easier to remember than the traditional alphabet. In Smith's study, seven of the eight subjects increased their reading age significantly over a fifteen-month period and experienced very little difficulty transferring back to traditional orthography. The i/t/a spelling disappeared rapidly in written work.

Downing (1967) reported on a survey of twenty-five schools where i/t/a had been used with educationally subnormal children. Generally, the teachers favored i/t/a as a means of improving reading skills, elevating self-confidence, and increasing motivation. The teachers reported that the children made an easy transition from i/t/a orthography to the traditional.

The results obtained by other investigators suggest that i/t/a is no better than traditional orthography for any group that is homogeneous with respect to intelligence. A comparison of the relative effectiveness of i/t/a versus traditional orthography in beginning reading instruction using educable mentally retarded children as subjects was reported by Mathias (1968). Forty children participated in the study, twenty being taught to read according to each method. At the end of the school year, the *Metropolitan Achievement Test* was administered to both groups in the appropriate orthography. The mean gain difference on the word knowledge subtest significantly favored the traditional orthography group. No other differences were found.

One year after the termination of treatment, both groups were administered the traditional orthography version of the *Metropolitan Achievement Test*. No differences were found on any of the subtests. The initial gain in word knowledge evidenced by the conventional group had disappeared. Both groups had learned to read at approximately the third month of the first year. It was concluded that the method of instruction did not differentially affect the success of beginning reading with educable mentally retarded children.

In a critical review of studies utilizing i/t/a instruction in special education, Gillooly (1967) cites three studies (Chasnoff, 1965; Hayes & Nemeth, 1966; Tanyzer, Alpert, & Sandel, 1965) involving children of low intelligence. A summary of their individual findings on the total *Stanford* and the *California Reading Tests* lends support to the conclusion that there are no i/t/a-traditional orthography differences in the reading achievement of retarded children.

Woodcock and Dunn (1967) compared six different

approaches for teaching reading to educable retarded children, including i/t/a. The six methods were: (1) a language-experience approach using traditional orthography, (2) a basal reader approach using traditional orthography, (3) a programmed text using traditional orthography, (4) a language-experience approach using the i/t/a, (5) a basal reader approach using the i/t/a, and (6) a basal reader approach using rebus symbols. Three hundred and sixty educable mentally retarded children from Chicago and Detroit special classes participated in the study. The mean IQ was 66; mean mental age, 5–6; and the mean chronological age, 8–8. After two years of instruction, all subjects were tested on the word knowledge, word discrimination and reading subtests of the *Metropolitan Reading Test* and the letter recognition, word reading, sentence reading and reading comprehension subtests of *Woodcock and Pfost's Beginning Reading Test*. No significant differences were found among the groups on any one of the seven measures of reading ability.

The fact that no single approach made any real difference in the subjects' overall reading achievement lends support to the conclusion that there is no *one* best way of teaching reading to retarded children. Individual differences among children as well as varying degrees of teacher effectiveness in implementing a particular reading method may be more important than the method itself.

Operant Conditioning Techniques and Programmed Instruction

Bijou (1965) conducted a three-year study using operant conditioning techniques to instruct seventeen mentally retarded children in reading, writing, and arithmetic. The chronological age of the subjects ranged from 8 to 14; the IQ from 44 to 77. Each child was presented with tasks specifically designed for him or her. The child received immediate feedback as to the appropriateness of the response. Marks given for correct responses could later be traded for candy or toys of the child's choice. The positive results of the study indicate that retarded children can be taught academic skills if the material is presented in a programmed manner and if reinforcement is immediate and meaningful to them.

Operant conditioning techniques and programmed instruction were also combined in a study by Kortas (1969), who tested the effects of a teacher-administered token system with a group of mentally retarded boys. Seventeen subjects considered to be poor readers (chronological age range: 8–10 to 12–5; IQ range: 53 to 86) from the Kennedy School, Palos Park, Illinois, participated in the seven-and-a-half-month study. Reinforcement was contingent on the correct solution of workbook items in the Sullivan Associates Programmed Reading Series. Percentage of items correct increased significantly under the token reinforcement system, whereas number of items completed decreased with the introduction of tokens. The subjects appeared to take more time to work out a correct solution and showed a decreased tendency to write random responses in the workbook without completing the required reading. After seven-and-a-half months of programmed reading, the *Metropolitan Achievement Tests: Reading* showed a group average gain of 1.0 years, attesting to the success of reinforcement and programmed instruction for the retarded.

Hewett and associates (1967) used a programmed approach successfully to teach basic reading skills to four groups of children—neurologically impaired, educable mentally retarded, emotionally disturbed, and normal. The IQ range of the twenty-five subjects was from 46 to 130; chronological age ranged from 4–10 to 21–6. The five-part lesson included oral reading review, vocabulary building, new oral reading, comprehension, and discrimination exercises. The effectiveness of the programmed approach is inferred from the fact that all subjects achieved an acceptable level of reading and gained more acceptance from parents and peers.

Stolurow (1963) reported on studies involving the use of programmed instruction in teaching sight vocabulary to retarded subjects as well as a sentence program using verbal prompts. Ellson and associates (1961) developed a teaching machine program found effective for producing rapid increases in the learning of a reading vocabulary. They reported one study in which thirty-eight retardates participated. Eighty-two words were selected from Gates' Reading Vocabulary for the Primary Grades. The program was branched in teaching each word, but the words themselves were not sequenced according to any programming rule. Each word was paired with a picture that the children were to name.

The statistically significant mean gain difference was 11.8 words in favor of the experimental group. After one month, a 43 percent loss in performance was reported. To determine the generalization of the programmed instruction, a vocabulary test consisting of words not previously employed in the program was administered before and immediately after a five-trial learning session. The experimental group gained on the average 7.1 words; the matched control group, 2.8 words. The difference was significant.

A sentence program was also developed by Ellson and associates (1961) and tested with normal first graders, slow first-grade readers, and retardates. A correction procedure was employed that provided a branch program in a sequential set of five decisions. The program was used in eight one-half-hour sessions, two per week for four weeks, followed one month later by a retention test. Normal children gained a mean of 30.5 words; slow learners, 20.0; and retarded children, 19.5 words. Retention was nearly 90 percent for all groups after one month.

An evaluation of programmed instruction using teaching machines with the mentally retarded was done by Blackman and Capobianco (1965). Nineteen experimental subjects and seventeen controls (mean chronological age approximately 14–0; mean IQ of approximately 54) took part in the study, which included both reading and arithmetic instruction. The experimental group was taught by means of teaching machines, whereas traditional special educational methods of instruction were used with the control subjects.

Results showed that both the experimental and control subjects improved significantly in reading and arithmetic; there were no significant differences between the groups' achievement. However, the experimental group showed greater improvement in out-of-school behavior. The authors hypothesized that: (a) the self-pacing provided by the machine instruction together with the absence of teacher pressure was less frustrating for the pupils, (b) the immediate feedback constituted consistent reinforcement, and (c) attention span and interest may have increased because of the mechanistic involvement of the machine.

Results such as these indicate that programmed instruction for educable mentally retarded children is clearly feasible. This method has been shown to be successful during the relatively short time it has been available and holds much hope for the future in special education.

The obvious conclusion to be drawn from studies on methodology is that no one single method of teaching reading has been found successful with all slow and disabled learners. Because of vast differences among individual children, an individualized program matched to the learning needs of each child that utilizes the most relevant aspects of various instructional methods may prove to be the most successful approach. Woodcock and Dunn (1967) have indicated that differences in teachers' ability to effectively implement a particular approach may be a more crucial factor in determining the method's success or failure than the instructional program itself.

These findings on methodology and teacher effectiveness accord with the results of the *National First Grade Reading Studies* (Bond & Dykstra, 1967), which compared the relative success of six programs of reading instruction. The combined data from twenty-seven individual studies were analyzed to determine the relative effectiveness of the various approaches for children who possessed high or low readiness characteristics. Pupils were blocked in three separate analyses on the basis of IQ, and on results in the *Durrell-Murphy Total Letters Test,* and the *Durrell-Murphy Phonemes Test.* Each analysis found no evidence that any particular program was especially effective for children with high or low IQ, high or low knowledge of letters, or high or low auditory discrimination. In most cases and on most measures, however, the children taught by a method emphasizing a direct decoding process outperformed children taught by other methods. This finding may have direct implications for teaching the retarded as well. The first-grade studies indicated, too, that the *teacher* was the single most important variable in teaching reading, and that children could learn to read under many widely differing conditions.

Perinatal Events as Causes of Reading and Learning Disabilities

Often cited as causes of reading disabilities or learning disabilities are perinatal factors, such as complications of the mother's pregnancy, difficulties during the birth process, and problems in early infancy. A critical review of the major studies that explore the relationship between reading disability and complications of pregnancy, birth, and early infancy was done by Balow, Rubin, and Rosen (1975–1976).

In all, these authors reviewed twenty-eight studies that analyzed the nature and extent of the relationship between problems of pregnancy, birth, early infancy, and reading performance. Their review showed that many of the studies had methodological problems. Consequently, the authors challenged conclusions made in many of the studies that they believe to be unfounded.

Balow, Rubin, and Rosen conclude that the evidence suggests that low birth weight and certain pregnancy and birth complications can indeed impair later reading ability. While additional research in this area is needed, they emphasize that such research must be carefully designed, comprehensive, and that the data must be collected to meet high standards of reliability and validity.

EEG Findings and Reading Disabilities

The results of the EEG (electroencephalogram) examination were among the variables analyzed in a follow-up study of high school students who were diagnosed as disabled readers at the elementary and junior high level (Muehl & Forrell, 1973–1974). Forty-three high school students were studied to determine the relationship of certain variables to high school reading performance.

The forty-three students were, on the average, about three grades retarded in reading when tested in high school. Only two subjects (4 percent) had reading scores above the fiftieth percentile. The evidence showed that children diagnosed as poor readers in the elementary and junior high school continued as a group to be poor readers later on in their schooling. This study showed a high incidence of EEG abnormality (63 percent) in the disabled reader group. However, the disabled readers with abnormal EEG patterns were as a group better readers than the disabled readers with normal EEG patterns.

Little relationship between EEG patterns and reading was found by Benton and Bird (1963) and Hartlage and Green (1971). Ayres and Torres (1967) found a greater incidence of abnormal EEGs among reading disability cases than in a control group.

These studies suggest that while there is a higher incidence of EEG abnormality among disabled learners who have reading difficulties, the precise nature of the relationship between EEG patterns and reading problems is not clear.

Correlates of Reading Failure

Correlates of learning failure were discussed in Chapters 1 and 2. These correlates are factors or components of learning that are thought to be highly correlated with learning to read. It is further contended that when these components of learning are not intact, they are highly related to difficulty in learning to read.

A comprehensive review of the research literature on components of associational learning relevant to reading was reported by Samuels (1973). Analyzed in this review were the correlates attention, visual discrimination, visual and auditory memory, and auditory discrimination. In addition to reviewing the research literature on these components, Samuels presented a model of learning that he believes can serve as a basis for further research on reading difficulty. The highlights of Samuels' review of correlates of reading failure are discussed in this section.

Attentional Deficits

Deficits in attention have been identified as one of the correlates that are highly related to difficulty in learning to read (Dykman, Ackerman, Clements, & Peters, 1971; Keogh & Margolis, 1976). Students who are low in academic achievement seem to be more distractible than high-achieving students (Baker & Madell, 1965; Brewer, 1967; Lahaderne, 1968; Samuels, 1967; Silverman, Davids, & Andrews, 1963). In his summary of the review of literature on attention, Samuels (1973) concludes that: (a) the correlate of attention is related to learning, (b) low-achieving students tend to be more distractible than high achievers, and (c) at the upper elementary level, a positive relationship exists between attention and achievement.

Visual Discrimination

The ability to discriminate letters and words visually is essential in learning to read. A deficit or disability in the area of visual discrimination is therefore viewed by many authorities as one of the most important causes of reading difficulty (Benton, 1962; Frostig, 1961; Goins, 1958).

However, several studies have shown that there is little difference between good and poor readers in their ability to visually discriminate forms (Bonsall & Dornbush, 1969; Goldmark, 1964; Olson, 1966). A strong relationship between visual perception and reading was reported in several other research studies (Busby & Hurd, 1968; Rosen, 1965; Spring, 1969). Busby and Hurd suggest that the relationship may be an artifact of the way the data were analyzed.

Summarizing the literature on form discrimination, Samuels (1973) concludes that: (a) some empirical evidence has been found to support a relationship between form discrimination difficulty and poor reading, but these studies have certain statistical flaws, (b) some researchers detected no differences in form discrimination abilities between good and poor readers, and (c) specific training approaches reported in the research literature suggest that training methods enhance visual discrimination and reading.

Visual and Auditory Memory

There is a strong belief that memory problems are related to reading difficulties. In a study of visual memory, Anderson and Samuels (1970) found that visual memory was significantly correlated with paired-associate learning and reading achievement. Samuels' (1973) review of current theory about auditory and visual memory and its relationship to reading concludes that: (a) visual memory may be stored both as a verbal image and as a visual image, (b) research on visual memory and reading indicates that poor reading is associated with inferior visual memory, and (c) visual memory may be improved if the learner is helped to discriminate and decode the distinctive features of visually presented stimuli.

Auditory Discrimination

According to Samuels (1973), the research on auditory perception is perplexing because auditory discrimination is defined differently in various studies. Some studies define it as the ability to discriminate between pairs of similar sounding words; some define it as the child's ability to name the letter of the sound that the teacher says; others define it as the ability to blend isolated sounds into words; still other studies define it as remembering some details of what has been said.

Some researchers contend that the link between auditory discrimination and reading achievement is tenuous and has not been clearly proven (Dykstra, 1962; Poling, 1953; Reynolds, 1953; Weiner, 1967; Wheeler & Wheeler, 1954). Other research studies show a strong positive relationship between auditory discrimination and reading (Bond, 1935; Gates, 1940; Harrington & Durrell, 1955; Monroe, 1932; Robinson, 1972; Wepman, 1960).

Samuels (1973) summarizes the research on auditory discrimination: (a) tests of auditory discrimination and testing methods are subject to criticism on several grounds, and (b) considering areas where intervention can produce changes, auditory discrimination does not seem to be particularly promising.

The Relationship of Central Processing Dysfunctions to Reading

Some researchers view correlates of reading failure such as those discussed above to be central processing dysfunctions.

Disabled learners are frequently defined as children having "disorders in one or more of the basic psychological processes" needed for school learning (Public Law 94–142, Section 5(b)(4), 1975). Various terms are used to refer to these psychological processes, including *perceptual modalities, learning style, cognitive processing, psycholinguistic abilities* (Chalfant & Scheffelin, 1969; Kirk & Kirk, 1971).

Central Processing Dysfunctions

The term *central processing dysfunctions* will be used here to convey the general idea implied by all of these terms. Children differ in their ability to process information, and these differences affect the child's learning—including learning to read. Children with processing dysfunctions are unable to learn from regular classroom instruction; therefore, they need special kinds of teaching. In other words, the premise is that certain children fail to learn efficiently in school because of deficits in central processing functions. Once these deficits are discerned or diagnosed, appropriate teaching can be prescribed.

A number of models of central processing dysfunction have been proposed (Chalfant & King, 1976; Chalfant & Scheffelin, 1969; Ensminger & Sullivan, 1974; Frostig, 1961; Johnson & Myklebust, 1967; Kirk & Kirk, 1971). While these models differ in certain respects, all of them specify underlying processing abilities such as auditory processing, visual processing, memory abilities, kinesthetic and tactile processing, language processing, and so on. The child's weaknesses and strengths in discrete central processing functions are assessed by use of formal tests, informal tests, and observational techniques. In reading, the processing concept suggests that children with auditory processing dysfunctions will have much difficulty with instructional approaches that are primarily auditory, such as phonics methods. Similarly, children who have difficulty with visual processing are likely to experience difficulty learning to read via visual approaches, such as the "sight method."

221
The Relationship
of Central
Processing
Dysfunctions to
Reading

According to the processing theory, once the child's strengths and weaknesses in central processing functions are ascertained, the teacher can develop an appropriate teaching plan. Three different teaching plans have been suggested, all of them based on the child's processing abilities and disabilities.

1. One approach is to help the child develop those processing functions that appear to be deficient. This is called the *building-the-deficits* or the *process-training* approach.

2. A second approach tries to match the child's strengths in learning to a method that uses those strengths. This is called *teaching-through-the-strengths,* the *preferred modality* approach, or the *ATI (aptitude-treatment-interaction)* approach.

3. The third approach is a kind of compromise. It advocates building the child's deficits and at the same time teaching the child through the areas of strength. This is called a *two-pronged* or *combined* approach.

Research on Central Processing Dysfunctions and Reading

The concept of central processing dysfunctions has been in existence since the early 1900s. However, there has been a relatively limited amount of research done on this subject. A review of current research on each of the three approaches to teaching based on the central processing dysfunction model is presented below.

Deficit Process Training

The theory underlying the process approach is that disabled learners exhibit certain weaknesses in discrete and specific processing functions that inhibit their ability to learn academic skills such as reading, arithmetic, spelling, or handwriting. In the case of reading, a poor auditory processing ability would cause a child to have difficulty learning to read. A similar case could be made for poor visual processing abilities or poor memory abilities. The theory contends that if the child's skills in the discrete deficit area are improved or built up through training, the deficit would be removed and the child would then be able to learn to read. The teaching method, then, trains the modality in which the child is deficient. It is similar to what some people refer to as *modality training, teaching-to-the-deficits,* or *psycholinguistic teaching.*

The efficacy of the process training approach for teaching disabled learners has been questioned seriously in recent research studies (Hammill & Larsen, 1974b; Newcomer & Hammill, 1976). The research method used in these studies was a review and statistical analysis of thirty-eight studies that attempted to train psycholinguistic functions. The reviewers concluded, "The idea that psycholinguistic constructs, as measured by the *ITPA*, can be trained by existing techniques remains nonvalidated" (Hammill & Larsen, 1947b, p. 11).

This review of the research has been criticized by Minskoff (1975) on methodological grounds and by Lund, Foster, and Perez (1977). After analyzing the primary studies reviewed by Hammill and Larsen, Lund and associates found positive results on six or more psycholinguistic functions measured by the *ITPA* and positive results when researchers concentrated on one psycholinguistic function. Some of the studies, of course, did not show significant results. Lund and associates reported that Hammill and Larsen drew unwarranted conclusions from the data.

Hammill and Larsen (1974a, 1974b), Hammill and Wiederholt (1973), Larsen and Hammill (1975), and Larsen, Rogers, and Sowell (1976) reviewed studies on visual and auditory modality training and have also studied the relationship of modality training and processes to good and poor readers. In general, they conclude that visual and auditory process training does not enhance the ability to learn to read and that some of the processes studied did not differentiate between good and poor readers.

These studies on the effects of modality training and on the differences between good and poor readers suffer from methodological problems, rendering the conclusions suspect. One can ask, "Does a major deficit in visual discrimination inhibit the ability to learn to read?" On the face of it, the obvious answer is yes. If a child is not able to discriminate between *A* and *B* or between *dog* and *man*, he or she will not be able to learn to read. However, there are very few children, who at the age of 6 do not have sufficient visual discrimination ability to learn to read. The studies reported tend to compare children having relatively minor visual discrimination problems with children who have normal visual discrimination. Children with minor visual problems or even children who have very severe visual problems can learn to read print. Eighty percent of children with 20/200 vision and less (legally blind) learn to read print.

This should suggest that the human organism is highly adaptable and that minor variations from the norm of one or even two standard deviations may not interfere with learning to read. From the study of exceptional children, we know that hard-of-hearing children learn to read but that deaf children have great difficulty learning to read due to their language disability.

Preferred Modality Approach

The second approach based on teaching through the preferred modality is sometimes called *aptitude-treatment-interaction* (ATI). In this approach the teacher first determines the child's intact, strong, or preferred modalities; then

223
The Relationship
of Central
Processing
Dysfunctions to
Reading

the teacher selects a teaching method that utilizes the child's modality of strength. In other words, the instructional technique will circumvent the child's processing weaknesses and exploit the child's intact functions. The modality of instruction is matched with the child's modality preference. Thus the child's aptitude for learning *interacts* with the treatment procedure. For instance, in reading, if the child learns easily through the auditory modality but has difficulty with the visual modality, a teaching method that uses auditory processing (such as the phonics method) would be selected.

A number of research studies have investigated the ATI or aptitude-treatment-interaction approach (Bateman, 1968; Bracht, 1970; Jones, 1972; Lilly & Kelleher, 1973; Newcomer & Goodman, 1975; Robinson, 1972; Sabatino & Dorfman, 1974; Ysseldyke, 1973). In these studies, children were given tests to determine their modality preference, and then they were given differential instruction in reading with a method that used each child's modality preference—either the visual or the auditory modality. The results of these studies showed that, in general, there was no significant interaction between modality preference and the method of reading instruction.

Explanations for the lack of significant interaction between modality preference and method of instruction have been given in the research literature (Cronbach, 1975; Jones, 1972; Lilly & Kelleher, 1973; Minskoff, 1975; Minskoff & Minskoff, 1976). The explanations include: (a) available tests of modality processing may not accurately measure the preferred perceptual modality, (b) there is no method of teaching a skill such as reading that relies on a single modality (perhaps both the visual and auditory modalities are so strongly involved in reading that learning to read without using both the auditory and visual functions is unlikely), (c) research has been marred by methodological and conceptual errors, (d) the preferred ability measured was not sufficiently different from the norm or deficit ability to warrant calling it a preferred modality (see discussion on this point in the previous section), and (e) the design of the aptitude-treatment-interaction studies obscured the interactions. For all of these reasons, these researchers suggest that the degree to which children can master reading through the use of their preferred modalities has not yet been determined.

Combined Methods

Advocates of combined methods suggest that teachers use knowledge about the child's central processing dysfunctions to design a combined teaching plan (Johnson & Myklebust, 1967; Minskoff & Minskoff, 1976). The teacher would attempt to build up the child's deficit areas while at the same time teaching the child through the processing areas of strength. Minskoff and Minskoff (1976) state:

> A child's disability and ability areas must both be simultaneously
> considered. . . . For example, if a child has a disability in the
> memory process, he should be given training to develop his recall

of auditory and visual material. If this child has a strength in the association process, aids such as meaningful associations and labeling are used until he shows improved recall (p. 218).

In the combined approach, several techniques are used simultaneously. In terms of research design, it is difficult to conduct research on such a method because it is hard to isolate the single variable being tested. Because of the interplay of several teaching methods, specifying the independent and dependent variables would be complicated. Thus, little or no research has been reported on the combined approach.

Tests of Central Processing Functions

There are a number of tests on the market that measure the child's central processing abilities. These include the *Illinois Test of Psycholinguistic Abilities (ITPA)*, the *Frostig Developmental Test of Visual Perception*, the *Wepman Test of Auditory Discrimination*, the *Detroit Tests of Learning Aptitude*, and the *Bender Visual-Motor Gestalt Test*. The value of these tests in measuring discrete abilities of mental functioning has been researched by several investigators (Hammill & Wiederholt, 1973; Hirshoren, 1969; Larsen, Rogers, & Sowell, 1976; Newcomer, Hare, Hammill, & McGettigan, 1975; Sedlack & Weener, 1973; Ysseldyke & Salvia, 1974).

These investigators raised the following kinds of objections to tests of central processing functions: (a) "perceptual processing" is only a theoretical construct that may not exist in reality (there is no agreement as to what constitutes a specific perceptual process, such as auditory discrimination), (b) there is little evidence that specific processing functions are necessary for learning to read, since many children who appear to have processing deficits have no difficulty, (c) the tests often do not measure the discrete processing area they purport to measure, and (d) specific tests of processing abilities demonstrate statistical shortcomings. Supporters of tests of processing functions have responded to these charges (Chalfant & King, 1976; Kirk & Kirk, 1977; Minskoff, 1975) as follows: (a) the tests are being used in ways and with populations for which they were not intended, (b) the tests were not designed as predictive instruments, (c) the critics give no alternative procedures for testing and teaching to replace those being criticized, and (d) the tests and methods have been found successful in clinical cases.

With respect to the *Illinois Test of Psycholinguistic Abilities,* Kirk and Kirk (1977, in press) summarized their response on its misuse:

1. The ITPA was not designed to solve all children's problems.
2. It was not designed to be used as a classification instrument.
3. It was not designed to predict academic achievement.
4. It was not designed to be used by untrained testers.

5. It was designed to be used as an intraindividual clinical tool to aid in the diagnosis of some relevant aspects of language, perception, and memory.
6. It was designed to be used primarily with young children.
7. It was designed to *help* ferret out relevant psychological abilities and disabilities in order to organize remedial material.
8. It was designed to help in differential diagnosis of different clinical types of children; also for the purpose of organizing differential remediation (pp. 25–26).

Three Approaches to Remedial Procedures

As indicated in the review of research, the results of studies on remedial procedures are fragmented and contradictory. These differences can be accounted for as owing to different samples and different remedial procedures. In attempting to reconcile different emphases in remediation, Kirk (1976) described three remedial approaches: (1) skill or task training, (2) process training, and (3) process-task training.

Skill or Task Training

Classroom teachers have always had the responsibility of finding out what a child can do and what he or she cannot do in content subjects. Procedures have been developed to help the teacher make an informal inventory of what a child can do in reading, writing, spelling, and arithmetic. For example, the teacher determines the child's independent, instructional, and frustration levels of reading. After inventorying the child's level and reading skills, the teacher organizes a corrective or developmental program. Good teachers diagnose children in the manner described, define daily objectives to be attained, and start the child at a comfortable but challenging level. They break down the lessons into subskills that would help the child develop that skill or content area.

The task training approach is a refinement of what a teacher normally does. This approach: (a) determines what the child can and cannot do in a skill, (b) analyzes the behaviors needed to succeed in the task, (c) defines the behavioral objectives, and (d) organizes a systematic remedial program using reinforcement techniques. Applied behavior analysts do not infer what processes underlie difficulties but rely solely on behavioral events and environmental conditions. They feel that their approach, which is task-oriented and observable, is the most parsimonious approach.

Process Training

Another common remedial method may be labelled *process training*. Process training is based on the assumption that what the child produces, that is, the child's products or skills, are dependent on psychological processes and that for these skills to develop it is necessary to train the underlying processes. For example, if a child is expected to learn to read, he or she must possess adequate processes of visual discrimination, sound-blending ability, and a host of other cognitive and perceptual skills. If children are to learn to talk, they must decode verbal language and encode their concepts into verbal expressive language. Some individuals attempt to train a process in isolation, hoping that the ability will facilitate the learning of a skill at a later date. For example, a child with poor visual discrimination is given visual discrimination exercises of circles and squares in the hope that this training will develop an ability that will facilitate learning to read later on. The opponents of process training state that research has not demonstrated that visual discrimination training or the training of other processes facilitates learning to read. Materials and methods that are currently used to train psychological processes in children have been challenged as worthless. Research in this area has been difficult to control, and most studies have dealt with children who already have sufficient visual discrimination ability or visual memory ability to learn to read.

The other approach to process training is to *train a process for its own sake,* without reference to how it facilitates learning at a later date. The child who does not decode language (has not learned to listen) is trained in the process of listening for its own sake. The child who does not discriminate objects in the environment is trained to discriminate objects in his or her immediate environment. If the child does not discriminate between touching a hot stove and a picture of a fire, he or she learns through pain to make this discrimination.

In other words, there is doubt about the usefulness of training processes in isolation in the hope that they will transfer to a skill at a later date. Few, however, question the training of a process for its own sake. The whole program, curriculum, and activities found in the kindergarten and nursery school involve the training of processes for their own sake as well as for later development. It is sometimes difficult to differentiate between a process and a product.

The Process-Task Approach
(aptitude-instructional-interaction)

Some specialists feel that for the ordinary child with problems arising from poor teaching or lack of opportunity, the skill- or task-training approach is adequate and effective. Children with severe disabilities, however, require "child analysis" as well as "task analysis." The resultant teaching approach will involve process- and task-training in the same remedial procedure. We can label this approach *process-task training* or *aptitude-instructional-interaction.* In this approach, instruction is matched to the aptitude or lack of aptitude in order to produce the best interaction; that is, process and task are integrated in remediation. Instead of teaching visual discrimination in isolation, we train visual discrimination of letters and words. This approach is generally used by those who analyze the child's abilities and disabilities and do a task analysis, that is, an analysis of the sequence of skills required by the task. Those who practice the process-task or aptitude-instructional-interaction approach are considered diagnostic prescriptive teachers since they do both child analysis and task analysis.

An example from reading may illustrate the process-task approach to remediation. A child who had attended school regularly up to the age of 9 was referred because he was unable to learn to read in spite of his tested IQ of 120 on the *WISC*. Analysis of the child's information-processing abilities showed a process deficit in visual memory. He was unable to reproduce in writing and from memory words presented to him visually. He demonstrated the visual memory deficit both on norm-referenced tests and on criterion-referenced tests. The process-task remediation procedure called for a program that would develop visual memory using the words and phrases the child needs in learning to read. This procedure of training the process of visual memory on the task itself is process-task training. Actually, Fernald's (1943) kinesthetic method trains memory for words *not* in the abstract but directly, using the words and phrases needed by the child in learning to read. The Fernald kinesthetic method, like other methods successful in children with severe disabilities, is a process-task approach, since it trains visual memory with words the child is learning to read.

The process-task approach is the procedure most commonly used by diagnostic prescriptive specialists, especially for children with severe learning disabilities. It seems there is merit in the flexibility permitted by the process-task approach in training children with learning disabilities.

Miscellaneous Studies

Several investigations have been concerned with the problem of choosing the proper reading instructional level for deviant learners. Should it be determined by the reading grade equivalent of a standardized reading test or by an informal assessment of the child's reading status based on predetermined criteria?

Cawley (1968) examined and compared the frequency of word recognition errors at levels determined by a standardized reading test with those at levels determined by Betts' (1946) criteria (95 percent word recognition in context and 75 percent comprehension). Forty-nine mentally retarded and fifty children of average intelligence were studied. Word recognition errors made during the reading of an Informal Reading Inventory were tallied. Errors were defined as substitutions, failure to recognize a word, omission, additions, and reversals. Errors were computed at two levels—the level determined by Betts' criteria and the level determined by the *SRA Reading Test*. In all instances among the retarded and young average children, the *SRA* instructional level was higher than that determined by the Informal Reading Inventory. The error scores among the older retarded children were nearly three times as great at the *SRA* oral reading level as at the level based upon Betts' criteria. Cawley (1968) contends that assigning a child to a reading level based on the reading grade equivalent of a standardized reading test tends to place the child in a very difficult instructional situation. The number of errors made is often so great as to make correction inefficient and new learning difficult.

Brown (1967) tested thirty educable mentally retarded children from fifteen intermediate-level classes in Kansas City, Missouri, to determine their instructional reading levels, using materials recommended for this purpose in special classes. The reading levels were then compared with teacher-assigned levels in the same material. Fifty percent of the children were considered to have been accurately placed; 23 percent were underplaced, that is, at a level that appeared to be too easy; and 27 percent were overplaced, that is, they were struggling with material that appeared to be too difficult for them. The author, therefore, suggested that the instructional level concept may need to be modified for special education. She feels it has been erroneously applied to the corrective or remedial situation. In the remedial context, instructional level indicates the point at which a halt should be called in the program. According to Brown, skills that are missing can then be brought up to a point of competence so that the developmental program can be resumed at an appropriate pace.

Many reading specialists have concluded that the grade equivalent score on standardized tests tends to overrate the student's reading performance, particularly that of the slow reader or slow learner. Thus, the pupils who are most frequently misplaced are the ones most in need of correct placement (Botel, 1959). Informal testing appears preferable for determining proper placement. Durrell (1956) proposes that "informal tests, based upon reading materials used in the classroom and observation . . . provide the best basis for planning classroom instruction" (p. 93).

The teaching of reading involves continuous diagnosis and treatment. It is the teacher's responsibility to plan a reading program that will allow for adjusting the instruction in relation to the child's performance.

Daley and Lee (1960) reported a reading experiment with retarded children to determine the efficacy of homogeneous grouping and its effect on reading speed changes. The groups, one homogeneous and one mixed, were selected from a school for the mentally retarded. The homogeneous group consisted of children of the same reading speed level; the mixed group was composed of children of different reading speed levels. Sixty hours of concentrated reading were included in the regular academic program of all subjects. The groups were evaluated before and after treatment with the *Durrell Analysis of Reading Difficulty*. Differences between the two groups in reading speed changes were not statistically significant, leading the authors to conclude that homogeneous grouping did not constitute a successful means of increasing reading speed for the retarded.

Summary

The studies reviewed in this chapter capsulize the contribution of research relative to the reading status of slow and disabled learners. The kinds of research studies undertaken in the last decade or two differ from those done earlier. In the earlier studies, researchers were concerned with: (a) the ability of atypical children to read up to their mental age-reading grade expectancy, (b) the mental age at which they should begin reading, and (c) comparisons of regular and special classes. Recent research has been concerned primarily with (a) the reading-teaching process, (b) the analysis of reading habits and abilities, and (c) instructional programming. The research findings are summarized below.

Regardless of age, slow-learning children tend to read below their mental age-reading grade expectancy except when special emphasis is placed on reading. Where special attention is given to reading, slow learners tend to read up to or beyond mental age expectancy. The studies indicate that mental age is important but that it is only one of the factors that determines reading achievement.

The optimum mental age at which reading should be taught has not been clearly determined. The wisdom of delaying the teaching of reading until a mental age of 6 has been attained has been questioned frequently.

A comparison of the reading achievement of slow-learning children and children of average or superior intelligence of the same mental age yielded inconclusive results.

Children with borderline intelligence learn to read at a higher level in the regular grades as compared with similar children assigned to special classes. However, mildly and moderately retarded children tend to read better in special classes.

The adequacy of the instructional program provided is more crucial than signs of organicity in predicting the reading success of disabled learners whether or not they are diagnosed as brain-injured children. No *one* method of instruction has been demonstrated to be clearly superior to others for teaching atypical children to read. New and unconventional methods (namely, the talking typewriter, Progressive Choice, i/t/a, operant conditioning, and programmed instruction) have been found successful in some instances in teaching atypical children to read.

Teacher enthusiasm for a method and teacher effectiveness in presenting it are of equal or greater importance than the method itself.

Complications in pregnancy, birth, and early infancy seem to be related to later reading disabilities. There is a higher incidence of abnormal EEG patterns among disabled readers. However, the exact relationship between reading difficulties and EEG patterns is not known. No relationship was found to exist between reading and lateral dominance.

Three approaches to teaching are based on the premise of central processing dysfunction: deficit process training, preferred modality training, and the combined approach. Research findings are conflicting on the relation between central processing dysfunction and reading. Additional research is needed.

Approaches to remediation include skill or task training, process training, and process-task training.

The research suggests that lack of progress in reading cannot be due to the child alone or to the method alone, but rather to the match between the child's characteristics and the methods and materials presented to him or her.

There may be some truth to the statement, "If a child hasn't learned to read, he hasn't been taught!"

Appendix A   Phonics

This appendix has two sections. The first part is a short phonics quiz to assess the teacher's knowledge of this subject area. The second part is a brief review of some phonic generalizations.

FŎN′ĬKS KWĬZ (Phonics Quiz)

The purpose of the phonics quiz is to give teachers the opportunity to evaluate their knowledge of phonics, structural or morphemic analysis, and phonic generalizations. Even among advocates of conflicting approaches to the teaching of reading, there is agreement that skills in word recognition and phonics are essential for effective reading. And all reading authorities agree that teachers of reading and language arts have the responsibility to help children acquire the skills that will enable them to unlock unknown words. Without phonics, most children cannot become self-reliant, discriminating, efficient readers.

In spite of this strong and united stand taken by the reading experts, many teachers and prospective teachers are not knowledgeable in this content area (Lerner & List, 1970). *The Torch Lighters* (Austin, 1961), an intensive and broad study of tomorrow's teachers of reading supported by the Carnegie Corporation, revealed that many prospective teachers do not know techniques or generalizations of phonics. A major recommendation resulting from the study was that college instructors make certain that students who will be teaching reading master the principles of phonics. Phonics and structural or morphemic analysis, then, should be part of the content area for the teacher of reading, language arts, and English.

It should be noted that recent research on the utility of phonic generalizations reveals that these rules have many exceptions. In fact, some are applicable less than half the time. Therefore, certain generalizations may have a limited utility value (Bailey, 1967; Burmeister, 1968; Clymer, 1963; Emans, 1967; Lerner, 1969; Winkley, 1966). Nevertheless, these generalizations do provide a helpful start in analyzing unknown words.

231

Although knowledge of rules and facts concerning phonics is part of the content area for the teacher, this is not a recommended way to teach phonics to a child. The strategies selected to teach a child the skill of unlocking words will depend on many factors.

To check your knowledge of phonics, select the correct answer for each of the following fifty questions. Compare your choices with the correct answers printed at the end of the "Phonics Quiz." Score two points for each correct answer. Check the table below the answers for your rating and classification.

Choose the Correct Answer

Consonants

1. Which of the following words ends with a consonant sound?
   a) piano   b) baby   c) relay   d) pencil   e) below
2. A combination of two or three consonants pronounced so that each letter keeps its own identity is called a
   a) silent consonant   b) consonant digraph   c) diphthong
   d) schwa   e) consonant blend
3. A word with a consonant digraph is
   a) stop   b) blue   c) bend   d) stripe   e) none of the above
4. A word with a consonant blend is
   a) chair   b) ties   c) thing   d) strict   e) where
5. A soft *c* is in the word
   a) city   b) cat   c) chair   d) Chicago   e) none of the above
6. A soft *g* is in the word
   a) great   b) go   c) ghost   d) rig   e) none of the above
7. A hard *c* is sounded in pronouncing which of the following nonsense words?
   a) cadur   b) ceiter   c) cymling   d) ciblent   e) chodly
8. A hard *g* would be likely to be found in which of the following nonsense words?
   a) gyfing   b) gesturn   c) gailing   d) gimber   e) geit
9. A *voiced* consonant digraph is in the word
   a) think   b) ship   c) whip   d) the   e) photo
10. An *unvoiced* consonant digraph is in the word
    a) those   b) thirteen   c) that   d) bridge   e) these

Vowels

11. Which of the following words contains a long vowel sound?
    a) paste   b) stem   c) urge   d) ball   e) off
12. Which of the following words contain a short vowel sound?
    a) treat   b) start   c) slip   d) paw   e) father

13. If *tife* were a word, the letter *i* would probably sound like the *i* in
    a) if b) beautiful c) find d) ceiling e) sing
    Why?
14. If *aik* were a word, the letter *a* would probably sound like the *a* in
    a) pack b) ball c) about d) boat e) cake
    Why?
15. If *ne* were a word, the letter *e* would probably sound like the *e* in
    a) fed b) seat c) batter d) friend e) weight
    Why?
16. A vowel sound represented by the alphabet letter name of that vowel is a
    a) short vowel b) long vowel c) diphthong d) digraph
    e) schwa
17. An example of the schwa sound is found in
    a) cotton b) phoneme c) stopping d) preview
    e) grouping
18. A diphthong is in the word
    a) coat b) boy c) battle d) retarded e) slow
19. Which of the following words contains a vowel digraph?
    a) toil b) amazing c) happy d) cape e) coat

Syllables

Indicate the correct way to divide the following nonsense words into syllables:

20. l i d b e r
    a) li-dber b) lidb-er c) lid-ber d) none of the above
    Why?
21. s e f u m
    a) se-fum b) sef-um c) s-efum d) sefu-m e) none
    Why?
22. s k e b l e
    a) skeb-le b) ske-ble c) sk-eble d) none of these
    Why?
23. g o p h u l
    a) gop-hul b) go-phul c) goph-ul d) none
    Why?
24. r e p a i n l y
    a) rep-ain-ly b) re-pai-nly c) re-pain-ly d) none of the above
    Why?
25. How many syllables are in the word *barked*?
    a) one b) two c) three d) four e) five
26. How many syllables are in the word *generalizations*?
    a) four b) five c) six d) seven e) eight
27. A word with an open syllable is
    a) pike b) go c) bend d) butter e) if
28. A word with a closed syllable is
    a) throw b) see c) why d) cow e) win

29. If *trigler* were a word, which syllable would probably be accented?
    a) trig   b) ler   c) neither   d) both
    Why?
30. If *tronition* were a word, which syllable would probably be accented?
    a) tro   b) ni   c) tion   d) none
    Why?
31. If *pretaineringly* were a word, which syllable would probably be accented?
    a) pre   b) tain   c) er   d) ing   e) ly
    Why?

Sound of Letter y

32. If *gly* were a word, the letter *y* would probably sound like
    a) the *e* in *eel*   b) the *e* in *pet*   c) the *i* in *isle*   d) the *i* in *if*   e) the *y* in *happy*
    Why?
33. If *agby* were a word, the letter *y* would probably sound like
    a) the *e* in *eel*   b) the *e* in *egg*   c) the *i* in *ice*   d) the *i* in *if*   e) the *y* in *cry*
    Why?

Silent Letters

34. *No* silent letters are found in which of the following nonsense words?
    a) knip   b) gine   c) camb   d) wron   e) shan
35. *No* silent letters are in
    a) nade   b) fruting   c) kettin   d) foat   e) pnam

Terminology

36. A printed symbol made up of two letters representing one single phoneme or speech sound is a
    a) schwa   b) consonant blend   c) phonetic   d) digraph   e) diphthong
37. The smallest sound-bearing unit, or a basic sound of speech, is a
    a) phoneme   b) morpheme   c) grapheme   d) silent consonant   e) schwa
38. A study of all the speech sounds in language and how these sounds are produced is
    a) phonics   b) semantics   c) orthography   d) etymology   e) phonetics
39. The application of speech sounds to the teaching of reading letters or groups of letters is called
    a) phonics   b) phonemics   c) orthography   d) etymology   e) phonetics

40. The study of the nature and function of human language utilizing the methodology and objectivity of the scientist is
    a) phonetics b) phonology c) linguistics d) morphology e) semantics
41. The approach to beginning reading that selects words that have a consistent sound-symbol relationship (CVC) is the
    a) basal reader approach b) phonics approach
    c) linguistics approach d) language-experience approach e) initial teaching alphabet approach
42. The approach to beginning reading that uses a simpler, more reliable alphabet to make the decoding of English phonemes less complex is the
    a) basal reader approach b) phonetic approach
    c) linguistic approach d) language-experience approach
    e) initial teaching alphabet approach
43. A *phonic element* is similar to which word in linguistic terminology?
    a) syntax b) phoneme c) morpheme d) grapheme
    e) intonation
44. The study of structural analysis is similar to what element of linguistics?
    a) syntax b) phonology c) morphology d) graphology e) intonation

The Utility of Phonic Generalizations

In examining both words that are exceptions to the rules and words that conform to the rules, researchers have found a varying percentage of utility to the generalizations in items 45 through 48. How frequently does each hold true?

45. When there are two vowels side by side, the long sound of the first one is heard and the second is usually silent.
    a) 25% b) 45% c) 75% d) 90%
    e) 100% of the time
46. When there are two vowels, one of which is final *e*, the first vowel is long and the *e* is silent.
    a) 30% b) 60% c) 75% d) 90%
    e) 100%
47. When a vowel is in the middle of a one-syllable word, the vowel is short.
    a) 30% b) 50% c) 70% d) 90%
    e) 100%
48. When a word begins with *kn*, the *k* is silent.
    a) 30% b) 50% c) 70% d) 90%
    e) 100%
49. The first American educator to advocate the teaching of phonics as an aid to word recognition and pronunciation was
    a) Noah Webster in *The American Blueback Spelling Book,* 1790

b) William McGuffey in *McGuffey's Readers,* 1879
c) Leonard Bloomfield, *Language,* 1933
d) Rudolph Flesch in *Why Johnny Can't Read,* 1955
e) Charles Fries, *Linguistics and Reading,* 1963
50. Most reading authorities agree that
   a) the sight word method is the best way to teach reading
   b) the phonics method is the best way to teach reading
   c) structural or morphemic analysis is the best way to teach reading
   d) there is no *one* best way to teach reading

Read the following nonsense words, applying phonic generalizations to determine their appropriate pronunciations.

bongtrike	crangle
plignel	magsletting
abcealter	phister
conborvement	flabinstate
gingabution	craipthrusher
recentively	wonaprint
fudder	knidderflicing
gentropher	

Answers to Phonics Quiz

1. d
2. e
3. e
4. d
5. a
6. e
7. a
8. c
9. d
10. b
11. a
12. c
13. c: long vowel with silent *e*
14. e: with two vowels, first is long, second is silent
15. b: one-syllable ending in vowel is long
16. b
17. a
18. b
19. e
20. c: divide between two consonants
21. a: vowel, consonant, vowel
22. b: words ending in *le*— consonant precedes the *le*
23. b: consonant digraphs are not divided
24. c: prefix and suffix are separate syllables
25. a
26. c
27. b
28. e
29. a: accent first of two syllables
30. b: accent syllables before *tion* ending
31. b: accent syllable with two adjacent vowels
32. c: *y* at end of one syllable word has a long *i* sound
33. a: *y* at end of multisyllable word has long *e* sound
34. e
35. b
36. d
37. a
38. e
39. a
40. c
41. c
42. e
43. b
44. c
45. b
46. b
47. c
48. e
49. a
50. d

Rating Scale

Score		Rating
92–100	EXCELLENT	Congratulations! You do know your phonics.

84–92   GOOD A brief refresher will help, though.
76–84   FAIR Study with your favorite third grader.
68–76   POOR You could be a case of the blind leading the blind.

A Review of Common Phonics Generalizations

Consonants

Consonants are the letters in the alphabet that are not vowels.
Consonant speech sounds are formed by modifying or altering
or obstructing the stream of vocal sound with the organs of
speech. These obstructions may be stops, fricatives, or res-
onants. Consonant sounds are relatively consistent and have
a regular grapheme-phoneme relationship. They include:
b, d, f, h, j, k, l, m, n, p, r, s, t, v, w, y (initial position).

Consonants c and g

Hard *c*: pronounced like *k* when followed by *a, o, u,* (cup,
cat).
Soft *c*: pronounced like *s* when followed by *i, e, y* (city,
cent).
Hard *g*: when followed by *a, o, u* (go, gay).
Soft *g*: when followed by *i, e, y,* sounds like *j* (gentle, gyp).

Consonant Blends

A combination of two or three consonant letters blended in
such a way that each letter in the blend keeps its own identity:
*bl, sl, cl, fl, gl, pl, br, cr, dr, fr, gr, pr, tr, sc, sk, sl, sw, sn, sp,
sm, spl, spr, str, scr, ng, nk, tw, dw.*

Consonant Digraphs

A combination of two consonant letters representing one
phoneme or speech sound that is not a blend of the two
letters: *sh, ch, wh, ck, ph, gh, th.*

Silent Consonants

Silent consonants are those consonants which, when combined
with specific other letters, are not pronounced. In the examples below, the silent consonants are the ones enclosed
in parentheses, and the letters shown with them are the specific
letters that cause them to be silent in combination. (There
are exceptions, however.)

i(gh)	sight, bright
m(b)	comb, lamb
(w)r	wren, wrong
(k)n	knew, knife
s(t)	listen, hasten
f(t)	often, soften

Vowels

The vowels of the alphabet are the letters *a, e, i, o, u,* and sometimes *y.* The vowel speech sounds are produced in the resonance chamber formed by the stream of air passing through in the oral cavity.

Short vowels: a, e, i, o, u, (sometimes y). A single vowel in a medial position usually has the short vowel sound: consonant, vowel, consonant (CVC). A diacritical mark called a *breve* ˘ may indicate the short vowel: *păt, săd, lĕd, sĭt, pŏt, cŭp, gўp.*

Long vowels: a, e, i, o, u, (sometimes y). The long vowel sounds the same as the alphabet letter name of the vowel. It is indicated with the diacritical mark ē called a *macron: gō, cāke, ēel, īce, nō, ūniform, crў.*

Double Vowels: Vowel Digraph

Frequently, when two vowels are adjacent, the first vowel has the long sound while the second is silent. Recent research has shown this generalization to hold true about 45 percent of the time: *tie, coat, rain, eat, pay.*

Final e

In words with a vowel-consonant-e pattern (VCe), the vowel frequently has the long sound while the *e* is silent. Research has shown this generalization to hold true about 60 percent of the time: *make, Pete, slide, hope, cube.*

Vowels Modified by r

Vowels followed by the letter *r* are neither long nor short, but the sound is modified by the letter *r.* This holds true about 85 percent of the time: *star, her, stir, horn, fur.*

Diphthongs

Two adjacent printed symbols representing two vowels, each of which contributes to a blended speech sound: *joy, toil, cow, house, few.*

Schwa Sound

This is the vowel sound in an unaccented syllable and is indicated with the symbol ə: *balloon, eaten, beautify, button, circus.*

Number of Syllables

There are as many syllables in a word as there are vowel sounds heard: *bruise* (one syllable), *beautiful* (three syllables).

Two Consonants (VC-CV)

If the initial vowel is followed by two consonants, divide the word between the two consonants. This rule holds true about 80 percent of the time: *con-tact, let-ter, mar-ket.*

Single Consonant (V-CV)

If the initial vowel is followed by one consonant, the consonant usually begins the second syllable. There are many exceptions to this rule. The generalization holds true about 50 percent of the time: *mo-tor, na-tion, stu-dent.*

Consonant-Le (C-le) Endings

If a word ends in *le*, the consonant preceding the *le* begins the last syllable. This generalization holds true about 95 percent of the time: *ta-ble, pur-ple, han-dle.*

Consonant Blends and Consonant Digraphs

Consonant blends and digraphs are not divided in separating a word into syllables. This holds true 100 percent of the time: *teach-er, graph-ic, de-scribe.*

Prefixes and Suffixes

Prefixes and suffixes usually form a separate syllable: *re-plac-ing, dis-appoint-ment.*

Suffix -ed

If the suffix *-ed* is preceded by *d* or *t*, it does form a separate syllable and is pronounced *-ed*. If the suffix *-ed* is not preceded by a *d* or *t*, it does not form a separate syllable. It is pronounced like *t* when it follows an unvoiced consonant, and it is pronounced like *d* when it follows a voiced consonant: *sanded (ed), patted (ed), asked (t), pushed (t), tamed (d), crazed (d).*

Open and Closed Syllables

Syllables that end with a consonant are closed syllables and the vowel is short: *can-*vass.

Syllables that end with a vowel are open syllables and the vowel is long: *ba-*by.

The y *Sound in One-Syllable Words*
and Multisyllable Words

When the *y* is the final sound in a one-syllable word, it usually has the sound of a long *i*: *cry, my, ply*.

When the *y* is the final sound of a multisyllable word, it usually has the long *e* sound: *funny, lady*.

Accent

When there is no other clue in a two-syllable word, the accent frequently falls on the first syllable. This generalization is true about 80 percent of the time: *pen'cil, sau'cer*.

In inflected or derived forms of words, the primary accent usually falls on or within the root word: *fix'es, un touched'*.

Two vowels together in the last syllable of a word gives a clue to an accented final syllable: *re main', re peal'*.

If two identical consonants are in a word, the syllable before the double consonant is usually accented: *big'ger, hal'low ed*.

The primary accent usually falls on the syllable preceding the suffixes *-ion, -ity, -ic, -ical, -ian, -ial, -ious*: *at ten' tion, hys ter' ical, bar bar' ian, bil' ious*.

Appendix B   Materials

Materials for Teaching Beginning Reading

Reading Readiness Skills

Auditory Perception Training. Developmental Learning Materials. A multimedia kit (cassette, spirit masters, etc.) for teaching auditory perception.

Dandy Dog's Early Learning Program. American Book Company. A readiness program.

Developing Learning Readiness Program. McGraw-Hill/ Webster Division. A motor and perceptual development program.

Children's World. Holt, Rinehart and Winston. A kit of multisensory materials for readiness.

Early Childhood Discovery Materials. Macmillan. Materials for readiness.

Early Learning. McGraw-Hill/Early Learning. Materials for readiness, beginning reading, and language.

Distar Language I and II. Science Research Associates. A program designed to teach basic language concepts and build vocabulary and communication skills.

The Fitzhugh PLUS Program. Allied Education Council. Perceptual training, spatial organization books for reading and arithmetic.

The Frostig Program for the Development of Visual Perception. Follett. Workbooks for training visual perception.

Goal Language Development Game. Milton Bradley. Games for developing language and psycholinguistic skills.

I Can Do It. Mafex Associates. Visual-motor activities.

The Language and Thinking Program. Follett. Materials to develop language and cognitive skills.

The MWM Program for Developing Language Abilities. Educational Performance Associates. A kit of remedial materials based on language disabilities as diagnosed by the *ITPA* (ages 3–11).

Matrix Games Package. Appleton-Century-Crofts. Games for readiness.

Peabody Language Development Kits. American Guidance Service. Kits of puppets, pictures, and lesson plans to develop oral language skills.

Semel Auditory Processing Program. Follett. A program for remediating deficits in auditory comprehension skills.

Sound-Order-Sense. Follett. A program to develop auditory perception abilities.

Phonics and Word Analysis

Conquests in Reading. Webster. Review of phonics and word attack skills, (4–6).

Decoding for Reading. Macmillan. Audiovisual program for older nonreaders.

Developmental and Remedial Reading Materials. Educator's Publishing Service.

Distar Reading I and II. Science Research Associates. Program to teach beginning reading; emphasis on cracking the code, (K–2).

Dr. Spello. McGraw-Hill/Webster Division. Phonics and spelling book, (4–8).

Durrell-Murphy Phonics Practice Program. Harcourt Brace Jovanovich. Self-directing phonics picture cards.

Edmark Reading Program. Edmark Associates. A programmed approach designed for students with extremely limited skills; teaches a 150-word vocabulary.

First Experiences with Consonants. First Experiences with Vowels. Instructo Corp. Materials to teach consonants and vowels.

Get Set Games. Houghton Mifflin. Games to teach decoding skills.

Ginn Word Enrichment Program. Ginn. Seven workbooks for word recognition skills.

Intersensory Reading Method. Book-Lab, Inc. Beginning phonics: books, cards, materials.

i/t/a Early-to-Read Program revised. Initial Teaching Alphabet. Uses i/t/a as a medium for beginning reading.

The Landon Phonics Program. Chandler. A phonics series.

Language Experiences in Reading Program. Encyclopaedia Britannica Education Corp. Language experience approach to beginning reading.

Lift-Off to Reading. Science Research Associates. A programmed beginning reading approach.

Macmillan Reading Spectrum. Macmillan. Six levels of word analysis, (4–6).

Merrill Linguistic Readers. Merrill. A linguistic-approach basal reader.

Michigan Language Program. Learning Research Associates. Individualized program for beginning reading books for listening, reading words, word attack and comprehension.

Mott Basic Language Skills Program. Allied Education Council. Reading program for adolescents. Levels 1–3, levels 4–6. Text-workbooks.

Open Court Correlated Language Arts Program. Open Court Publishing Co. Basal reader series stressing phonics.

The Palo Alto Reading Program: Sequential Steps in Reading. Harcourt Brace Jovanovich. A programmed and linguistic approach to beginning reading.

Peabody Rebus Reading Program. American Guidance Service. The use of rebus pictures for teaching beginning reading.

Phonetic Keys to Reading. Economy Company. A phonic approach to beginning reading. Books, cards, charts, (1–4).

Phonics Skill Builders. McCormick-Mathers. Set of six workbooks for teaching phonics skills, (1–6).

Phonics We Use. Lyons and Carnahan. A series of phonics workbooks, (1–8).

The Phonovisual Method. Phonovisual Products. A series of books, charts, manuals, and cards for teaching phonics, (primary).

Programmed Reading. McGraw-Hill. Twenty-one books of programmed instruction in reading.

The Reading Experience and Development Series (READ). American Book Co.

Reading Helper Books. Book-Lab, Inc. Five activities books for beginning reading, (K–2).

Reading in High Gear. Science Research Associates. A programmed reading program for adolescent nonreaders.

Reading with Phonics. Lippincott. Workbooks and phonics cards for teaching phonics skills, (primary).

Remedial Reading Drills (Hegge, Kirk, Kirk). George Wahr Publishing Co. Exercises to develop skills in phonics and word recognition, (1–3).

Speech-to-Print Phonics. Harcourt Brace Jovanovich. Cards and manual for developing phonics skills.

SRA Reading Program. Science Research Associates. A basal reading series with a linguistic emphasis, (1–6).

Structural Reading Program. L. W. Singer Co. A structured basal program with emphasis on phonics, (prereading 2).

Sullivan Remedial Reading Program. Behavioral Research Laboratories. Series of programmed workbooks.

Weekly Reading Practice Books. American Guidance Service. Beginning reading phonics program.

Wenkart Phonics Readers. Wenkart Publishing Co. A set of readers with a phonics emphasis.

Word Attack Series. Teachers College Press. Three workbooks to teach word-analysis skills.

Wordland Series. Continental Press. A phonics program on reprinted ditto masters.

Words in Color. Xerox Education Division. Use of color to teach initial reading.

Write and See. Appleton-Century-Crofts, New Century Publications. Self-correcting phonics materials with reappearing ink process, (1–4).

Reading Comprehension

Be a Better Reader, Foundations. Prentice-Hall. Designed for practice in reading in content areas, (4–6).

Developmental Reading Text-Workbooks. Bobbs-Merrill. Six workbooks to give training and practice in several programs in reading, (K–6).

Diagnostic Reading Workbooks Series. Charles E. Merrill. Workbooks designed for developmental or remedial programs in reading, (K–6).

Gates-Peardon Reading Exercises. Teachers College Press. Reading exercises to develop the ability to read for general significance, to predict outcomes, to understand directions, to note details.

New Practice Readers. McGraw-Hill/Webster Division. Reading selections and questions designed to improve comprehension skills in reading, (2–8).

New Reading Skilltext Series. Charles E. Merrill. Reading comprehension workbooks, (1–6).

Reading Skills Builders. Reader's Digest Services. Magazine format with short reading selections and accompanying comprehension skills, (1–8).

Reading Success Series. My Weekly Reader. Scholastic Magazine and Book Service. Six booklets of high-interest level to teach basic reading skills.

Reading Thinking Skills. Continental Press. Preprinted masters for liquid duplicating, (PP–6).

Specific Skills Series. Barnell-Loft. Exercise booklets designed for practice in specific reading comprehension skills: locating the answer, following directions, using the context, getting the facts, working with sound, drawing conclusions, getting the main idea, (1–8).

SRA Reading Laboratory. Science Research Associates. Boxed materials consisting of multilevel and color-cued reading matter and answer keys. Reading rate and comprehension, (1–12).

Standard Test Lessons in Reading (McCall-Crabbs). Teachers College Press. Paperback booklets with short reading selections and comprehension questions, (3–7).

Materials for Teaching Advanced Reading

Materials to Develop Comprehension

Action Reading System and *Double Action*. Scholastic Book Services. Reading levels 2.0–5.0. Kit of reading material for secondary school students who are seriously behind in reading.

Activity-Concept English (ACE). Scott, Foresman. A kit of many reading components for students deficient in language skills.

Activities of Reading Improvement. Steck-Vaughn. Three workbooks of specific reading skills for junior high students.

Advanced Reading Skills. Reader's Digest. Magazine format of short stories, (R.L. 4–8).

Basic Reading Skills for Junior High School Use. Scott, Foresman. Workbook for developing reading skills. Designed for remedial reading pupils at junior high level.

Be a Better Reader. Prentice-Hall. Reading improvement in the content areas, (4–6 and junior high).

Breakthrough. Allyn & Bacon. Stories especially designed for the problem reader; stories of mature interest but low reading level.

Building Reading Skills in the Content Areas. Educational Activities. Cassettes for subject areas of geography, history, science, and mathematics, (R.L. 2–6).

Classroom Reading Clinic. McGraw-Hill/Webster Division. A variety of reading materials. Elementary reading level. Skill building and high-interest, low-vocabulary books.

The Clues Program. Clues Magazines. Educational Progress. *Clues Magazines,* instructional tapes. (R.L. 2–6; interest level, grade 5 and up.)

Contact. Scholastic. Series of anthologies for secondary students at the 4–6 reading level. Designed to motivate the hard-to-reach student.

Developing Reading Efficiency. Burgess. A workbook for junior-high level containing lessons for a variety of reading skills.

Developmental Reading Text Workbooks. Bobbs-Merrill, (R.L. 1–6).

Diagnostic Reading Workbooks Series. Charles E. Merrill. R.L. 1–6 for remedial reading programs.

Directions. Houghton Mifflin. Short anthologies, reading skill booklets, for the reluctant reader.

Effective Reading. Globe Book. Exercises and materials for levels 4–8.

Gaining Independence in Reading. Charles E. Merrill. Three hard-covered textbooks, (4–12).

Gates-Peardon Reading Exercises. Teachers College Press. Reading exercises to develop the ability to read for general significance, to predict outcomes, to understand directions, and to note details, (3–6).

Improve Your Reading Ability. Charles E. Merrill. Text-workbook for developing comprehension skills and rate. Intermediate difficulty level.

McCall-Crabbs Standard Test Lessons in Reading. Teachers College Press. Paperback booklets with short reading selections and comprehension questions, (3–7).

New Goals in Reading. Steck-Vaughn. Reading workbooks, (4–6).

New Practice Readers. McGraw-Hill/Webster Division. Reading selections and questions designed to improve comprehension skills in reading, (2–8).

Open Highways Program. Scott, Foresman. Basal reading series for poor readers at secondary level, reading 3–4 years below grade level.

Reading Developmental Kits. Addison-Wesley. Boxed kits of cards that can be used for junior and senior high levels, (primary–10).

Reading Essential Series. Steck-Vaughn. (1–8).

Reading for Concepts. McGraw-Hill. Series of books for reading for concepts, (R.L. 1.6–8.9).

Reading for Meaning Series. Lippincott. A series of workbooks designed to improve comprehension skills, vocabulary, central thought, details, organization, and summarization, (4–6 and 7–10).

Reading for Understanding. Science Research Associates. Boxed multilevel selections graduated in difficulty. Designed to develop comprehension skills, (5–12).

Reading Improvement Material. Reader's Digest Services. Workbooks for reading improvement at advanced levels, (7–10).

Reading Skills Builders. Reader's Digest. Magazine format with short reading selections and accompanying comprehension questions, (1–8).

The Reading Skills Lab Program. Houghton Mifflin. Nine workbooks to teach specific comprehension skills, (4–6).

Reading Spectrum. Macmillan. Variety of individualized supplementary materials for skills and recreational reading, (junior high).

Read-Understand-Remember Books. Allied Education Council. For developing understanding and retention. Self-correction, (R.L. 2.7–7.2).

Remediation Reading (RR). Modern Curriculum Press. Word-recognition skills workbook designed for older student.

SCOPE/Skills and SCOPE/Visuals. Scholastic. Series of high-interest/low-reading-level skills workbooks, 4–6.

SCORE. Scholastic. Weekly news magazine for grades 8–12, (R.L. 4–6).

Specific Reading Skills. Jones-Kenilworth. Wordbuilding, comprehension, critical and creative reading, (PP–8.5).

Specific Skills Series. Barnell-Loft. Exercise books designed for practice in specific reading comprehension skills, locating the answer, following directions, using the context, getting the facts, working with sound, drawing conclusions, getting the main idea, (1–8).

SRA Reading Laboratory. Science Research Associates. Boxed materials consisting of multilevel reading matter. Comprehension questions and rate improvement materials, (1–12; kit 3a for 7–9).

Step Up Your Reading Power. McGraw-Hill/Webster Division. Five workbooks for remedial secondary school level; six fact questions and two thought questions after each selection.

Study Skills Library. Educational Developmental Laboratories, Division of McGraw-Hill. Reading skills focusing on content subjects. Material is boxed by subject area and difficulty level, (4–9).

Study Type Reading Exercises. Teachers College Press. Reading exercises at the secondary level, (high school).

The Thinking Box. Benefic Press. Designed to develop critical thinking skills. Boxed material, individualized to teach twelve thinking skills, (upper intermediate to junior high).

High-Interest, Low-Vocabulary Reading Materials

Many books are written specifically for poor readers. They are books with a relatively easy vocabulary and style but with an interest level that would maintain the interest of the older reader. It is important for the teacher to find books with subject matter that interests the older reader yet is easy enough for the slow or disabled reader. The following books are designed for this purpose. Descriptive material on easy-reading-level materials with more mature interest can be obtained from the publishers. Estimated reading level and interest level are shown.

Publisher	Title	Reading Grade Level	Interest Grade Level
Allyn & Bacon	*Breakthrough Series*	1–6	7–12
Benefic Press	*Animal Adventure Series*	PP–1	1–4
	Butternut Bill Series	PP–1	1–6
	Button Family Adventures	PP–3	1–3
	Cowboys of Many Races	PP–5	1–6
	Cowboy Sam Series	PP–3	1–6
	Dan Frontier Series	PP–4	1–7
	Mystery Adventure Series	2–6	4–9
	Moonbeam Series	PP–3	1–6
	Racine Wheels Series	2–4	4–9
	Sailor Jack Series	PP–3	1–6
	Space-Age Books	1–3	3–6
	Space Science Fiction	2–6	4–9
	Sports Mystery Stories	2–4	4–9
	What Is It Series	1–4	1–8
	World of Adventure	2–6	4–9
Book-Lab	*The Hip Reader*	PP–3	4–9
	Young Adult Sequential Reading Action Program	6	6–9
Bobbs-Merrill	*Childhood of Famous Americans*	4–5	4–9
Children's Press	*About Books*	1–4	2–8
	Fun to Read Classics	5–8	5–12
	The Frontiers of America Series	3	3–8
	I Want To Be Series	2–4	4–6
	Rally Series	4–5	7–10
	True Book Series	2–3	3–6
John Day Publishing	*Reading Fundamentals for Teenagers*	3–4	6–8
	Let's Visit Series	4–7	7–10
Doubleday	*Signal Books*	4	5–9
Field Educational Publications	*Americans All Series*	4	3–9
	Checkered Flag Series	2–4	6–12
	Deep Sea Adventures	2–5	3–11
	Jim Forest Readers	1–3	1–7
	The Morgan Bay Mysteries	2–4	4–11
	The Reading-Motivated Series	4–5	4–10
Fearon Publishers	*Pacemaker Classics*	2	7–12
	Pacemaker True Adventures	2	5–12
	Pacemaker Story Books	2	7–12
Finney Co.	*Finding Your Job*	2–5	4–10
Follett	*Interesting Reading Series*	2–3	7–12
	Turner Career Guidance Series	5–6	8–10
	Turner-Livingston Communication Series	5–6	11–12
	Turner-Livingston Reading Series	4–6	7–9
	Vocational Reading Series	4–6	9–12

Publisher	Title	Reading Grade Level	Interest Grade Level
Frank Richards	*The Getting Along Series*	3–5	4–8
	Getting and Holding a Job	3–5	4–10
Garrard Publishing	*American Folktales*	3–4	2–6
	Basic Vocabulary Series	1–2	1–4
	Discovery Books	2–3	2–5
	Junior Science Books	4–5	6–9
	Folklore of the World Series	3–4	2–8
	First Reading Books	1–2	1–4
	Myths, Tales, and Legends	5	4–7
	Pleasure Reading Series	4–5	3–7
	Regional American Stories	4	3–6
	Sports	4	3–6
Globe Book	*Stories for Teenagers*	6	6–12
Grosset & Dunlap	*We Were There Series*	4–7	7–9
	How and Why Wonder Books	4–7	7–9
E. M. Hale	*Getting to Know Books*	4–5	4–9
	How and Why Series	4–5	4–9
	Story Of Series	3–4	3–9
Harper & Row	*American Adventure Series*	3–6	4–8
Harr Wagner	*Jim Forest Readers*	3–6	4–8
	Reading Motivated Series	2–6	3–8
	Deep Sea Adventure Series	4–8	5–10
	Wildlife Adventure Series	4–6	5–10
	Morgan Bay Mysteries	4–6	5–10
D. C. Heath	*Teen-Age Tales*	4–6	6–11
	Reading Caravan Series	3–6	5–10
Longmans, Roberts & Green	*Tempo Books*	7–8	9–11
Mafex Associates	*Magpie Series*	1–3	4–8
	Target Series	2–4	4–9
	Citizens All	1–3	4–8
William Morrow	*Morrow's High Interest/ Easy Reading Books*	1–8	4–10
Oxford University Press	*Wildrush Books*	3–4	5–9
Pyramid Books	*Hi-Lo Reading Series*	3–8	5–12
Random House	*All About Books*	4–6	4–11
	Gateway Books	2–3	3–8
	Landmark Books	5–7	5–11
	Step-up Books	2–3	3–9
	World Landmark Books	5–6	5–11
Reader's Digest Services	*Reading Skill Builders*	1–4	2–5
	Adult Readers for Slow Learners	3–7	4–10
Scholastic Magazine and Book Services	*Action Libraries*	2–3	4–7

Publisher	Title	Reading Grade Level	Interest Grade Level
Steck-Vaughn	*Reading Essential Series*	1–8	4–10
	Read Better With Jim		
	King Series	2–8	4–10
Watts Franklin	*First Book Series*	4–7	7–9
	Let's Find Out Series	2–4	5–6
Xerox Educational Publications	*Know Your World*	3–5	4–8

Appendix C   Tests

The purpose of this appendix is to serve as a reference for widely used tests. Most of the tests have been mentioned elsewhere in this book. Descriptive information about each test, such as the age of the subject, time required, whether it is a group or individual test, who can administer it, and so on, is given in this appendix. However, the descriptive material is very brief and not designed to be evaluative. Detailed descriptions and critical evaluation of tests can be obtained from the *Mental Measurement Yearbook,* O. K. Buros, editor (1975), Gryphon Press (see Appendix D for address). The book is available in reference libraries.

The reader is also referred to articles on tests of factors that inhibit learning to read by Mavrogenes, Hanson, and Winkley (1976) and by Harris and Sipay (1975).

Test publisher appears after the test name: each publisher's address is listed in Appendix D.

In this appendix, tests are grouped as follows:

1. Tests of Intelligence or Potential for Learning
2. Tests of Visual Acuity
3. Tests of Auditory Acuity
4. Motor Development Tests
5. Tests of Mental Processing
6. Visual Perception Tests
7. Auditory Perception Tests
8. Speech and Language Tests
9. Reading Tests: Survey
10. Reading Tests: Diagnostic
11. Reading Tests: Criterion-referenced

Tests of Intelligence or Potential for Learning

Tests of intelligence assess the child's capacity or potential for learning. Some of these tests must be given by trained examiners; others can be administered by the clinician or teacher.

Goodenough-Harris Drawing Test. Harcourt Brace Jovanovich.
Ages: 3–15. *Time:* ten to fifteen minutes. Individual or group. Administered by a person with some training. Provides a score of nonverbal intelligence obtained through an objective scoring of a child's drawing of a human figure.

Peabody Picture Vocabulary Test. American Guidance Service.
Ages: 2–8. *Time:* fifteen minutes. Individual. An individually administered test of receptive language vocabulary and intelligence.

Slosson Intelligence Test. Slosson Educational Publications.
Ages: 4 and up. *Time:* twenty to thirty minutes. Group or individual. Administered by classroom teacher or clinician. Brief test of verbal intelligence.

Stanford-Binet Intelligence Scale. Houghton Mifflin.
Ages: 2 to adult. *Time:* one hour. Individual. Administered by trained examiner or psychologist. Test of general intelligence.

Wechsler Intelligence Scale for Children—Revised (WISC-R). Psychological Corporation.
Ages: 5–15. *Time:* one hour. Individual. Administered by trained examiner or psychologist. Test of general intelligence; giving scores for Verbal IQ, Performance IQ, and Full IQ.

Tests of Visual Acuity

These tests evaluate the child's ability to see clearly. They screen for near- and far-point acuity as well as binocular vision. They are used as visual screening tests by the trained diagnostician or school nurse. If visual difficulties are found, the child should be referred to an eye care specialist.

Keystone Visual Survey. Telebinocular. Keystone View Co.
Ages: 5 and up. *Time:* four to eight minutes. Individual test. Administered by person with some training.

Ortho-Rater. Bausch and Lomb.
Ages: 5 and up. *Time:* six to eight minutes. Individual test. Administered by person with some training.

School Vision Tester. Bausch and Lomb.
Ages: Grade K and up. *Time:* two to three minutes. Individual test. Administered by person with some training.

Titmus Vision Test. Titmus Optical Co.
Ages: 3 and up. *Time:* two to five minutes. Individual test. Layman can administer.

The audiometer is used to screen for hearing loss. An audiogram is obtained to indicate hearing in terms of frequency and intensity. Several manufacturers of audiometers are: Audivox, Belltone, Maico, and Zenith. *Ages:* Grade K and up. *Time:* ten to twenty minutes for screening. Individual and some group tests. Administered by clinician who has had training in the use of the audiometer, speech pathologist, or school nurse.

Motor Development Tests

Lincoln-Oseretsky Motor Development Scale. C. H. Stoelting Co.
Ages: 6–14. *Time:* thirty to sixty minutes. Individual test. Administered by clinician. Assesses a variety of motor skills.

Oseretsky Tests of Motor Proficiency. American Guidance Service.
Ages: 4–16. *Time:* twenty to thirty minutes. Individual test. Administered by clinician. Measures gross and fine motor skills according to a developmental scale.

Purdue Perceptual-Motor Survey. Charles E. Merrill.
Ages: 6–10. *Time:* twenty to thirty minutes. Individual test. Administered by clinician.

Southern California Sensory Integration Tests. Western Psychological Service.
A battery consisting of the following separate tests: Southern California Kinesthesia and Tactile Perception Test, Southern California Motor Accuracy Test, Southern California Perceptual-Motor Tests, Figure-Ground Visual Perception Tests, Ayres Space Test, Position in Space, Design Copying.
Ages: 3–10. *Time:* varying, running from five to sixty minutes for each test. Individual or group test. Administered by trained clinician.

Tests of Mental Processing

Detroit Tests of Learning Aptitude. Bobbs-Merrill.
Ages: 3–adult. *Time:* variable dependent upon subtests given. Individual test. Administered by trained clinician. There are nineteen subtests of various areas of general mental processing.

Illinois Test of Psycholinguistic Abilities. University of Illinois Press.
Ages: 2½–10. *Time:* variable, dependent upon subtests given; full test, about ninety minutes. Individual test. Administered by trained clinician. Twelve subtests of various areas of mental processing.

Screening Tests for Identifying Children with Specific Language Disability (Slingerland). Educator's Publishing Service.
Ages: Grades one to two, two to three, three to four, and five to six. *Time:* sixty minutes. Individual or group test. Administered by classroom teacher or clinician. Tests visual copying, memory, and discrimination; three auditory group tests, one individual auditory test.

Search. Walker Educational Book Corp.
Ages: 5–6. *Time:* twenty minutes. Individual test. Administered by classroom teacher or specialist. Ten subtests— visual perception, auditory perception, body image.

Tests of Visual Perception

Bender Gestalt Test. Western Psychological Services.
Ages: 4–10. *Time:* ten minutes. Individual test. For the Developmental Scoring system, see E. Koppitz, *Bender Gestalt Test for Young Children,* New York: Grune & Stratton, 1963. Developmental Koppitz scoring can be done by a trained clinician. Other scoring systems for mental dysfunction and projective scoring can be done by a psychologist. A test of copying designs.

Benton Visual Retention Test. Psychological Corporation.
Ages: 6 and up. *Time:* five to ten minutes. Individual test. Administered by trained clinician. To assess memory of visual designs.

Developmental Test of Visual-Motor Integration (Beery-Buktenica). Follett.
Ages: 2–15. *Time:* ten minutes. Individual or group test. Administered by clinician or classroom teacher. A test of copying designs.

Marianne Frostig Test of Visual Perception. Consulting Psychological Press.
Ages: 3–8. *Time:* thirty to sixty minutes. Individual or group test. Administered by trained clinician. Consists of five subtests of visual perception: eye-motor coordination, figure-ground, constancy of shape, position in space, spatial relationships.

Perceptual Forms Test. Winter Haven Lions Research
Foundation.
Ages: 5–8. *Time:* ten minutes. Group or individual test.
Administered by classroom teacher or clinician.

Tests of Auditory Perception

Goldman-Fristoe-Woodcock Auditory Skills Test Battery.
American Guidance Service.
Ages: 3–8 and up. *Time:* ten to fifteen minutes for each test.
Individual test. Administered by clinician. Consists of
twelve tests and five kits: auditory selective attention test,
diagnostic auditory discrimination tests, parts I, II, and III,
auditory memory tests, and sound-symbol tests.

*Goldman-Fristoe-Woodcock Test of Auditory Discrimina-
tion*. American Guidance Service.
Ages: 4 and up. *Time:* fifteen to twenty minutes. Individual test. Administered by clinician. Test of ability to discriminate speech sounds in quiet and in noise.

Wepman Auditory Discrimination Test. Language Research Associates.
Ages: 5 and up. *Time:* five to ten minutes. Individual test.
Administered by clinician. Test of ability to hear single
phoneme differences in words.

Speech and Language Tests

The tests listed in this section assess speech and language.
Speech is examined with the articulation tests; language
ability, with the language tests. In analyzing the reading difficulty, the child's language skills are a very important factor
to consider.

Articulation

Goldman-Fristoe Test of Articulation. American Guidance
Service.
Ages: 2 and up. *Time:* ten minutes. Individual test. Administered by speech clinician. Articulation of speech
sounds.

Templin-Darley Test of Articulation. University of Iowa,
Bureau of Education Research and Service.
Ages: 3 and up. *Time:* five to fifteen minutes for screening;
twenty to forty minutes for total diagnosis. Individual.
Administered by speech clinician. Articulation of speech
sounds.

Carrow Elicited Language Inventory. Learning Concepts.
Ages: 3–8. *Time:* five minutes. Individual test. Administered by trained person or speech clinician. The child imi-
tates a sequence of sentences.

Developmental Sentences Analysis. Northwestern University
Press.
Ages: 3–7. *Time:* one or more hours. Individual test.
Administered by speech clinician or trained person. A
corpus of the child's utterances are taped and then analyzed.

Houston Test of Language Development. Houston Test Co.
Ages: 6 months to 6 years. *Time:* thirty minutes. Individual
test. Administered by clinician. Measures comprehension
and use of language.

Northwestern Syntax Screening Test. Northwestern University Press.
Ages: 3–8. *Time:* fifteen to twenty minutes. Individual
test. Administered by trained person or speech and language clinician. Measures receptive and expressive syntac-
tical structures (comprehension and formulation of basic
sentence structures, transformations, and morphological
forms).

Picture Story Language Test. Grune & Stratton.
Ages: 7–17. *Time:* fifteen to thirty minutes. Individual test.
Administered by clinician. Measures written language skills
in terms of productivity of words and sentences, syntax,
and abstract-concrete scores.

Test for Auditory Comprehension of Language (Carrow).
Learning Concepts.
Ages: 3–6. *Time:* five to twenty minutes. Individual test.
Administered by clinician. Measures receptive language in
the areas of vocabulary, morphology, and syntax.

Utah Test of Language Development. Communication
Research Associates.
Ages: 1½–14½. *Time:* thirty to forty-five minutes. Individual test. Administered by person with some training.
Measures expressive and receptive language skills of children, including sequencing, reproducing figures, verbal
repetition, and so on.

Reading Tests: Survey

Reading tests are classified into three groups in this listing:
survey reading tests, diagnostic reading tests, and criterion-
referenced reading tests. Tests most frequently used are described in this section. The purpose of the survey reading
achievement test is to give the teacher an idea of the level at

which the child is reading. Most survey tests require about forty-five minutes to one hour to administer.

California Reading Tests. California Test Bureau/McGraw-Hill.
Ages: Level 1, grades one to two; *Level 2,* grades two to four; *Level 3,* grades four to six; *Level 4,* grades six to nine; *Level 5,* grades nine to twelve. Tests vocabulary and comprehension (Levels 1 and 2 also test word attack). Group test. Administered by classroom teacher.

Gates-MacGinitie Reading Tests. Teachers College Press.
Ages: Primary A, grade one; *Primary B,* grade two; *Primary C,* grade three. Each contains two parts: vocabulary and comprehension. *Primary CS,* speed and accuracy for grades two, three; *Survey D,* grades four to six; *Survey E,* grades seven to nine; *Survey F,* grades ten to twelve. Each survey test contains subtests of vocabulary, comprehension, speed and accuracy. Group test. Administered by classroom teacher.

Metropolitan Reading Tests. Harcourt Brace Jovanovich.
Ages: Primer, grades K.7–1.4 (listening for sounds, word knowledge, comprehension); *Primary I,* grades 1.5–2.4; *Primary II,* grades 2.5–3.4 (word knowledge, word analysis, comprehension). *Elementary,* grades 3.5–4.9; *Intermediate,* grades 5–6.9; *Advanced,* grades 7–9.5 (word knowledge, comprehension). Group test. Administered by classroom teacher.

Peabody Individual Achievement Test (PIAT). American Guidance Service.
Ages: Kindergarten through adult. Reading is included in two of the five subtests: mathematics, reading recognition, reading comprehension, spelling, general information. Individual test. Administered by clinician.

SRA Assessment Survey: Reading. Science Research Associates.
Ages: Primary I, grades 1–2.5; *Primary II,* grades 2.5–3; *Multilevel Blue,* grades 4–5; *Multilevel Green,* grades 6–7; *Multilevel Red,* grades 8–9.5. Vocabulary and comprehension subtests. Group test. Administered by classroom teacher.

Stanford Reading Tests. Harcourt Brace Jovanovich.
Ages: Primary I, grades 1.5–2.4; *Primary II,* grades 2.5–3.4; *Primary III,* grades 3.5–4.4; *Intermediate I,* grades 4.5–5.4; *Intermediate II,* grades 5.5–6.9 (vocabulary, reading, comprehension, and word-study skills subtests); *Advanced,* grades 7–9.5 (vocabulary and reading comprehension). Group test. Administered by classroom teacher.

Wide Range Achievement Test (WRAT). Guidance Associates of Delaware.

Ages: Level I, 5–12; *Level II,* 5–adult. *Time:* Brief tests (fifteen minutes) of word recognition, spelling, and arithmetic computation. Individual test. Administered by clinician.

Reading Tests: Diagnostic

The following group of tests gives more analytic information than the survey tests. They measure a variety of specific reading skills. The time required will vary depending on the number of subtests given.

Botel Reading Inventory. Follett.
Ages: grades one to twelve. Consists of several subtests to determine reading instructional levels. Tests of phonics, word recognition, word opposites reading, and word opposites listening. Group test. Administered by clinician or teacher.

Doren Diagnostic Reading Test. American Guidance Service.
Ages: grades two to eight. Test of word-attack skills including beginning sounds, sight words, rhyming, whole-word recognition, words within words, speech consonants, blending, vowels, ending sounds, discriminate guessing, letter recognition, and spelling. Group test. Administered by clinician, reading specialist.

Durrell Analysis of Reading Difficulty. Harcourt Brace Jovanovich.
Ages: nonreaders to students in grade six and older. Three levels of reading: nonreader, primary grade, intermediate grade. A battery of diagnostic subtests of oral reading, silent reading, listening comprehension, word recognition and word analysis, visual memory of word forms, auditory analysis of word elements, spelling, handwriting. Checklists of errors. Individual test. Administered by reading specialist or trained clinician.

Gates-McKillop Reading Diagnostic Test. Teachers College Press.
Ages: nonreaders and up. A complete battery of diagnostic reading tests. The subtests include oral reading (accompanied by an analysis of errors in reading words), words (flash presentation and untimed presentation), phrases (flash presentation), knowledge of word parts (recognizing and blending word parts, letter sounds, naming capital and lower-case letters), recognizing the visual form of sounds (nonsense words, initial letters, final letters, vowels), auditory blending, and supplementary tests (spelling, oral vocabulary, syllabication, auditory discrimination). Individual test. Administered by reading specialist or trained clinician.

Gilmore Oral Reading Test. Harcourt Brace Jovanovich.
Ages: grades one to eight. Test of oral reading. Scores for
accuracy, comprehension, and rate. Individual test. Administered by clinician.

Gray Oral Reading Tests. Bobbs-Merrill.
Thirteen oral reading passages. Accuracy and rate in a
combined score. Individual test. Administered by reading
specialist or trained clinician.

Group Diagnostic Reading Aptitude and Achievement Tests
(Monroe-Sherman). Nevins Printing Co.
Ages: grades three to nine. Battery of diagnostic tests including: *Part I. Achievement Tests:* Paragraph Understanding, Reading Speed, Word Discrimination; Consonants; Reversals; Reading Additions and Omissions; Arithmetic Computation; Spelling. *Part II. Aptitude Tests:* Visual Tests (letter memory and form memory); Auditory Tests
(letter memory and discrimination and orientation); Motor
Tests (copying and crossing out letters); Language Tests
(vocabulary). Group or individual test. Administered by
reading specialist or trained clinician.

Spache Diagnostic Reading Scales. California Test Bureau/
McGraw-Hill.
Ages: grades 1.5–8; disabled readers, grades nine to twelve.
Battery of tests including three word lists, twenty-two
graded reading passages, and eight supplementary phonics
tests. Reading passages give instructional, independent, and
potential reading levels. Individual test. Administered by
reading specialist or trained clinician.

Stanford Diagnostic Reading Test. Harcourt Brace Jovano-
vich.
Ages: Level I, grades 2.5–4.5; *Level II,* grades 4.5–8.5.
Separate measures of comprehension, vocabulary, syllabica-
tion, auditory skills, phonic analysis, and rate. Group test.
Administered by clinician or teacher.

Woodcock Reading Mastery Tests. American Guidance
Service.
Ages: K–12. Five subtests of reading: letter identification,
word identification, word attack, word comprehension,
passage comprehension. Scores are given in two ways: grade
level and mastery level (criterion-referenced). Individual
test. Administered by trained clinician.

Reading Tests: Criterion-Referenced

The following group of tests provides information about the
pupil's reading in terms of mastery levels of specific skills
(rather than grade level). They are referred to as criterion-
referenced tests because progress is measured in terms of

specific skills criteria. A number of commercial publishers have tests and materials that fit in this category. They are designed for regular classroom use to monitor growth of all pupils but are also useful for problem readers. The specific sequence of skills as well as the number of skills tested differs in each of these programs.

Croft In-Service Reading Program. Croft Educational Services.

Fountain Valley Teacher Support System in Reading. Richard L. Zweig.

Individual Pupil Monitoring System—Reading. Houghton Mifflin.

Prescriptive Reading Inventory. California Test Bureau/ McGraw-Hill.

Read-On. Random House.

Skills Monitoring System—Reading. Harcourt Brace Jovanovich.

Wisconsin Design for Reading Skills Development. National Computer System.

Appendix D   Addresses of Publishers

The following list contains, in alphabetical order, the names and addresses of the publishers and manufacturers of materials mentioned elsewhere in this book, as well as some producers of materials that were not mentioned. The purpose of this listing is to provide a convenient directory for the reader. The rapidity of changes in names and addresses makes it inevitable that some of the entries below will become out of date during the life of this textbook.

Academic Therapy Publications, 1539 Fourth St., San Rafael, Calif. 94901

Adapt Press, Inc., 808 West Avenue North, Sioux Falls, S.D. 57104

Addison-Wesley Publishing Co., 2725 Sand Hill Rd., Menlo Park, Calif. 94025

Allied Education Council, P.O. Box 78, Galien, Mich. 49113

Allyn & Bacon, 470 Atlantic Ave., Boston, Mass. 02210

American Book Co., 450 W. 33 St., New York, N.Y. 10001

American Education Publications, 245 Long Hill Rd., Middletown, Conn. 06457

American Guidance Associates, 1526 Gilpin Ave., Wilmington, Del. 19899

American Guidance Service, Inc. (AGS), Publishers' Building, Circle Pines, Minn. 55014

American Speech and Hearing Association, 9030 Old Georgetown Rd., Washington, D.C. 20014

Ann Arbor Publishers, P.O. Box 338, Worthington, Ohio 43085

Appleton-Century-Crofts, 440 Park Avenue South, New York, N.Y. 10016

Arrow Book Club (Scholastic Book Services), 50 West 44 St., New York, N.Y. 10036

Association for Childhood International, 3615 Wisconsin Ave. N.W., Washington, D.C. 20036

Baldridge Reading Instructional Materials, 14 Grigg St., Greenwich, Conn. 06830

Bantam Books, Inc., 666 Fifth Ave., New York, N.Y. 10019

Barnell-Loft, 958 Church St., Baldwin, N.Y. 11510

Basic Books, Inc., 10 E. 53 St., New York, N.Y. 10022

Bausch & Lomb Optical Co., Rochester, N.Y. 14602

Beckley-Cardy, 1900 N. Narragansett, Chicago, Ill. 60639

Behavioral Research Laboratories, P.O. Box 577, Palo Alto, Calif. 94302

Bell and Howell, 7100 McCormick Rd., Chicago, Ill. 60645

Benefic Press, 10300 W. Roosevelt Rd., Westchester, Ill. 60153

Bobbs-Merrill Co., 4300 W. 62 St., Indianapolis, Ind. 46206

Book-Lab, Inc., 1449 37 St., Brooklyn, N.Y. 11218

Borg-Warner Educational Systems, 7450 N. Natchez Ave., Niles, Ill. 60648

Bowmar, Box 3623, Glendale, Calif. 91201

William C. Brown Co., 2460 Kerper Blvd., Dubuque, Iowa 52001

Burgess Publishing, 7108 Olms Lane, Minneapolis, Minn. 55435

California Test Bureau, A Division of McGraw-Hill, Del Monte Research Park, Monterey, Calif. 93940

Center for Applied Linguistics, 1717 Massachusetts Ave. N.W., Washington, D.C. 20036

Children's Press, 1224 West Van Buren St., Chicago, Ill. 60607

Communication Research Associates, P.O. Box 11012, Salt Lake City, Utah 84111

Consulting Psychologists Press, 577 College Ave., Palo Alto, Calif. 94306

Continental Press, Inc., Elizabethtown, Pa. 17022

Council for Exceptional Children, 1920 Association Dr., Reston, Va. 22091

Craig Corp., 921 W. Artesia Blvd., Compton, Calif. 90220

Creative Playthings, Inc., Edinburg Rd., Cranbury, N.J. 08540

Creative Publications, P.O. Box 10328, Palo Alto, Calif. 94303

Crippled Children and Adults of Rhode Island, The Meeting Street School, 33 Grotto Ave., Providence, R.I. 02901

Cuisenaire Company of America, Inc., 12 Church St., New Rochelle, N.Y. 10885

The John Day Co., 666 5th Ave., New York, N.Y. 10019

Developmental Learning Materials, 7440 N. Natchez Ave., Niles, Ill. 60648

Devereau Foundation, Devon, Pa. 19333

Dexter & Westbrook, Ltd., 958 Church St., Rockville Centre, N.Y. 11510

DIAL, Inc., Box 911, Highland Park, Ill. 60035

Doubleday & Co., Garden City, N.Y. 11530

The Economy Company, 1901 N. Walnut Ave., Oklahoma City, Okla. 74103

Easier-to-Learn Materials, Box 329, Garden City, N.Y. 11530

Edmark Associates, 655 S. Orcas St., Seattle, Wash. 98108

Educational Activities, Inc., 1937 Grand Ave., Baldwin, N.Y. 11520

Educational Development Laboratories, A Division of McGraw-Hill, 1221 Avenue of the Americas, New York, N.Y. 10020

Educational Performance Associates, 563 Westview Ave., Ridgefield, N.J. 07657

Educational Progress Corp., P.O. Box 4563, Tulsa, Okla. 74145

Educational Service, Inc., P.O. Box 219, Stevensville, Mich. 49127

Educational Teaching Aids Division, A. Daigger & Co., 159 W. Kinzie St., Chicago, Ill. 60610

Educational Testing Service, Princeton, N.J. 08540

Educator's Publishing Service, 75 Moulton St., Cambridge, Mass. 02138

Edukaid of Ridgewood, 1250 E. Ridgewood Ave., Ridgewood, N.J. 07450

Electronic Future, Inc., 57 Dodge Ave., North Haven, Conn. 06473

Encyclopaedia Britannica Educational Corp., 425 N. Michigan Ave., Chicago, Ill. 60611

Essay Press, Box 5, Planetarium Station, New York, N.Y. 10024

Fearon Publishers, 6 Davis Dr., Belmont, Calif. 94002

Field Educational Publications, Inc., 2400 Hanover St., Palo Alto, Calif. 94002

Finney Co., 3350 Gorham Ave., Minneapolis, Minn. 55426

Follett Educational Corp., 1010 W. Washington Blvd., Chicago, Ill. 60607

Frank Richards Pub., Inc., 330 1st St., Box 370, Liverpool, N.Y. 13088

Alvyn M. Freed, 391 Munroe St., Sacramento, Calif. 95825

Garrard Publishing Co., 1607 N. Market St., Champaign, Ill. 61820

General Learning Corp., 250 James St., Morristown, N.J. 07960

Ginn & Co., 191 Spring St., Lexington, Mass. 02173

Globe Book Co., 175 Fifth Ave., New York, N.Y. 10010

Grosset & Dunlap, Inc., 51 Madison Ave., New York, N.Y. 10010

Grune & Stratton, 111 Fifth Ave., New York, N.Y. 10003

Gryphon Press, 220 Montgomery St., Highland Park, N.J. 08904

Guidance Associates, 1526 Gilpin Ave., Wilmington, Del. 19800

E. M. Hale & Co., 1201 S. Hastings Way, Eau Claire, Wisc. 54701

C. S. Hammond & Co., 515 Valley St., Maplewood, N.J. 07040

Harcourt Brace Jovanovich, Inc., 757 Third Ave., New York, N.Y. 10017

Harper & Row Publishers, Inc., 10 East 53 St., New York, N.Y. 10022

D. C. Heath & Co., 125 Spring St., Lexington, Mass. 02173

Marshall S. Hiskey, 5640 Baldwin, Lincoln, Neb. 68507

Hoffman Information Systems, Inc., 5632 Peck Rd., Arcadia, Calif. 91006

Holt, Rinehart and Winston, Inc., 383 Madison Ave., New York, N.Y. 10017

Houghton Mifflin Co., One Beacon St., Boston, Mass. 02107

Houston Press, University of Houston, Houston, Tex. 77000

Ideal School Supply Co., 11000 South Lavergne, Oak Lawn, Ill. 60453

Initial Teaching Alphabet Publications, Inc., 6 E. 43 St., New York, N.Y. 10017

Instructional Industries, Inc., Executive Park, Ballston Lake, N.Y. 12019

Instructo Corp., 200 Cedar Hollow Rd., Paoli, Pa. 19301

The Instructor Publications, 7 Bank St., Dansville, N.Y. 14437

International Reading Association, 800 Barksdale Rd., Newark, Del. 19711

Jones-Kenilworth Co., 8301 Ambassador Row, Dallas, Tex. 75247

Journal of Learning Disabilities, 101 East Ontario St., Chicago, Ill. 60611

Journal of Special Education, 111 Fifth Ave., New York, N.Y. 10003

The Judy Co., 310 N. Second St., Minneapolis, Minn. 55401

Kenworthy Educational Service, P.O. Box 3031, 138 Allen St., Buffalo, N.Y. 14201

Keystone View Co., 2212 E. 12 St., Davenport, Iowa 52803

Laidlaw Bros., Thatcher & Madison Sts., River Forest, Ill. 60305

Language Research Associates, Box 95, 950 E. 59 St., Chicago, Ill. 60637

Learning Concepts, 2501 N. Lamar, Austin, Tex. 78705

Learning Corporation of America, 1350 Avenue of the Americas, New York, N.Y. 10019

Learning Research Associates, 1501 Broadway, New York, N.Y. 10036

Learning Resource Division, EDL, 202 Miriam Dr., Lakeland, Fla. 33803

Learning Through Seeing, LTS Bldg., Box 368, Sunland, Calif. 91040

J. P. Lippincott Co., E. Washington Square, Philadelphia, Pa. 19105

Longmans, Roberts, and Green, Burnt Mill, Harlow, Essex, England

Love Publishing Co., 6635 E. Villanova Pl., Denver, Colo. 80222

Lyons and Carnahan Educational Publishers, 407 E. 25 St., Chicago, Ill. 60616

The Macmillan Co., 866 Third Ave., New York, N.Y. 10022

Mafex Associates, Inc., 111 Barron Ave., Johnstown, Pa. 16906

McCormick-Mathers Publishing Co., 450 W. 33rd St., New York, N.Y. 10001

McGraw-Hill Book Co., 1221 Avenue of the Americas, New York, N.Y. 10020

McGraw-Hill/Early Learning, Paoli, Pa. 19301

David McKay Co., 750 Third Ave., New York, N.Y. 10017

Charles E. Merrill, 1300 Alum Creek Dr., Columbus, Ohio 43216

Milton Bradley Co., 74 Park St., Springfield, Mass. 01101

Modern Curriculum Press, 13900 Prospect Rd., Cleveland, Ohio 44136

William C. Morrow, 105 Madison Ave., New York, N.Y. 10016

The C. V. Mosby Co., 11830 Westline Industrial Dr., St. Louis, Mo. 63141

Motivational Research Inc., P.O. Box 140, McLean, Va. 22101

National Council of Teachers of English, 1111 Kenyon Rd., Urbana, Ill. 61801

National Education Association Publications, 1201 16 St. N.W., Washington, D.C. 20036

National Reading Conference, Inc., Reading Center, Marquette University, Milwaukee, Wisc. 53233

New Readers Press, Box 131, Syracuse, N.Y. 13210

New York Association for Brain Injured Children, 305 Broadway, New York, N.Y. 10007

Noble & Noble, Publishers, 1 Dag Hammarskjold Plaza, New York, N.Y. 10017

Northwestern University Press, 1735 Benson Ave., Evanston, Ill. 60201

Open Court Publishing Co., Box 599, 1039 Eighth St., LaSalle, Ill. 61301

Orton Society, 8415 Bellona Lane, Towson, Md. 21204

F. A. Owen Publishing Co., 7 Bank St., Dansville, N.Y. 14437

Oxford U. Press, 200 Madison Ave., New York, N.Y. 10016

Peek Publications, P.O. Box 11065, Palo Alto, Calif. 94303

Perceptual Development Laboratories, 6767 Southwest Ave., St. Louis, Mo. 63143

Phonovisual Products, 12216 Parklawn Dr., Rockville, Md. 20852

Prentice-Hall, Inc., Englewood Cliffs, N.J. 07632

J. A. Preston Corp., 71 Fifth Ave., New York, N.Y. 10003

Priority Innovations, P.O. Box 792, Skokie, Ill. 60076

The Psychological Corp., 304 E. 45 St., New York, N.Y. 10017

Psychological Test Specialists, Box 1441, Missoula, Mont. 59801

Psychotechnics, 1900 Pickwick Ave., Glenview, Ill. 60025

G. P. Putnam Sons, 200 Madison Ave., New York, N.Y. 10016

Pyramid Books, 919 Third Ave., New York, N.Y., 10016

Rand McNally & Co., P.O. Box 7600, Chicago, Ill. 60680

Random House, 201 E. 50 St., New York, N.Y. 10022

Reader's Digest Services, Educational Division, Pleasantville, N.Y. 10570

Rheem Califone, 5922 Bancroft St., Los Angeles, Calif. 90016

Scholastic Magazine and Book Services, 50 W. 44 St., New York, N.Y. 10036

Science Research Associates, 259 E. Erie St., Chicago, Ill. 60611

Scott, Foresman and Co., 1900 East Lake Ave., Glenview, Ill. 60025

Silver Burdett Co., A Division of General Learning Corp., 250 James St., Morristown, N.J. 07960

The L. W. Singer Co., A Division of Random House, 201 E. 50 St., New York, N.Y. 10022

Sullivan Associates, Webster Division, McGraw-Hill Book Co., New York, N.Y. 10022

Slosson Educational Publications, 140 Pine St., East Aurora, N.Y. 14052

Society for Visual Education, 1356 Diversey Parkway, Chicago, Ill. 60614

Special Child Publications, 4635 Union Bay Place N.E., Seattle, Wash. 98105

Steck-Vaughn Co., Box 2028, Austin, Tex. 78767

C. H. Stoelting Co., 424 N. Homan Ave., Chicago, Ill. 60624

Teachers College Press, Teachers College, Columbia University, 1234 Amsterdam Ave., New York, N.Y. 10027

Teachers Publishing Corp., 22 W. Putnam Ave., Greenwich, Conn. 06830

Teaching Aids, 159 W. Kinzie St., Chicago, Ill. 60610

Teaching Resources Corp., 100 Boylston St., Boston, Mass. 02116

Teaching Technology Corp., 7471 Greenbush Ave., North Hollywood, Calif. 91609

Charles C. Thomas Publisher, 301–27 E. Lawrence Ave., Springfield, Ill. 62717

3 M Visual Products, 3 M Center, St. Paul, Minn. 55101

Tweedy Transparencies, 207 Hollywood Ave., East Orange, N.J. 07018

United States Department of Health, Education and Welfare, Washington, D.C. 20025

United States Government Printing Office, Superintendent of Documents, Washington, D.C. 20025

University of Chicago Press, 5801 Ellis Ave., Chicago, Ill. 60637

University of Illinois Press, Urbana, Ill. 61801

George Wahr Publishing Co., 316 State St., Ann Arbor, Mich. 41808

Walker Educational Book Corp., 720 Fifth Ave., New York, N.Y. 10019

Watts Franklin, Inc., 845 3rd Ave., New York, N.Y. 10022

Webster, 1221 Avenue of the Americas, New York, N.Y. 10020

Webster Division, McGraw-Hill, Manchester Rd., Manchester, Mo. 63011

Weekly Reader Paperback Book Club, American Education Publications, A Xerox Company, 55 High St., Middletown, Conn. 06457

Wenkart Publishing Co., 4 Shady Hill Square, Cambridge, Mass. 02138

Western Psychological Services, 12031 Wilshire Blvd., Los Angeles, Calif. 90025

Western Publishing Education Services, 1220 Mound Ave., Racine, Wisc. 53404

Westinghouse Learning Corp., P.O. Box 30, Iowa City, Iowa 52240

Wheeler Press, 17 Ferguson Rd., Warren, N.J. 07060

Wheeler Publishing Co., 10 E. 53 St., New York, N.Y. 10022

John Wiley & Sons, 605 Third Ave., New York, N.Y. 10016

Winston Press, Inc., 25 Groveland Terrace, Minneapolis, Minn. 55403

Winter Haven Lions Research Foundation, Box 1112, Winter Haven, Fla. 33880

Xerox Education Publications, Education Center, Columbus, Ohio 43216

Zaner-Bloser Co., 612 North Park St., Columbus, Ohio 43215

Richard L. Zweig Associates, 20800 Beach Blvd., Huntington Beach, Calif. 92648

Glossary

Auditory Blending The ability to synthesize the phonemes of a word, when they are pronounced with separations between phonemes, so that the word can be recognized as a whole.

Auditory Closure The ability to form an entire word when only part of the word is heard.

Auditory Perception The ability to interpret or organize the sensory data received through the ear.

Basal Reader Approach A method of teaching reading in which instruction is given through the use of a series of basal readers. Sequence of skills, content, vocabulary, and activities is determined by the authors of the series. Teacher's manuals and children's activity books accompany the basal reading series.

Behavior Modification A technique of changing human behavior based on the theory of operant behavior and conditioning. Careful observation of events preceding and following the behavior in question is required. The environment is manipulated to reinforce the desired responses, thereby bringing about the desired change in behavior.

Borderline Child Child who is borderline in intellectual functioning, between the mentally retarded and average range. (IQ range of 68–85)

Body Image An awareness of one's own body and the relationship of the body parts to each other and to the outside environment.

Brain-injured Child A child who before, during, or after birth has received an injury to or suffered an infection of the brain. As a result of such organic impairment, there are disturbances that prevent or impede the normal learning process.

Cerebral Dominance The dominant control of an individual's activities by one hemisphere of the brain. In most individuals, the left side of the brain controls language function, and the left side is considered the dominant hemisphere.

Clinical Teaching An approach to teaching that attempts to tailor learning experiences to the unique needs of a particular child. Consideration is given to the child's individual ways of learning and processing information.

Closure The ability to recognize a whole or gestalt, especially when one or more parts of the whole are missing or when the continuity is interrupted by gaps.

Cloze Procedure   A technique used in testing, teaching reading comprehension, and determining readability. It involves deletion of words from the text and leaving blank spaces. Measurement is made by rating the number of blanks that can be filled correctly.

Code-Emphasis Approaches to Reading   Approaches that emphasize decoding the printed word or the sound-symbol relationship of the phonemes.

Cognition   The act or process of knowing. The various thinking skills and processes are considered cognitive skills.

Concept   An abstract idea generalized from particular instances.

Conceptual Disorders   A disturbance in the thinking process and in cognitive activities, or a disturbance in the ability to formulate concepts.

Context Clues   Recognizing a word in a sentence or paragraph from clues in the balance of the sentence or paragraph.

Correlates of Reading Failure   Factors that inhibit learning to read.

Criterion-Referenced Tests   Mastery tests in which achievement is determined by assessing the pupil's performance on an orderly sequence of specific skills.

Cross-Modality Perception   The neurological process of converting information received through one input modality to another system within the brain. The process is also referred to as *intersensory transfer, intermodal transfer,* and *transducing.*

Developmental Reading   The pattern and sequence of normal reading growth and development in a child in the learning-to-read process.

Diagnostic Teaching   Teaching a child in a way that provides diagnostic information about the student.

Diagnostic Reading Test   A test designed to give a detailed analysis of specific reading skills and difficulties.

Disabled Learners   Individuals whose learning pattern deviates from the norm to such a degree that it is difficult to acquire academic skills through ordinary classroom instruction.

Dyslexia   A disorder of children who, despite conventional classroom experience, fail to attain the skills of reading. The term is frequently used when neurological dysfunction is suspected as the cause of the reading disability.

Educability of Intelligence   Acceleration of child's mental maturity through home and school training.

Educable Mental Retardation   Condition of an individual whose IQ is in the range of 67 to 52. Similar to the term *mildly retarded* as it is used in the most recent definition of mental retardation.

Etiology   The cause or origin of a condition.

Fernald Method   The reading method developed by Grace Fernald, incorporating both language and tracing techniques in a multisensory procedure.

Frustration Reading Level The oral reading level that is too difficult for the individual.

Functional Literacy That level of reading ability that enables the individual to participate fully in our society.

Function Word See *Structural Words*.

Gillingham Method Method for teaching reading developed by Anna Gillingham; a multisensory alphabetic method.

Grapheme A written language symbol that represents an oral language code.

Hegge-Kirk-Kirk Remedial Reading Drills A method of teaching reading that incorporates phonics and principles of minimal change.

Hemispheric Dominance See *Cerebral Dominance*.

Hyperactivity An extreme amount of activity. Also, impulsive or driven activity.

Hyperkinesis Constant and excessive movement and motor activity.

Incidental Method Presentation of words and phrases in conversation relating to the immediate experiences of the child.

Independent Reading Level The oral reading level at which the student is able to read independently.

Individualized Reading The method of teaching reading that utilizes the child's interest; learning is structured through the child's own reading selections, using a variety of books. The teacher acts as a consultant, aide, and counselor.

Informal Reading Inventory A method of determining the child's reading level by judging oral reading of graded reading passages.

Initial Teaching Alphabet (i/t/a) A method of beginning reading instruction based on twenty-two characters representing the sounds of English.

Instructional Reading Level The oral reading level at which the pupil is able to read with some supportive instructional help from the teacher.

Interindividual Testing Testing that determines an individual's level of functioning compared with that of others of the same age.

Intraindividual Testing Testing that permits a comparison of the child's various abilities to one another rather than to other children of the same age.

Language Human communicative behavior, usually reflecting a particular linguistic system.

Language Disorder Atypical language patterns developed by children, despite the fact that they live in a standard English language environment.

Language Difference The language patterns of an individual that reflect the language of his or her environment, but are different from the standard English pattern of the school.

Language-Experience Method A method of teaching reading and other language skills, based on the experiences of children. The method frequently involves the generation of experienced-based materials that are dictated by the child, written down by the teacher, then used in class as the material for teaching reading.

Lateral Confusion   See *Mixed Laterality*.

Laterality   Involves the awareness of the two sides of one's body and the ability to identify them as left or right correctly.

Learning Disabilities (as defined by Congress in Public Law 94–142)   Those children who have a disorder in one or more of the basic psychological processes involved in understanding or in using language, spoken or written, which disorder may manifest itself in imperfect ability to listen, think, speak, read, write, spell, or do mathematical calculations. Such disorders include such conditions as perceptual handicaps, brain injury, minimal brain dysfunction, dyslexia, and developmental aphasia. Such term does not include children who have learning problems which are primarily the result of visual, hearing, or motor handicaps, of mental retardation, of emotional disturbance, or environmental, cultural, or economic disadvantage.

Least Restrictive Environment   To the maximum extent appropriate, handicapped children are to be educated with children who are not handicapped. Special classes, separate schooling, or other removal of handicapped children from the regular educational environment should occur only when the nature or severity of the handicap is such that education in regular classes with the use of supplementary aids and services cannot be achieved satisfactorily (from Public Law 94–142).

Lexical Words   Content words, class words. Words that have referential meaning, as opposed to words with relationship values (see *Structural Words*). Lexical words are roughly equivalent to verbs, nouns, adjectives, and adverbs.

Linguistics   The scientific study of the nature and function of human language.

Linguistic Method   A method of teaching reading based on helping children learn to "break the written language code."

Mainstreaming   Placing of children with handicaps in the regular education system, particularly in the regular classroom.

Maturational Lag   A slowness in certain specialized aspects of neurological development.

Meaning-Emphasis Approaches to Reading   The collection of reading methods that emphasize understanding and comprehension.

Memory   The ability to store and retrieve upon demand previously experienced sensations and perceptions, even when the stimulus that originally evoked them is no longer present. Also referred to as *imagery* and *recall*.

Mental Maturity   The overall intelligence level of the individual.

Mental Retardation   (a) Subaverage general intellectual functioning which originates during the developmental period and is associated with impairment in adaptive behavior (*AAMD Manual,* Heber, 1961, p. 3). (b) IQ 70 and below, significantly subaverage general intellectual functioning, existing concurrently with deficits in adaptive behavior, and manifested during the developmental period *(AAMD Manual,* Grossman, 1973, p. 5). IQs of 67 or less.

Mildly Retarded Individuals with subnormal mental development, IQ range of 67 to 52. (*a*) Minimal academic educability; (*b*) potential for social acceptance in community; (*c*) minimal occupational adequacy for self-support. This type of child is also referred to as *educable mentally retarded.*

Minimal Brain Dysfunction A mild or minimal neurological abnormality that causes learning difficulties in the child with near-average intelligence.

Mixed Laterality (Lateral Confusion) Tendency to perform some acts with a right preference and others with a left, or the shifting from right to left for certain activities.

Modality The pathways through which an individual receives information and thereby learns. The "modality concept" postulates that some individuals learn better through one modality than through another. For example, a child may receive data better through the visual modality than the auditory modality.

Moderately Retarded Individual whose IQ is in the range of 51 to 36. Not educable in the areas of academic achievement, ultimate social adjustment in the community, or independent occupational adjustment at adult level. The child can learn self-help skills, social adjustment in the family, economic usefulness in structured workshop setting. This type of child is sometimes referred to as *trainable mentally retarded.*

Neurological Impress Method A method of teaching reading by means of unison reading by student and instructor.

Norm-Referenced Tests Formal tests that have been standardized by administration to a large group of children.

Perception The process of organizing or interpreting the raw data obtained through the senses.

Phoneme The smallest unit of sound in any particular language.

Phonetics A study of all the speech sounds in language and how these sounds are produced.

Phonics The application of portions of phonetics to the teaching of reading in English. The establishment of the sound (or phoneme) of the language with the equivalent written symbol (or grapheme).

Phonology The linguistic system of speech sounds in a particular language.

Programmed Instruction A method of teaching reading that uses programmed self-instructional and self-corrective materials.

Psycholinguistics The field of study that blends aspects of two disciplines—psychology and linguistics—to examine the total picture of the language process.

Reading Comprehension The understanding of the meaning of what is read.

Reading Readiness The collection of integrated abilities,

traits, and skills that the child needs in order to learn the complex process called reading.

Rebus   Picture or symbol of a printed word.

Remedial Reading   Special reading methods used with the atypical learner.

Sensory-Motor   A term applied to the combination of the input of sensations and the output of motor activity. The motor activity reflects what is happening to the sensory organs such as the visual, auditory, tactual, and kinesthetic sensations.

Slow Learners   A generalized term referring to individuals who have a reduced rate of learning.

Soft Neurological Signs   Neurological abnormalities that are mild or slight and difficult to detect, as contrasted with the gross or obvious neurological abnormalities.

Standardized Tests   See *Norm-Referenced Tests.*

Structural Words   Function words, linguistic referents for words of a sentence that show the relationship between parts of the sentence, as opposed to content words. Structure words include these elements of traditional grammar: prepositions, conjunctions, modal and auxiliary verbs, and articles.

Syntax   The grammar system of a language. The linguistic rules of word order and the function of words in a sentence.

Trainable Mental Retardation   Condition of an individual with an IQ of less than 52. Similar to the term *moderately retarded* as it is used in the most recent definition of mental retardation.

VAKT Method   A multisensory approach to teaching reading: visual, auditory, kinesthetic, and tactile.

Vision   A variety of functions, including acuity and perception, dealing with the ability to see.

Visual-Motor Coordination   The ability to coordinate vision with the movements of the body or parts of the body.

Visual Perception   The identification, organization, and the interpretation of sensory data received by the individual through the eye.

References

Ahmann, J. Stanley. "An Exploration of Survival Levels of Achievement by Means of Assessment Techniques." In D. Nielsen and H. Hjelm, eds. *Reading and Career Education*. Newark, Del.: International Reading Association, 1975.

Ainsworth, S. H. *An Exploratory Study of Educational, Social, and Emotional Factors in the Education of Mentally Retarded Children in Georgia Public Schools.* U.S. Office of Education Research Program, Project No. 171. Athens, Ga.: University of Georgia, 1959.

Allen, Roach Van. "Three Approaches to Teaching Reading." *Proceedings of the International Reading Association,* 7 (1964), 153–54.

Allen, Roach Van. "How a Language Experience Program Works." In Elaine C. Vilscek, ed. *Decade of Innovations: Approaches to Beginning Reading.* Newark, Del.: International Reading Association, 1968, pp. 1–8.

Allen, Roach Van. *Language Experiences in Communication.* Boston: Houghton Mifflin Company, 1976.

Anastasi, Anne. *Psychological Testing.* New York: The Macmillan Co., 1975.

Anderson, R., and S. J. Samuels. "Relationship Between Visual Recognition, Memory, Paired-Associate Learning, and Reading." Paper presented at the meeting of the American Educational Research Association. Minneapolis, Minn., 1970.

Austin, Mary C. *The Torch Lighters: Tomorrow's Teachers of Reading.* Cambridge, Mass.: Harvard University Press, 1961.

Ayres, A. Jean. *Sensory Integration and Learning Disorders.* Los Angeles: Western Psychological Services, 1973.

Ayres, F. W., and Fernando Torres. "The Incidence of EEG Abnormalities in a Dyslexic and Control Group." *Journal of Clinical Psychology,* 23 (July 1967), 334–336.

Bailey, Mildred H. "The Utility of Phonic Generalizations in Grades One Through Six." *Reading Teacher,* 20 (February 1967), 413–418.

Baker, R. W., and T. O. Madell. "Continued Investigation of Susceptibility to Distraction in Academically Underachieving and Achieving Male College Students." *Journal of Educational Psychology,* 56 (October 1965), 254–258.

Bakwin, H. "Reading Disability in Twins." *Developmental Medicine and Child Neurology,* 5 (1973), 184–187.

Balow, Bruce, Rosalyn Rubin, and Martha J. Rosen. "Perinatal Events as Precursors of Reading Disability." *Reading Research Quarterly,* 11 (1975–1976), 36–71.

Bangs, Tina. *Language and Learning Disorders of the Pre-Academic Child.* New York: Appleton-Century-Crofts, 1968.

Barrett, Thomas C. "Visual Discrimination Tasks as Predictors of First Grade Reading Achievement." *Reading Teacher,* 18 (January 1965), 276–282.

Barsch, Ray H. *Achieving Perceptual-Motor Efficiency.* Vol. 1. Seattle: Special Child Publications, 1967.

Bateman, Barbara. "Efficacy of an Auditory and a Visual Method of First Grade Reading Instruction with Auditory and Visual Learners." In H. K. Smith, ed. *Perception and Reading,* pp. 105–111. Newark, Del.: International Reading Association, 1968.

Bateman, Barbara. "Implications of a Learning Disability Approach for Teaching Educable Retardates." In D. Hammill and N. Bartel, eds. *Educational Perspectives in Learning Disabilities,* pp. 293–296. New York: John Wiley & Sons, 1971.

Bateman, Barbara, and Jan Wetherell. "Psycholinguistic Aspects of Mental Retardation." *Mental Retardation,* 3 (April 1965), 8–13.

Becker, John T. "Language Experience Approach in a Job Corps Reading Lab." *Journal of Reading,* 13 (January 1970), 281–284, 319–321.

Becker, John T. "Language Experience Attack on Adolescent Illiteracy." *Journal of Reading,* 15 (November 1972), 115–119.

Becker, W. C., and S. E. Engelmann. *Technical Report, 1976–1.* Eugene, Oregon: University of Oregon, 1976.

Bender, Loretta. "Specific Reading Disability as a Maturational Lag." *Bulletin of the Orton Society,* 7 (January 1957), 9–18.

Bennett, Annette. "Reading Ability in Special Classes." *Journal of Educational Research,* 20 (April 1929), 236–238.

Bennett, Annette. *A Comparative Study of Subnormal Children in the Elementary Grades.* New York: Teachers College, Columbia University, Bureau of Publications, 1932.

Benton, Arthur L. "Dyslexia in Relation to Form Perception and Directional Sense." In J. Money, ed. *Reading Disability,* pp. 81–102. Baltimore: Johns Hopkins Press, 1962.

Benton, Arthur L., and Joseph W. Bird. "The EEG and Reading Disability." *American Journal of Orthopsychiatry,* 33 (April 1963), 529–531.

Berry, Mildred M. *Language Disorders in Children: The Basis and Diagnosis.* New York: Appleton-Century-Crofts, 1969.

Betts, Emmett A. *The Prevention and Correction of Reading Difficulties.* Evanston, Ill.: Row, Peterson and Co., 1936.

Betts, Emmett A. *Foundations of Reading Instruction.* New York: American Book Co., 1946.

Bijou, S. W. "Application of Operant Principles to the Teaching of Reading, Writing, and Arithmetic to Retarded Children." In *New Frontiers in Special Education.* Washington, D.C.: Council for Exceptional Children, 1965, pp. 1–5.

Blackman, L. S., and R. J. Capobianco. "An Evaluation of Programmed Instruction with the Mentally Retarded Utilizing Teaching Machines." *American Journal of Mental Deficiency,* 70 (September 1965), 262–269.

Blake, Kathryn, Ira Aaron, and Helen Westbrook. "Learning of Basal Reading Skills by Mentally Handicapped and Non-Mentally Handicapped Children." *Journal of Research and Development in Education,* 2 (Winter 1969), 1–138.

Blatt, B. "The Physical, Personality, and Academic Status of Children Who Are Mentally Retarded Attending Regular Classes." *American Journal of Mental Deficiency*, 62 (1958), 810–818.

Blau, H., and Harriet Blau. *A Theory of Learning to Read by 'Modality Blocking' or 'Non-Visual' AKT*. 1969.

Bliesmer, E. P. "Reading Abilities of Bright and Dull Children of Comparable Mental Ages." *Journal of Educational Psychology*, 45 (October 1954), 321–331.

Bloomer, R. H. "The Cloze Procedure as a Remedial Reading Exercise." *Journal of Developmental Reading*, 5 (Spring 1962), 173–181.

Bloomfield, Leonard, and C. L. Barnhart. *Let's Read, A Linguistic Approach*. Detroit: Wayne State University Press, 1961.

Bloomfield, Leonard, and C. L. Barnhart. *Let's Read*. Bronxville, N.Y.: C. L. Barnhart, Inc., 1963.

Bond, G. L. "Auditory and Speech Characteristics of Good and Poor Readers." *Teachers College Contributions to Education*, No. 954. New York: Columbia University, 1935.

Bond, Guy L., and Robert Dykstra. "The Cooperative Research Program in First Grade Reading Instruction." *Reading Research Quarterly*, 2 (Summer 1967), entire issue.

Bond, Guy L., and Miles A. Tinker. *Reading Difficulties: Their Diagnosis and Correction*. 2d ed. New York: Appleton-Century-Crofts, 1967.

Bonsall, C., and R. L. Donbush. "Visual Perception and Reading Ability." *Journal of Educational Psychology*, 60 (June 1969), 294–299.

Bormuth, John. "The Cloze Readability Procedure." *Elementary English*, 45 (April 1968), 429–436.

Botel, M. *How to Teach Reading*. Chicago: Follett Publishing Co., 1959.

Boyd, John E. "Teaching Children with Reading Problems." In D. Hammill and N. Bartel, eds. *Teaching Children with Learning and Behavior Problems*, pp. 15–60. Boston: Allyn & Bacon, Inc., 1975.

Bracht, G. H. "Experimental Factors Related to Aptitude-Treatment Interaction." *Review of Educational Research*, 40 (December 1970), 627–645.

Brewer, W. F. "Paired-Associate Learning of Dyslexic Children." Unpublished doctoral dissertation, University of Iowa, 1967.

Brown, Virginia. "Reading Instruction." *Exceptional Children*, 34 (November 1967), 197–199.

Burke, Carolyn, and Yetta Goodman. *Reading Miscue Inventory: Manual Procedure for Diagnosis and Evaluation*. London: Collier-MacMillan, 1972.

Burmeister, Lou D. "Usefulness of Phonic Generalizations," *Reading Teacher*, 21 (1968), 349–356.

Buros, Oscar K., ed. *Reading Tests and Reviews I*. Highland Park, N.J.: Gryphon Press, 1968.

Buros, Oscar K., ed. *Reading Tests and Reviews II*. Highland Park, N.J.: Gryphon Press, 1975.

Burt, C. *Mental and Scholastic Tests*. London: King, 1921.

Burt, C., and R. B. Lewis. "Teaching Backward Readers." *British Journal of Educational Psychology*, 16 (1946), 116–132.

Busby, W. A., and D. E. Hurd. "Relationship Between Auditory and Visual Perceptual Ability and Reading Achievement." Paper presented at the meeting of the American Educational Research Association, Chicago, 1968.

Capobianco, R. J., and D. Y. Miller. *Quantitative and Qualitative Analyses of Exogenous and Endogenous Children in Some Reading Processes.* U.S. Office of Education Cooperative Research Program. Syracuse, N.Y.: Syracuse University Research Institute, 1958.

Cassidy, V. M., and J. E. Stanton. *An Investigation of Factors Involved in the Educational Placement of Mentally Retarded Children: A Study of Differences Between Children in Special and Regular Classes in Ohio.* U.S. Office of Education Cooperative Research Project, No. 032. Syracuse, N.Y.: Syracuse University Research Institute, 1959.

Cawley, J. F. "Word Recognition Performance of Mentally Handicapped and Average Children: Implications for Classroom Diagnosis." *Mental Retardation,* 6 (June 1968), 28–31.

Cawley, J. F., H. A. Goodstein, and W. H. Burrow. *Reading and Psychomotor Disability Among Mentally Retarded and Average Children.* Storrs, Conn.: The University of Connecticut, 1968.

Cawley, J. F., H. A. Goodstein, and W. H. Burrow. *The Slow Learner and the Reading Problem.* Springfield, Ill.: Charles C Thomas, 1972.

Cegelka, Patricia, and Walter Cegelka. "A Review of Research: Reading and the Educable Mentally Handicapped." *Exceptional Children,* 37 (November 1970), 187–200.

Celebre, G. "Psycholinguistic Abilities and Oral Word Recognition Associated with Relative Level of Personality Adjustment in Primary School Age Children with Minimal Brain Dysfunction." Unpublished doctoral dissertation, Temple University, 1971.

Chalfant, James C., and Frank S. King. "An Approach to Operationalizing the Definition of Learning Disabilities." *Journal of Learning Disabilities,* 9 (April 1976), 228–243.

Chalfant, James C., and Margaret Scheffelin. *Central Processing Dysfunctions in Children: A Review of Research.* NINDS Monograph No. 9. Bethesda, Md.: U.S. Department of Health, Education, and Welfare, 1969.

Chall, Jeanne. *Learning to Read: The Great Debate.* New York: McGraw-Hill Book Co., 1967.

Chapman, Carrie S. "A Study of the Reading Ability of Special Class Pupils." Unpublished master's thesis, University of Oregon, 1939.

Chasnoff, R. E. *Comparison of the Initial Teaching Alphabet with the Traditional Alphabet in First-Grade Reading.* Report of Cooperative Research Project No. S210 of the U.S. Office of Education, 1965.

Clymer, Theodore L. "The Utility of Phonic Generalizations in the Primary Grades." *Reading Teacher,* 16 (January 1963), 252–258.

Clymer, Theodore L., et al. *Reading 720.* Lexington, Mass.: Ginn and Co., 1976.

Codebook Series. Philadelphia, Pa.: J. B. Lippincott Co., 1975.

Coghill, George E. *Anatomy and the Problem of Behaviour.* New York: The Macmillan Co., 1929.

Coleman, James S., et al. *Equality of Educational Opportunity.* Washington, D.C.: Government Printing Office, 1966.

Cowen, P. A. "Special Classes vs. Grade Group for Subnormal Pupils." *School and Society* 48 (1938), 27–28.

Cratty, Bryant. *Intelligence in Action.* Englewood Cliffs, N.J.: Prentice-Hall Inc., 1973.

Critchly, MacDonald. *Developmental Dyslexia.* Springfield, Ill.: Charles C Thomas, 1964.

Cronbach, L. J. "Beyond the Two Disciplines of Scientific Psychology." *American Psychologist,* 30 (1975), 116–127.

Curriculum Motivation Series. Chicago: Rand McNally & Co., 1972.

Daley, W., and R. Lee. "Reading Disabilities in a Group of Mentally Retarded Children." *Training School Bulletin,* 57 (November 1960), 85–93.

Dallman, M., Roger Rouche, L. Chang, and J. DeBoer. *The Teaching of Reading.* New York: Holt, Rinehart and Winston, Inc., 1974.

Davidson, Helen P. "An Experimental Study of Bright, Average, and Dull Children at the Four-Year Mental Level." *Genetic Psychology Monograph,* 9 (1931), 119–290.

Davis, Frank B. "Criterion-Referenced Testing: A Critique." In W. Blanton, R. Farr, and J. Tuinman, eds. *Measuring Reading Performance,* pp. 44–50. Newark, Del.: International Reading Association, 1974.

Davy, Ruth Ann. "Adaptation of Progressive Choice Method for Teaching Reading to Retarded Children." *American Journal of Mental Deficiency,* 67 (September 1962), 274–280.

Dechant, E. V. *Improving the Teaching of Reading.* 2d ed. Englewood Cliffs, N.J.: Prentice-Hall Inc., 1970.

Dobzhansky, T. *Evolution, Genetics, and Man.* N.Y.: John Wiley & Sons, 1955.

Dolch, Edward. *Problems in Reading.* Champaign, Ill.: Garrard Publishing Co., 1948.

Dolch, Edward. *The Psychology and Teaching of Reading.* Boston: Ginn and Co., 1931, 1951.

Downing, J. "E.S.N. School Teachers Assessment i/t/a." *Special Education,* 56 (1967), 12–16.

Dunn, Lloyd M. "A Comparison of the Reading Processes of Mentally Retarded and Normal Boys of the Same Mental Age." *Studies of Reading and Arithmetic in Mentally Retarded Boys.* Lafayette, Ind.: Society for Research in Child Development, Inc., 1956.

Dunn, Lloyd M. "Special Education for the Mildly Retarded—Is Much of It Justifiable?" In D. Hammill and N. Bartel, eds. *Educational Perspectives in Learning Disabilities,* pp. 231–250. New York: John Wiley & Sons, 1971.

Dunn, Lloyd M. "Special Education for the Mildly Retarded: Is It Justifiable?" *Exceptional Children,* 35 (September 1968), 5–22.

Durkin, Dolores. *Children Who Read Early.* New York: Teachers College Press, 1966.

Durkin, Dolores. *Teaching Young Children to Read.* Boston: Allyn & Bacon, Inc., 1972.

Durrell, Donald. *Improving Reading Instruction.* New York: Harcourt, Brace & World, Inc., 1956.

Dyer, Henry S. "Research Issues on Equality of Educational Opportunities: School Factors." *Harvard Education Review,* 38 (Winter
1968), 38–56.

Dykman, Roscoe A., Peggy T. Ackerman, Sam D. Clements, and John
Peters. "Specific Learning Disabilities: An Attentional Deficit
Syndrome." In H. Myklebust, ed. *Progress in Learning Disabilities,*
Vol. II, pp. 56–93. New York: Grune & Stratton, Inc., 1971.

Dykstra, R. "The Relationship Between Selected Reading Readiness
Measures of Auditory Discrimination and Reading Achievement at
the End of First Grade." Unpublished doctoral dissertation, University of Minnesota, 1962.

Dykstra, R. *The Cooperative Research Program in First Grade
Reading Instruction.* Minneapolis: University of Minnesota Press,
1967.

Early-to-Read, i/t/a Program, Book 4. *fiend a wae.* New York: Initial Teaching Alphabet Publications, Inc., 1966.

Edmark Associates. *Edmark Reading Program, Teacher's Guide.*
Seattle: Edmark Associates, 1972.

Elenbogen, M. L. "A Comparative Study of Some Aspects of Aca-
demic and Social Adjustment of Two Groups of Mentally Retarded
Children in Special Classes and in Regular Grades." *Dissertation
Abstracts,* 17 (1957), 2497.

Elkins, John. "Some Psycholinguistic Aspects of the Differential
Diagnosis of Reading Disability in Grades I and II." Unpublished
doctoral dissertation, University of Queensland, Australia, 1972.

Ellson, D. G., et al. "Programmed Teaching and Elementary Reading—A Progress Report." Paper presented at the Great Lakes
Regional Meeting of the American Association on Mental Deficiency, Indiana University, 1961.

Emans, Robert. "When Two Vowels Go Walking and Other Such
Things." *Reading Teacher,* 21 (December 1967), 262–269.

Engelmann, Siegfried. "Classroom Techniques: Teaching Reading to
Children with Low Mental Age." *Educational Training of the
Mentally Retarded,* 2 (January 1967), 77–127.

Engelmann, Siegfried, and E. C. Bruner. *Distar Reading: An Instructional System.* Chicago: Science Research Associates, 1969.

Ensminger, Eugene, and Margaret M. Sullivan. "Information-Processing Models Applied to Educating Handicapped Children." In
L. Mann and D. Sabatino, eds. *Second Review of Special Education,* pp. 51–78. New York: Grune & Stratton, Inc., 1974.

Farr, Roger. *Reading: What Can Be Measured?* Newark, Del.:
International Reading Association, 1969.

Federal Register. *Assistance to States for Education of Handicapped
Children,* Procedures for Evaluating Specific Learning Disabilities.
December 29, 1977.

Fernald, Grace. *Remedial Techniques in Basic School Subjects.*
New York: McGraw-Hill Book Co., 1943.

Flesch, Rudolf. *Why Johnny Can't Read.* New York: Harper and
Brothers, 1955.

Frey, R. M. "Reading Behavior of Public School Brain-Injured and
Non-Brain-Injured Children of Average and Retarded Mental
Development." Unpublished doctoral dissertation, University of
Illinois, 1961.

Fries, Charles C. *Linguistics and Reading.* New York: Holt, Rinehart and Winston, Inc., 1963.

Frostig, M. *Frostig Developmental Test of Visual Perception.* Palo Alto: Consulting Psychologist Press, 1961.

Frostig, M. "The Needs of Teachers for Specialized Information on Reading." In W. M. Cruickshank, ed. *The Teaching of Brain-Injured Children,* pp. 87–110. Syracuse, N.Y.: Syracuse University Press, 1966.

Frostig, M., et al. "A Developmental Test of Visual Perception for Evaluating Normal and Neurologically Handicapped Children." *Perceptual and Motor Skills,* 12 (December 1961), 383–394.

Fry, Edward. "Developing a Word List for Remedial Reading." *Elementary English,* 34 (November 1957), 456–458.

Gaier, Eugene L., and Mary Jeffrey Collier. "The Latency-Stage Story Preferences of American and Finnish Children." *Child Development,* 31 (September 1960), 431–451.

Gallagher, J. J. "The Future Special Education System." In E. Meyen, ed. *Conference on the Categorical/Non-categorical Issue in Special Education.* Columbia, Mo.: University of Missouri Press, 1971, pp. 1–13.

Gates, A. I. *Interest and Ability in Reading.* New York: The Macmillan Co., 1930.

Gates, A. I. "The Necessary Mental Age for Beginning Reading." *Elementary School Journal,* 37 (March 1937), 497–508.

Gates, A. I. "A Further Evaluation of Reading Readiness Tests." *Elementary School Journal,* 40 (April 1940), 577–591.

Gates, A. I. *The Improvement of Reading.* 3d ed. New York: The Macmillan Co., 1947.

Getman, Gerald. "Visualmotor Complex in the Acquisition of Learning Skills." In J. Helmuth, ed. *Learning Disorders,* Vol. 1, pp. 49–76. Seattle: Special Child Publications, 1965.

Gillespie, Patricia H., and Lowell Johnson. *Teaching Reading to the Mildly Retarded Child.* Columbus, Ohio: Charles E. Merrill Books, Inc., 1974.

Gillingham, Anna, and Bessie Stillman. *Remedial Teaching for Children with Specific Disability in Reading, Spelling, and Penmanship.* Cambridge, Mass.: Educator's Publishing Service, 1968.

Gillooly, W. B. "The Use of i/t/a in Special Education: A Critical Review." *Journal of Special Education,* 1 (1967), 127–134.

Glass, Gerald G. *Teaching Decoding as Separate from Reading.* Garden City, N.Y.: Adelphi University Press, 1973.

Glass, Gerald G., and Elizabeth H. Burton. "How Do They Decode? Verbalizations and Observed Behaviors of Successful Decoders." *Education,* 94 (September-October, 1973), 58–63.

Goddard, H. H. *Feeblemindedness: Its Causes and Consequences.* N.Y.: The Macmillan Co., 1916.

Goins, J. T. *Visual Perceptual Abilities and Early Reading Progress.* Supplementary Educational Monographs, No. 87. Chicago: University of Chicago Press, 1958.

Goldmark, B. "The Relation of Visual Perception, Auditory Perception, and One Aspect of Conceptualization to Word Recognition." Unpublished doctoral dissertation, University of Arizona, 1964.

Goldstein, H., J. W. Moss, and Laura J. Jordan. *The Efficacy of Special Class Training on the Development of Mentally Retarded Children.* U.S. Office of Education Cooperative Research Project No. 619. Urbana, Ill.: University of Illinois, 1965.

Goodman, Kenneth. "A Linguistic Study of Cues and Miscues in Reading." *Elementary English Review,* 42 (1965), 639–643.

Goodman, Kenneth. "Analysis of Oral Reading Miscues." *Reading Research Quarterly,* 5 (Fall 1969), 9–30.

Goodman, Yetta. "Reading Diagnosis—Qualitative and Quantitative." *The Reading Teacher,* 25 (1972), 32–37.

Gove, Mary K. "Using the Cloze Procedure in a First Grade Classroom." *The Reading Teacher,* 29 (October 1975), 36–38.

Grossman, H., ed. *Manual on Terminology and Classification of Mental Retardation.* Washington, D.C.: American Association on Mental Deficiency, 1973.

Guszak, Frank J. *Diagnostic Reading Instruction in the Elementary School.* New York: Harper & Row, 1972.

Hallahan, D., and J. Kauffman. *Introduction to Learning Disabilities.* Englewood Cliffs, N.J.: Prentice-Hall, Inc., 1976.

Hallgren, B. "Specific Dyslexia: A Clinical and Genetic Study." *Acta Psychiatrica Neurologia,* Supplement 65 (1950).

Hammill, Donald, and N. Bartell. *Teaching Children with Learning and Behavior Problems.* Boston: Allyn & Bacon, Inc., 1975.

Hammill, Donald D., and Stephen C. Larsen. "Relationship of Selected Auditory Perceptual Skills and Reading Ability." *Journal of Learning Disabilities,* 7 (August/September 1974a), 282–291.

Hammill, Donald D., and Stephen C. Larsen. "The Effectiveness of Psycholinguistic Training." *Exceptional Children,* 41 (September 1974b), 5–15.

Hammill, Donald D., and J. Lee Wiederholt. "Review of the Frostig Visual Perception Test and Related Training Program." In L. Mann and D. Sabatino, eds. *First Review of Special Education,* pp. 33–48. New York: Grune & Stratton, Inc., 1973.

Harrington, M., and D. D. Durrell. "Mental Maturity vs. Perceptual Ability in Primary Reading." *Journal of Educational Psychology,* 46 (March 1955), 131–138.

Harris, Albert. *How to Increase Reading Ability.* 4th ed. New York: David McKay, 1961; 5th ed., 1970.

Harris, Albert, and Edward Sipay. *How to Increase Reading Ability.* 6th ed. New York: David McKay Co., Inc., 1975.

Hartlage, Lawrence C., and Joseph Green. "EEG Differences in Children's Reading, Spelling and Arithmetic Abilities." *Perceptual and Motor Skills,* 32 (February 1971) 133–134.

Hayes, R. B., and J. Nemeth. *An Attempt to Secure Additional Evidence Concerning Factors Affecting Learning to Read.* Report of Cooperative Research Project No. 2697. Washington, D.C.: U.S. Office of Education, 1966.

Heber, R. F. *A Manual on Terminology and Classification in Mental Retardation.* 64 Monograph Supplement. *American Journal of Mental Deficiency,* 1959; rev. ed., 1961.

Heber, Rick, H. Barber, S. Harrington, C. Hoffman, and C. Fallander. "Rehabilitation of Families at RISK for Mental Retardation." *Rehabilitation Research and Training Center in Mental Retardation Progress Report.* Madison, Wis.: University of Wisconsin, 1972.

Heckelman, R. G. "The Neurological Impress Method of Remedial Reading Instruction." *Academic Therapy,* 4 (Summer 1969), 277–282.

Hegge, T. G. "Special Reading Disability with Particular Reference to the Mentally Deficient." *Proceedings, American Association Mental Deficiency,* 39 (1934), 297–343.

Hegge, Thorleif, Samuel A. Kirk, and Winifred Kirk. *Remedial Reading Drills.* Ann Arbor, Mich.: George Wahr, 1936.

Hermann, Knud. *Reading Disability: A Medical Study of Word-Blindness and Related Handicaps.* Springfield, Ill.: Charles C. Thomas, 1959.

Hewett, F. M., D. Mayhew, and Ethel Robb. "An Experimental Reading Program for Neurologically Impaired, Mentally Retarded, and Severely Emotionally Disturbed Children." *American Journal of Orthopsychiatry,* 37 (1967), 35–48.

Hill, Iverna. "A Survey of Reading Difficulties of Mentally Retarded Children in Schenectady, N.Y." Unpublished master's thesis, N.Y. State College for Teachers, Albany, 1939.

Hill, Walter R. "Reading Testing for Reading Evaluation." In W. Blanton, R. Fall, and J. Tuinman, eds. *Measuring Reading Performance,* pp. 1–14. Newark, Del.: International Reading Association, 1974.

Hillerich, Robert L. "Word Lists—Getting It All Together." *The Reading Teacher,* 27 (January 1974), 353–360.

Hinshelwood, James. *Congenital Word Blindness.* London: H. K. Lewis, 1917.

Hirshoren, A. A. "A Comparison of the Predictive Validity of the Revised Stanford-Binet Intelligence Scale and the Illinois Test of Psycholinguistic Abilities." *Exceptional Children,* 35 (March 1969), 517–521.

Hobbs, N. *The Futures of Children.* San Francisco: Jossey-Bass, 1975.

Hoyt, Mildred. "Mental Age and School Attainment of 1007 Retarded Children in Massachusetts." *Journal of Educational Psychology,* 15 (December 1924), 297–301.

Johnson, Dale D. "The Dolch List Reexamined." *The Reading Teacher,* 24 (February 1971), 449–457.

Johnson, Doris, and Helmer Myklebust. *Learning Disabilities: Educational Principles and Practices.* New York: Grune & Stratton, Inc., 1967.

Johnson, G. O. *Education for the Slow Learners.* Englewood Cliffs, N.J.: Prentice-Hall, Inc., 1963.

Johnson, Marjorie, and Roy Kress. *Informal Reading Inventories.* International Reading Association, 1965.

Jones, Carroll. "Very Bright and Feebleminded Children: The Study of Qualitative Differences." *Training School Bulletin,* 16 (1919–1920), 137–141, 153–164, 169–180.

Jones, Jon Paul. *Intersensory Transfer, Perceptual Shifting, Modal Preference and Reading.* Newark, Del.: International Reading Association. ERIC/CRIER, 1972.

Jongsma, Eugene. *The Cloze Procedure as a Teaching Technique.* Newark, Del.: International Reading Association, 1971.

Jordan, Laura. "Reading and the Young Mentally Retarded Child." *Mental Retardation,* 1 (February 1963), 21–27.

Jordan, Laura. "Verbal Readiness Training for Slow Learning Children." *Mental Retardation,* 3 (April 1965), 19–22.

Jordan, Laura. "Building the Readiness Program." *Mental Retardation,* 5 (1967), 28–31.

Karlin, Robert. *Teaching Elementary Reading.* New York: Harcourt Brace Jovanovich, 1971.

Karlin, Robert. "Evaluation for Diagnostic Teaching." In Walter MacGinitie, ed. *Assessment Problems in Reading.* Newark, Del.: International Reading Association, 1973.

Karnes, Merle B. *The Karnes Early Language Activities.* Champaign, Ill.: GEM Materials Enterprises, 1975.

Kass, C. E. "Psycholinguistic Disabilities of Children with Reading Problems." *Exceptional Children,* 32 (April 1966), 533–539.

Kauffman, J., and D. Hallahan, eds. *Teaching Children with Learning Disabilities: Personal Perspectives.* Columbus, Ohio: Charles E. Merrill Books, Inc., 1976.

Kelly, Elizabeth M. "The Improvement of Reading in Special Classes for Mentally Retarded Children." *Proceedings, American Association Mental Deficiency,* 39 (July 1934), 67–73.

Keogh, Barbara, and Marc L. Levitt. "Special Education in the Mainstream: A Confrontation of Limitations." *Focus on Exceptional Children,* 8 (March 1976), 1–11.

Keogh, Barbara K., and Judith Margolis. "Learn to Labor and Wait: Attentional Problems of Children with Learning Disorders." *Journal of Learning Disabilities,* 9 (May 1976), 276–286.

Kephart, Newell C. *The Slow Learner in the Classroom.* 2d ed. Columbus, Ohio: Charles E. Merrill Books, Inc., 1971.

Kirk, Samuel A. "The Influence of Manual Training on the Learning of Simple Words in the Case of Subnormal Boys." *Journal of Educational Psychology,* 24 (1933), 525–535.

Kirk, Samuel A. "A Study of the Relation of Ocular and Manual Preference to Mirror Reading." *Pediatric Seminar and Journal of Genetic Psychology,* 44 (1934), 192–205.

Kirk, Samuel A. *Manual of Directions for Use with the Hegge-Kirk-Kirk Remedial Reading Drills.* Ann Arbor, Mich.: George Wahr, 1936.

Kirk, Samuel A. *Teaching Reading to Slow Learning Children.* Boston: Houghton Mifflin Co., 1940.

Kirk, Samuel A. *Early Education of the Mentally Retarded.* Urbana, Ill.: University of Illinois Press, 1958.

Kirk, Samuel A. "Research in Education." In H. Stevens, and R. Heber, eds. *Mental Retardation,* pp. 57–99. Chicago: University of Chicago Press, 1964.

Kirk, Samuel A. "Diagnostic, Cultural and Remedial Factors in Mental Retardation." In Sonia F. Osler and R. E. Cooke, eds. *Biosocial Basis of Mental Retardation.* Baltimore: Johns Hopkins Press, 1965.

Kirk, Samuel A. "The Education of Intelligence," *The Slow Learning Child,* 20 (July 1973), 67–83.

Kirk, Samuel A. Chapter 8, "Samuel A. Kirk." In J. M. Kauffman and Daniel P. Hallahan, *Teaching Children with Learning Disabilities: Personal Perspectives,* pp. 238–269. Columbus, Ohio: Charles E. Merrill Books, Inc., 1976.

Kirk, Samuel A. "Learning Disabilities: Reopening Pandora's Box." Speech delivered at the 27th annual conference of the Orton Society, New York, December 14, 1976.

Kirk, Samuel A., and John Elkins. "Characteristics of Children Enrolled in the Child Service Demonstration Centers." *Journal of Learning Disabilities,* 8 (December 1975), 630–637.

Kirk, Samuel A., and Winifred D. Kirk. "How Johnny Learns to Read." *Exceptional Children,* 22 (January 1956), 158–160.

Kirk, Samuel A., and Winifred D. Kirk. *Psycholinguistic Learning Disabilities.* Urbana, Ill.: University of Illinois Press, 1971.

Kirk, Samuel A., and Winifred D. Kirk. "The Uses and Abuses of the ITPA." *Journal of Speech and Hearing Disorders,* in press.

Kirk, Samuel A., and Francis Lord. *Exceptional Children: Educational Resources and Perspectives.* Boston: Houghton Mifflin Co., 1974.

Kirk, Samuel A., and James J. McCarthy. "The Illinois Test of Psycholinguistic Abilities—An Approach to Differential Diagnosis." *American Journal of Mental Deficiency,* 66 (November 1961), 399–412.

Kirk, Samuel A., James J. McCarthy, and Winifred Kirk. *The Illinois Test of Psycholinguistic Abilities.* Urbana, Ill.: University of Illinois Press, 1968.

Kirk, Winifred D., and Samuel A. Kirk. "The Influence of the Teacher's Handedness on Children's Reversal Tendencies in Writing." *Pediatric Seminar and Journal of Genetic Psychology,* 47 (1935), 473–477.

Kolburne, L. L. *Effective Education for the Mentally Retarded Child.* New York: Vantage Press, 1965.

Kortas, Sister Maureen. "The Effects on Programmed Reading of a Token Contingency System with a Class of Educable Retarded Boys." Unpublished doctoral dissertation, University of Illinois, 1969.

Kucera, H., and W. Francis. *Computational Analysis of Present-Day American English.* Providence, R.I.: Brown University Press, 1967.

Lahaderne, H. M. "Attitudinal and Intellectual Correlates of Attention: A Study of Four Sixth-grade Classrooms." *Journal of Educational Psychology,* 59 (October 1968), 320–324.

Langford, Kenneth, K. Slade, and A. Barnett. "An Explanation of Impress Techniques in Remedial Reading." *Academic Therapy,* 9 (Spring 1974), 309–319.

Larsen, Stephen C., and Donald D. Hammill. "Relationship of Selected Visual Perceptual Abilities to School Learning." *Journal of Special Education,* 9 (Fall 1975), 282–291.

Larsen, Stephen C., Dorothy Rogers, and Virginia Sowell. "The Use of Selected Perceptual Tests in Differentiating Between Normal and Learning Disabled Children." *Journal of Learning Disabilities,* 9 (February 1976), 85–90.

Lawson, Gary D. *Newspaper Reading.* Elk Grove, Calif.: Elk Grove Unified School District, 1960.

Lee, Dorris M., and Roach Van Allen. *Learning to Read through Experience.* 2nd ed. New York: Appleton-Century-Crofts, 1963.

Lee, Laura, R. Koenigskecht, and S. Mulern. *Interactive Language Development Teaching.* Evanston, Ill.: Northwestern University Press, 1975.

Lenneberg, Eric. *The Capacity for Language Acquisition in the Structure of Language.* J. A. Foder, and Jerrold J. Katz, eds. Englewood Cliffs, N.J.: Prentice-Hall, Inc., 1964.

Lent, James R. "Mimosa Cottage Experiment in Hope." *Psychology Today,* 2 (June 1968), 51–58.

Lerner, Janet W. "The Utility of Phonic Generalizations—A Modification." *The Journal of the Reading Specialist,* 8 (March 1969), 117–118.

Lerner, Janet W., and Lynne List. "The Phonics Knowledge of Prospective Teachers, Experienced Teachers, and Elementary Pupils." *Illinois School Research,* 7 (Fall 1970), 39–42.

Lerner, Janet W. *Children with Learning Disabilities: Theories, Diagnosis, and Teaching Strategies.* 2d ed. Boston: Houghton Mifflin Co., 1976.

Levitt, Edith. "Higher-Order and Lower-Order Reading Responses of Mentally Retarded and Nonretarded Children at the First-Grade Levels." *American Journal of Mental Deficiency,* 77 (July 1972), 13–20.

Lewitter, Frances I. "A Genetic Analysis of Specific Reading Disability." Unpublished master's dissertation, University of Colorado, 1975.

Lilly, M. Stephen, and John Kelleher. "Modality Strengths and Aptitude-Treatment Interaction." *Journal of Special Education,* 7 (Spring 1973), 5–14.

Lindsley, Ogden R. "Precision Teaching in Perspective." In Samuel A. Kirk and Francis Lord, eds. *Exceptional Children: Educational Resources and Perspectives,* pp. 477–482. Boston: Houghton Mifflin Co., 1974.

Linn, J. R., and Thomas J. Ryan. "The Multisensory-Motor Method of Teaching Reading." *Journal of Experimental Psychology,* 36 (January 1968), 57–59.

Lopardo, Genevieve S. "LEA—Cloze Reading Material for the Disabled Reader." *The Reading Teacher,* 29 (October 1975), 42–44.

Lund, Kathryn, Georgiana E. Foster, and Frederick C. McCall Perez. "The Effectiveness of Psycholinguistic Training: A Reevaluation." *Exceptional Children,* November 1977, in press.

Macione, J. R. "Psychological Correlates of Reading Disability as Defined by the Illinois Test of Psycholinguistic Abilities." Unpublished doctoral dissertation, University of South Dakota, 1969.

MacMillan, D. L., R. L. Jones, and G. F. Aloia. "The Mentally Retarded Label: A Theoretical Analysis and Review of Research." *American Journal of Mental Deficiency,* 79 (November 1974), 241–261.

Manning, Ardelle. *Magazines.* Palo Alto: Ardelle Manning Productions, 1964.

Mathias, D. C. "Teaching Reading to Retardates: A Comparison of i/t/a with Traditional Orthography." *Bureau Memorandum,* 9 (3). Madison, Wis.: Department of Public Instruction, 1968.

Mavrogenes, Nancy A., Earl F. Hanson, and Carol K. Winkely. "A Guide to Tests of Factors that Inhibit Learning to Read." *The Reading Teacher,* 29 (January 1976), 343–358.

McCarthy, W., and J. Oliver. "Some Tactile-Kinesthetic Procedures for Teaching Reading to Slow-Learning Children." *Exceptional Children,* 31 (April 1965), 419–421.

McCracken, R. "Standardized Reading Tests and Informal Reading Inventories," *Education,* 82 (February 1962), 366–369.

McCracken, Robert A. *Standard Reading Inventory.* Klamath Falls, Ore.: Klamath Printing Co., 1966.

McKee, Paul. *Reading. A Program of Instruction for the Elementary School.* Boston: Houghton Mifflin Co., 1966.

McKee, Paul, M. Lucile Harrison, Annie McCowen, and Elizabeth Lehr. *High Roads.* Boston: Houghton Mifflin Co., 1962, p. 228.

Melcher, Ruth T. "Developmental Progress in Young Mentally Handicapped Children Who Receive Prolonged Pre-Academic Training." *American Journal of Mental Deficiency,* 45 (1940), 265–273.

Merrill, Maud A. "The Ability of the Special Class Children in the Three R's." *Pediatric Seminars,* 25 (1918), 88–96.

Merrill, Maud A. "The Relation of Intelligence to Ability in the Three R's in the Case of Retarded Children." *Pediatric Seminars,* 28 (1921), 249–274.

Merrill, Maud A. "On the Relation of Intelligence to Achievement in the Case of Mentally Retarded Children." *Comparative Psychology Monographs,* 2 (1924), 1–100.

Meyen, E., ed. *Proceedings—The Missouri Conference on the Categorical/Non-categorical Issue in Special Education.* Columbia, Mo.: University of Missouri Press, 1971.

Minskoff, Esther H. "Research on Psycholinguistic Training: Critique and Guidelines." *Exceptional Children,* 42 (November 1975), 136–143.

Minskoff, Esther H., and J. Gerald Minskoff. "A Unified Program of Remedial and Compensatory Teaching for Children with Process Learning Disabilities." *Journal of Learning Disabilities,* 9 (April 1976), 215–222.

Mintz, A. "Reading Reversals and Lateral Preferences in a Group of Intellectually Subnormal Boys." *Journal of Educational Psychology,* 37 (1946), 487–501.

Money, John, ed. *The Disabled Reader: Education of the Dyslexic Child.* Baltimore: Johns Hopkins Press, 1966.

Monroe, Marion. *Children Who Cannot Read.* Chicago: University of Chicago Press, 1932.

Monroe, Marion. "Reading Aptitude Tests for the Prediction of Success and Failure in Beginning Reading," *Education,* 56 (September 1935), 7–14.

Moore, O. K. "Autotelic Responsive Environments and Exceptional Children." In J. Hellmuth, ed. *The Special Child in Century 21,* pp. 87–138. Seattle: Special Child Publications, 1964.

Morphett, Mabel V., and C. Washburne. "When Should Children

Begin to Read?" *Elementary School Journal,* 31 (April 1931), 496–503.

Muehl, Siegmar, and Elizabeth R. Forrell. "A Follow-Up Study of Disabled Readers: Variables Related to High School Reading Performance." *Reading Research Quarterly,* 9 (1) (1973–1974), 110–122.

Mullen, F. A., and W. Ilken. *The Reading Ability of the Older Ungraded Pupil.* Chicago: Chicago Public Schools, 1952.

Murphy, Richard T. "Assessment of Adult Reading Competence." In D. Nielsen and H. Hjelm, eds. *Reading and Career Education,* pp. 50–61. Newark, Del.: International Reading Association, 1975.

Myers, Patricia, and Donald Hammill. *Methods of Learning Disorders.* New York: John Wiley & Sons, 1976.

Myklebust, H. "Learning Disabilities: Definition and Overview." In *Progress in Learning Disabilities.* Vol. I, pp. 1–15. New York: Grune & Stratton, 1968.

Neufeld, Rose G. *Reading Fundamentals for Teenagers.* New York: John Day Co., 1963.

Newcomer, Phyllis L., and Libby Goodman. "Effect of Modality Instruction on the Learning of Meaningful and Nonmeaningful Material by Auditory and Visual Learners." *Journal of Special Education,* 9 (Fall 1975), 261–268.

Newcomer, Phyllis, and Donald D. Hammill. *Psycholinguistics in the Schools.* Columbus, Ohio: Charles E. Merrill Books, Inc., 1976.

Newcomer, Phyllis, B. Hare, D. Hammill, and J. McGettigan. "The Construct Validity of the Illinois Test of Psycholinguistic Abilities." *Journal of Learning Disabilities,* 8 (April 1975), 220–231.

New Phonics Workbook. Cleveland, Ohio: Modern Curriculum Press, 1976.

New York Times, October 4, 1975.

Northcutt, Norvell W. "Functional Literacy for Adults." In D. Nielsen and H. Hjelm, eds. *Reading and Career Education,* pp. 43–49. Newark, Del.: International Reading Association, 1975.

Olson, A. V. "School Achievement, Reading Ability, and Specific Visual Perception Skills in the Third Grade." *The Reading Teacher,* 19 (April 1966), 490–492.

Orman, J. "Introduction to Reading Through the Initial Teaching Alphabet." *Teaching and Training,* 4 (1966), 109–113.

Orton, June L. "The Orton Gillingham Approach." In J. Money and G. Shiffman, eds. *Disabled Reader,* pp. 119–145. Baltimore: Johns Hopkins Press, 1966.

Orton, Samuel T. *Reading, Writing, and Speech Problems in Children.* New York: W. W. Norton & Co., Inc., 1937.

Otto, Wayne. "Evaluating Instruments for Assessing Needs and Growth in Reading." In E. McGinitie, ed. *Assessment Problems in Reading,* pp. 14–20. Newark, Del.: International Reading Association, 1973.

Otto, W., R. McMenemy, and R. Smith. *Corrective and Remedial Teaching.* 2d ed. Boston, Mass.: Houghton Mifflin Co., 1973.

Park, George E. "The Etiology of Reading Disabilities: An Historical Perspective." *The Journal of Learning Disabilities,* 1 (May 1968), 318–330.

Parker, Don, and Genevieve Scallell. *SRA Reading Laboratory I Word Games.* Chicago: Science Research Associates, Inc., 1962.

Pertsch, C. F. "A Comparative Study of the Progress of Subnormal Pupils in the Grades and in Special Classes." Unpublished doctoral dissertation, Columbia University, 1936.

Poling, D. L. "Auditory Deficiencies of Poor Readers." *Clinical Studies in Reading II. Supplementary Educational Monographs,* 77 (1953), 107–111.

Powell, William R. "Reappraising the Criteria for Interpreting Informal inventories." In D. DeBoer, ed. *Reading Diagnosis and Evaluation,* pp. 100–109. Newark, Del.: International Reading Association, 1967.

Powell, William R. "The Validation of the Instructional Reading Level." In R. Leibert, ed. *Diagnostic Viewpoints in Reading,* pp. 121–133. Newark, Del.: International Reading Association, 1971.

Proger, Barton B. "Test Review #18. Woodcock Reading Mastery Tests." *Journal of Special Education,* 9 (4)(Winter 1975), 439–444.

Programmed Reading. New York: Sullivan Associates, McGraw-Hill Book Co., 1973.

Public Law 94-142. Education of All Handicapped Children Act of 1975. 94th Congress, November 29, 1975.

Quay, Herbert C. "The Facets of Educational Exceptionality: A Conceptual Framework for Assessment, Grouping, and Instruction." In D. Hammill and N. Bartel, eds. *Educational Perspectives in Learning Disabilities,* pp. 329–341. New York: John Wiley & Sons, 1971.

Ragland, G. G. "The Performance of Educable Mentally Handicapped Students of Differing Reading Ability on the Illinois Test of Psycholinguistic Abilities." Unpublished doctoral dissertation, University of Virginia, 1964.

Ramanauskas, S. *Oral Reading Errors and Cloze Comprehension of Mentally Retarded Children.* Storrs, Conn.: University of Connecticut, 1970.

Rankin, E. F., and Joseph W. Culhane. "Comparable Cloze and Multiple-Choice Comprehension Test Scores." *Journal of Reading,* 13 (December 1969), 193–198.

Reading 720 Series. Boston: Ginn & Co., 1976.

Remington, F. A. "A Unit Method of Teaching Reading to Mentally Retarded Children." *Training School Bulletin,* 53 (April 1956), 40–43.

Renshaw, S. "The Abilities of Pupils in Detroit Prevocational Classes." *Journal of Educational Psychology,* 10 (February 1919), 83–94.

Reynolds, M. C. "A Study of the Relationships Between Auditory Characteristics and Specific Silent Reading Abilities." *Journal of Educational Research,* 46 (February 1953), 439–449.

Right to Read. Report of Forum 7, White House Conference on Children. Washington, D.C.: Superintendent of Documents, U.S. Government Printing Office, 1970.

Ring, Shirley B. "A Comparison of Achievement and Mental Ages of Ninety-Eight Special Class Children." Unpublished master's thesis, Boston University, 1951.

Robinson, Helen M. *Why Pupils Fail in Reading*. Chicago: University of Chicago Press, 1946.

Robinson, Helen M. "Visual and Auditory Modalities Related to Methods for Beginning Reading." *Reading Research Quarterly,* 8 (Fall 1972), 7–41.

Rosen, C. I. "A Study of Visual Perception Capabilities of First Grade Pupils and the Relationship Between Visual Perception Training and Reading Achievement." Unpublished doctoral dissertation, University of Minnesota, 1965.

Ross, Alan O. *Psychological Aspects of Learning Disabilities and Reading Disorders*. New York: McGraw-Hill Book Co., 1976.

Roswell, Florence, and Gladys Natchez. *Reading Disability: Diagnosis and Treatment*. New York: Basic Books, 1971.

Rude, Robert. "Objective-Based Reading Systems: An Evaluation." *Reading Teacher,* 28 (November 1974), 169–175.

Ruhly, Velma. "A Study of the Relationship of Self-Concept, Socioeconomic Background, and Psycholinguistic Abilities to Reading Achievement of Second Grade Males Residing in a Suburban Area." Unpublished doctoral dissertation, Wayne State University, 1970.

Sabatino, David A. "Auditory Perception: Development, Assessment, and Intervention." In L. Mann and D. Sabatino, eds. *The First Review of Special Education*. New York: Grune & Stratton, 1973.

Sabatino, David A., and Nancy Dorfman. "Matching Learning Aptitude to Two Commercial Reading Programs." *Exceptional Children,* 4 (October 1974), 85–90.

Samuels, S. J. "The Effect of Simultaneous Versus Successive Similarity and the Van Restoroff Effect." *Journal of Educational Psychology,* 58 (December 1967), 337–342.

Samuels, S. Jay. "Success and Failure in Learning to Read: A Critique of the Research." *Reading Research Quarterly* 8, 2 (Winter 1973), 200–239.

Sawyer, Diane J. "Readiness Factors for Reading: A Different View." *The Reading Teacher,* 28 (April 1975), 620–624.

Scarborough, Willie H. "The Incidence of Reading Retardation Among 1182 Mentally Handicapped Children." Paper read at American Association for Mental Deficiency Convention, fall, 1951.

Sceats, John. *i.t.a. and the Teaching of Literacy*. New York: Pitman Publishing Corp., 1967.

Schiefelbusch, Richard L., Ross H. Copeland, and James O. Smith. *Language and Mental Retardation*. New York: Holt, Rinehart and Winston, 1967.

Sedlack, R., and P. Weener. "Review of Research on the ITPA." In L. Mann and D. Sabatino, eds. *The First Review of Special Education,* pp. 113–164. New York: Grune & Stratton, 1973.

Sheperd, G. "Selected Factors in the Reading Ability of Educable Mentally Retarded Boys." *American Journal of Mental Deficiency,* 71 (November 1967), 563–570.

Shotick, A. L. "A Comparative Investigation of the Performance of Mentally Retarded and Intellectually Normal Boys on Selected Reading Comprehension and Performance Tasks." Unpublished doctoral dissertation, Syracuse University, 1960.

Siegenthaler, Bruce M., J. B. Sallade, and J. S. Tordibuona. "Speech Hearing Measurement in an Intellectually Average to Below-Average Group of Children." *American Journal of Mental Deficiency,* 76 (February 1972), 427–433.

Silberberg, Norman E., and Margaret Silberberg. "The Bookless Curriculum: An Educational Alternative." *Journal of Learning Disabilities,* 2 (June 1969), 302–307.

Silverman, M., A. Davids, and J. Andrews. "Powers of Attention and Academic Achievement." *Perceptual and Motor Skills,* 17 (1963), 243–249.

Sipay, Edward R. "A Comparison of Standard Reading Scores as Functional Reading Levels." *Reading Teacher,* 17 (January 1964), 265–268.

Sivaroli, Nicholas J. *Classroom Reading Inventory.* 2d ed. Dubuque, Iowa: William C. Brown, 1973.

Skeels, Harold M. "A Study of the Effects of Differential Stimulation on Mentally Retarded Children: A Follow-Up Study." *American Journal of Mental Deficiency,* 46 (January 1942), 340–350.

Skeels, Harold M. "Adult Status of Children with Contrasting Early Life Experiences." *Monographs of the Society for Research in Child Development,* No. 31. Chicago: University of Chicago Press, 1966.

Skeels, Harold M., and H. B. Dye. "A Study of the Effects of Differentiated Stimulation on Mentally Retarded Children." *Proceedings and Addresses of the Sixty-Third Annual Session of the American Association on Mental Deficiency,* 44 (No. 1, 1939), 114–130.

Slaughter, Stella S. *The Educable Mentally Retarded Child and His Teacher.* Philadelphia, Pa.: F. A. Davis Co., 1964.

Slingerland, Beth H. *A Multi-sensory Approach to Language Arts for Specific Language Disability Children.* Cambridge, Mass.: Educator's Publishing Service, 1974.

Smith, M. "Eight Backward Pupils and i/t/a." *Special Education,* 55 (3, 1960), 19–22.

Smith, Nila B. *American Reading Instruction.* Newark, Del.: International Reading Association, 1965.

Smith, Robert M. *Clinical Teaching.* New York: McGraw-Hill Book Co., 1974.

Spache, George D., and Evelyn B. Spache. *Reading in the Elementary School.* Boston: Allyn & Bacon, 1973.

Spalding, Romalda B. *The Writing Road to Reading.* New York: Whiteside and Morrow, 1962.

Spring, C. "Same-different Reaction Time for Letters in Dyslexic and Normal Children." Unpublished doctoral dissertation, University of California, Davis, 1969.

Stauffer, Russell. *Directing Reading Maturity as a Cognitive Process.* New York: Harper & Row, 1969.

Stevens, G., and R. Orem. *The Case for Early Reading.* St. Louis, Mo.: Warren H. Green, Inc., 1968.

Sticht, Thomas G., and Howard H. McFann. "Reading Requirements for Career Entry." In D. Nielsen and H. Hjelm, eds. *Reading and Career Education,* pp. 62–76. Newark, Del.: International Reading Association, 1975.

Sticht, Thomas, John S. Caylor, Richard Kern, and Lynn C. Fox. "Project REALISTIC: Determination of Adult Literacy Skill Levels." *Reading Research Quarterly,* 7 (Spring 1972), 424–465.

Stolurow, L. M. "Programmed Instruction for the Mentally Retarded." *Review of Educational Research,* 33 (February 1963), 126–136.

Stone, Clarence R. *Better Primary Reading.* St. Louis: Webster Publishing Co., 1936.

Strang, Ruth. *Reading Diagnosis and Remediation.* Newark, Del.: International Reading Association, 1968.

Strang, Ruth. *Diagnostic Teaching of Reading.* New York: McGraw-Hill Book Co., 1969.

Sucher, Floyd, and Ruel A. Allred. *Reading Placement Inventory.* Oklahoma City: Economy Co., 1973.

Tanyzer, H. J., H. Alpert, and L. Sandel. *Beginning Reading—The Effectiveness of Different Media.* Report of the Nassau School Development Council. Mineola, N.Y., 1965.

Taylor, J., ed. *Selected Writings of Hughlings Jackson.* London: Hadden and Straughton, 1932.

Taylor, Sanford E., Helen Frackenpohl, and James L. Pettee. "Grade Level Norms for the Components of the Fundamental Reading Skills." *Research Information Bulletin, No. 3.* Huntington, N.Y.: Educational Development Laboratories, Inc., a division of McGraw-Hill Book Co., 1960.

Thomas, G. I. "A Study of Reading Achievement in Terms of Mental Ability." *Elementary School Journal,* 47 (September 1946), 28–33.

Thompson, R., and C. Dziuban. "Criterion-Reference Reading Tests in Perspective." *Reading Teacher,* 27 (December 1973), 292–294.

Thorndike, Robert L. "Dilemmas in Diagnosis." In E. McGinitie, ed. *Assessment Problems in Reading,* pp. 55–67. Newark, Del.: International Reading Association, 1973.

Thurstone, L. L. *The Nature of Intelligence.* Patterson, N.J.: Littfield, Adams and Co., 1960.

Thurstone, T. G. *An Evaluation of Educating Mentally Handicapped Children in Special Classes and in Regular Grades.* U.S. Office of Education Cooperative Research Program, Project No. OE. SAE-6452. Chapel Hill: University of North Carolina, 1959.

Traub, Nina, and Francis Bloom. *Recipe for Reading.* Cambridge, Mass.: Educator's Publishing Service, 1970.

Vance, H. S. "Psychological and Educational Study of Brain-Damaged and Non-Brain-Damaged Mentally Retarded Children." *Dissertation Abstracts,* 17 (1956), 1033.

Vogel, Susan A. "Syntactic Abilities in Normal and Dyslexic Children." *Journal of Learning Disabilities,* 7 (February 1974), 103–109.

Vogel, Susan A. *Syntactic Abilities in Normal and Dyslexic Children.* Baltimore: University Park Press, 1975.

Wassmann, Katherine. "A Comparative Study of Mentally Deficient Children in Regular and in Special Classes." Unpublished master's thesis, George Washington University, 1933.

Weiner, Bluma B. "A Report on the Final Academic Achievement of Thirty-Seven Mentally Handicapped Boys Who Had Been Enrolled in a Prolonged Pre-Academic Program." *American Journal of Mental Deficiency,* 59 (September 1954), 210–219.

Weiner, P. S. "Auditory Discrimination and Articulation." *Journal of Speech and Hearing Disorders,* 32 (February 1967), 19–28.

Wepman, J. M. "Auditory Discrimination, Speech, and Reading." *Elementary School Journal,* 3 (March 1960), 245–247.

Wepman, J. M. "The Perceptual Basis of Learning," In H. Alan Robinson, ed. *Meeting Individual Differences in Reading,* pp. 25–43. Chicago: University of Chicago Press, 1964.

Wheeler, L. R., and V. D. Wheeler. "A Study of the Relationship of Auditory Discrimination to Silent Reading Abilities." *Journal of Educational Research,* 48 (October 1954), 103–113.

Winkley, Carol K. "Which Accent Generalizations Are Worth Teaching?" *Reading Teacher,* 20 (December 1966), 219–224.

Wiseman, D. E. "The Effects of an Individual Remedial Program on Mentally Retarded Children with Psycholinguistic Disabilities." Unpublished doctoral dissertation, University of Illinois, 1965.

Witty, P. A., and Estelle McCafferty. "Attainment by Feebleminded Children." *Education,* 50 (1930), 588–597.

Woodcock, Richard W., and Charlotte R. Clark. *Peabody Rebus Reading Program.* Circle Pines, Minn.: American Guidance Service, 1969.

Woodcock, R. W., and L. M. Dunn. *Efficacy of Several Approaches for Teaching Reading to the Educable Mentally Retarded.* U.S. Office of Education Project No. 5-0392. Nashville: George Peabody College for Teachers, 1967.

Wormer, Frank S. "What Is Criterion-Referenced Measurement?" In W. Blaton, R. Farr, and J. Tuinman, eds. *Measuring Reading Performances,* pp. 44–50. Newark, Del.: International Reading Association, 1974.

Ysseldyke, James E. "Diagnostic-Prescriptive Teaching: The Search for Aptitude-Treatment Interaction." In L. Mann and D. Sabatino, eds. *First Review of Special Education.* New York: Grune & Stratton, Inc., 1973.

Ysseldyke, James E., and John Salvia. "Diagnostic-Prescriptive Teaching: Two Models." *Exceptional Children,* 41 (November 1974), 181–186.

Index of Names

Index of Subjects